WORSHIP IN ISLAM

The Essential Mawdūdī Series

First Principles of Islamic Economics
Four Key Concepts of the Qur'ān
Islamic Civilization: Its Foundational Beliefs and Principles
Let Us Be Muslims
The Islamic Movement: Dynamics of Values, Power and Change
The Islamic Way of Life
Towards Understanding Islam
Towards Understanding the Qur'ān, Vols 1–10, 14
Towards Understanding the Qur'ān (single abridged volume)
Worship in Islam

Forthcoming
Towards Understanding the Qur'ān, Vols 11–13

WORSHIP IN ISLAM

An In-Depth Study of *ʿIbādah, Ṣalāh* and *Ṣawm*

Sayyid Abul Aʿlā Mawdūdī

Translated and edited by
Ahmad Imam Shafaq Hashemi

THE ISLAMIC FOUNDATION

Worship in Islam: An In-Depth Study of ʿIbādah, Ṣalāh and Ṣawm

Published by
THE ISLAMIC FOUNDATION,
Markfield Conference Centre,
Ratby Lane, Markfield, Leicestershire
LE67 9SY, United Kingdom
E-mail: publications@islamic-foundation.com
Website: www.islamic-foundation.com

Quran House, PO Box 30611, Nairobi, Kenya

PMB 3193, Kano, Nigeria

Distributed by
KUBE PUBLISHING LTD.
Tel: +44(0)1530 249230, Fax: +44(0)1530 249656
E-mail: info@kubepublishing.com

Cataloguing-in-Publication Data is available from the British Library

ISBN: 978-0-86037-605-7 *casebound*
ISBN: 978-0-86037-571-5 *paperback*

Typeset by: N.A.Qaddoura
Cover design by: Nasir Cadir
Printed by: Imak Ofset – Turkey

Contents

PART TWO
ʿ*IBĀDAH*: ITS SIGNIFICANCE IN THE ISLAMIC SOCIAL ORDER

Transliteration Table

Arabic Consonants

Initial, unexpressed medial and final: ء ’

ا	a	د	d	ض	ḍ	ك	k
ب	b	ذ	dh	ط	ṭ	ل	l
ت	t	ر	r	ظ	ẓ	م	m
ث	th	ز	z	ع	‘	ن	n
ج	j	س	s	غ	gh	هـ	h
ح	ḥ	ش	sh	ف	f	و	w
خ	kh	ص	ṣ	ق	q	ي	y

With a *shaddah*, both medial and final consonants are doubled.

Vowels, diphthongs, etc.

Short:	ـَ	a	ـِ	i	ـُ	u
Long:	ـَا	ā	ـِي	ī	ـُو	ū
Diphthongs:			ـَوْ	aw		
			ـَيْ	ay		

Introduction

Anis Ahmad[1]

In one form or another, worship is a common phenomenon in most of the world's known religions, cultures and civilizations. Not only did so-called primitive man, perhaps fascinated by the enormity of nature, bow down and prostrate in front of natural objects and offered flowers and food to befriend nature, but, even in the developed religions and also in secular societies, certain acts of devotion and ritual have become an integral part of life and society. Religiously-conscious communities in the east and the west, even in the so-called less developed cultures, carry highly articulated systems of worship. Often worship is performed through bodily gestures and postures, mental and bodily discipline, animal sacrifice and dedicated pilgrimages to 'holy' places. Those who call themselves liberated and irreligious have their own secular rituals, acts of devotion and offerings that are earnestly and meticulously observed. Examples of such rituals are observed on Valentine's Day, the Olympic torch procession, New Year celebrations, saluting and standing respectfully when the national anthem is played or placing wreaths on the graves of national heroes on designated memorial days.

Is worship the projection of an overactive mind? Is it a psychological need or a cultural hang-up? Do we need worship in an age of science and technology? Does worship help in seeking mental peace? These and many other similar questions persuade us to look critically into the meaning and relevance of worship (*'ibādah*) in Islam and other religio-cultural traditions.

Followers of the world religions observe elaborate rituals, performed to celebrate the human cycle of birth, maturity and death, which are known as 'rites of passage'. There are also non-cyclic 'crisis' rituals such as 'fertility rituals'. Modern anthropological studies of religion often associate these rituals with

---

[1] Professor Anis Ahmad is Meritorious Professor of Ethics and Comparative Religion and Vice-Chancellor at Riphah International University, Islamabad, Pakistan and is the general editor of the Essential Mawdūdī series.

myth and myth-making, as symbolic dramatizations of certain fundamental human needs in a society, whether 'biological', 'social' or 'theological'.[2]

Rituals, ceremonies and festivals are generally manifestations of the concept of worship in a religion. To the contrary, the Arabic term *ʿibādah,* usually translated as worship, servitude or remembrance in order to serve the ultimate Creator, refers to a wider and more comprehensive phenomenon. It is essentially a spiritual encounter of a believer with his or her Creator, the Eternal, All-Knowing, All-Powerful and All-Merciful Allah, Most Glorified and Exalted. Whilst it is an intimate personal experience, it can assume an overt and manifest articulation, in conscious yet visible or not-so-visible forms. It is an acknowledgement as well as a manifestation of an attitude of thankful attachment with and commitment towards the Transcendent, Allah Most Glorified and Exalted.

Worship, in this sense, is a matter of dialogue between the finite and the Infinite; it is a subject–Object relationship. It is a unique way of relating with the Ultimate Reality and Truth through adoration, glorification, love, veneration, praise and submission. It is an earnest effort of bewildered followers to open up their hearts to the All-Hearing, All-Seeing and All-Caring. It is an on-going spiritual interaction between the seeker and the Sought.

In many religions this dialogue may take place at a sacrificial level, wherein offerings are made as an individual or collective partaking in religious experience. It may take place at a mystical level, where certain chanting and disciplining of the heart, mind, soul and self may culminate in a spiritual communion with the Ultimate, resulting in enlightenment, elation of spirit and experience of the ineffable and an incommunicable ecstasy. Individual prayers, meditations, prostrations and kneeling down only express humility and obedience to the One Most High.

In the ancient Sumerian religion prostration and kneeling do not appear in their orthodox service, but there is evidence of their use among the Babylonians and the Assyrians as acts of worship. Worship in the form of *puja* does not have a place in the Buddhist path or *marga.* However, worship as *dāna* or giving or gifting is a known practice in Buddhism. Chinese religions have a special place for ancestral veneration and filial piety with elaborate rituals. Religion, according to Jesus (peace be upon him), consists in filial trust and love towards

[2] Richard B. Pilgrim, 'Ritual' in T. William Hall (ed.), *Introduction to the Study of Religion* (New York: Harper and Row, 1978), pp. 64–7; Clyde Kluckhohn, 'Myth and Ritual: A General Theory' in William Lassa and Evan Vogt (eds.) *Reader in Comparative Religion* (New York: Harper and Row, 1965), pp. 144–58.

God, and loyalty to His Will for His Kingdom 'on earth as it is in heaven'. Thus the Christian norm of worship is the Lord's Prayer.[3] Jewish worship done in the synagogue includes prayers and the reading of scripture. Rabbis are essentially learned men who guide and educate their community in religious matters. Worship in Judaism appears to be popular and democratic. There are three daily services in the synagogue: evening prayer at sunset, morning, prayer at around 6 am and afternoon prayers. Public services can only be offered in synagogues if ten males are present. Traditionally, women sit in a separate section in a gallery or marked off by a partition. In reformed synagogues, the gallery is open and men and women may sit together.[4] In Judaism, the rabbi has no organic connection with the priesthood, while worship in Hinduism does have an organic connection with it. Nearly all functions are performed by priests belonging to the Brahmanical caste. Worship in Hinduism includes the reverence of nature, animals, plants, mythical gods and goddesses and holy men, places and symbols.

This brief review indicates that worship in one form or another has been an integral part of man's quest for the Ultimate, his search for purpose in life and his yearning to relate with the Transcendent.

Does Islam, like other religions, prescribe certain offerings, devotions, celebrations and festivals or does it have a different view of worship? What does the Qur'an mean when it says: *And We did not create Jinn and human except for worship* (*ʿibādah*) (*al-Dhāriyāt* 51: 54)? In this verse, does *ʿibādah* mean only prayer, fasting, *zakāh* and hajj, the four main obligatory *ʿibādāt*? Or, as elaborated elsewhere in the Qur'an, does it mean total commitment to Allah in all aspects of one's life and behaviour: *Say, surely my prayer, all my acts of devotion (worship) and my living and my dying are only for Allah the Lord of the whole universe* (*al-Anʿām* 6: 162)? Serving Allah stands here for the discharge of all possible human activities in personal, social, political, economic and cultural domains in order to follow Allah's Will and to seek His Pleasure alone. The Qur'an wants the Messengers of Allah to become *ʿibād,* or servants, in order to serve their Rabb and Lord alone. Does *ʿibādah,* therefore, mean worship only at certain times and in specific forms or it is a matter of conducting one's whole life according to Allah's direction and guidance? This critical question and many more deserve to be resolved in order to understand basic features and forms of worship in Islam.

[3] Geoffrey Parrinder, *Worship in the World Religions* (London: Sheldon Press, 1974), p. 223.

[4] Ibid, pp. 174–5.

The Qur'anic statement mentioned earlier says that the jinn and humans are both created in order to serve Allah. But how is He to be served? The Qur'an answers the question and elaborates that the Creator of the universe and mankind, Allah Most Glorified and Exalted is by nature Kind (al-Karīm), Loving (al-Wudūd), Merciful (al-Raḥmān) and Mercy-giving (al-Raḥīm), and that He therefore not only created humanity and jinn out of His love and kindness but He also did not leave them without guidance (*hidāyah*), a blessing that has illuminated all the pathways of life, and a source of unlimited favour. The straight path (*al-ṣirāṭ al-mustaqīm*) has been clearly spelled out, enabling humans to be successful here and in the Hereafter. This and other favours of Allah call for thanking Him for His kindness and concern for His servants. Worship or *ʿibādah* in Islam, therefore, is first and foremost a way of thankfulness (*shukr*) to Allah Most Glorified and Exalted for His unlimited favours and blessings that all human beings receive day and night throughout their lifespans. This is why those who are called Allah's servants (*ʿibād*) are known for their observance of the regular prescribed prayers as well for those late at night and other optional prayers and devotions to their Creator. In this framework, *ʿibādah* manifests itself in the discharge of what has been laid down as obligations towards Allah (*ḥuqūq Allāh*) that are the foundation for social obligations (*ḥuqūq al-ʿibād*), which include helping the needy, orphans, debtors and prisoners. The fulfilment of social responsibilities therefore constitutes a core dimension of *ʿibādah* or worship and thankfulness to Allah in the Qur'an and the Sunnah.

> *The true servants* (ʿibād) *of the Merciful One are those who walk on the earth gently and when the foolish ones address them, they simply say: 'peace unto you', who spend the night prostrating themselves before their Lord. ... The true servants of the Merciful One are those who are neither extravagant nor niggardly in their spending but keep the golden mean between the two ... who do not bear witness to any falsehood and who, when they pass by frivolity, pass by it with dignity.*
>
> (*al-Furqān* 25: 63–72)

It is worth noting that there is no concept of 'personal salvation' in isolation from social existence in the Islamic scheme of *ʿibādah*. Salvation is an integral part of a total and all-embracing response to holding fast to Allah in intimate and personal as well as social behaviour. This is in contrast to the concept of salvation in some other religious traditions wherein the personal dimension overrides the social one, as conceptualized in *moksha* and *nirvana* in Hinduism or redemption in Christianity.

The Social Dimension of Worship

In Islam, man's success in the Hereafter is linked directly to the fulfilment of social responsibility (*ḥuqūq al-ʿibād*). Whilst our personal relationship with Allah is the soul and breath of *ʿibādah* and right motivation its hallmark, it is equally important to act ethically in economic, social and political life, in respect of all matters relating to the family in order to attain Allah's pleasure and achieve felicity in the Hereafter. In a hadith related by Abū Hurayrah, the Prophet is reported to have said:

> Seven categories of people will be under a special shade on the Day when there will be no shade except that of Allah Most Glorified and Exalted: (1) a just ruler; (2) one whose heart is always attached to the mosque; (3) two persons who befriend each other only for Allah and His *dīn*; (4) one who sheds tears privately when remembering Allah; (5) one who is charmed by a woman of beauty and status but refuses to act immorally out of fear of Allah; (6) one who spends money in the way of Allah in such a way that his left hand does not know what his right has done; and (7) a youth who grew up serving Allah.[5]

This hadith directly links our success in the Hereafter with firm attachment and unceasing loyalty to Allah together with our social attitudes and our behaviour and conduct in society. Another hadith focuses on economic behaviour in this world. It affirms that no person shall leave on the Day of Judgment until he is asked about three deeds he did in the world: (1) did he practise what he knew of Islam?; (2) how did he earn his wealth and where did he spend it?; and (3) how did he use the good health given to him by Allah?[6] The Qur'an advises believers to pray to Allah Most Glorified and Exalted to bestow upon them good in this world and good in the Hereafter (*al-Baqarah* 2: 201). Wealth generation through ethical and moral economic activity is considered to be part of *ʿibādah* by the Qur'an and so is its just and fair use.

In Islam, the concept of *ʿibādah* goes far beyond ritual. It envelops all possible activities of life and behaviour. The conventional understanding of duality between *dīn* and *dunyā* (the worldly life) has no place in the vision of *ʿibādah*: the two are inextricably *integrated* in this concept, and embedded in a *holistic* worldview. *ʿIbādah* stands for realization of Allah's commands in personal, familial, social, financial, economic, political and cultural matters. This is why the

[5] Narrated by ʿAbdullāh ibn ʿUmar, *Saḥīḥ al-Bukhārī*, hadith no. 6,308.

[6] Reported by ʿAbdullāh ibn Masʿūd, *Sunan al-Tirmidhī*, hadith no. 2,340.

hadith mentioned above qualifies success in the Hereafter, *even* for a leader conscious of Allah, in terms of applying good and fair governance in this world.

The social dimension of *ʿibādah* in Islam is also reflected in the fact that all obligatory *ʿibādāt* (worship) in Islam is ideally performed in congregation and not privately or in isolation from society. This is borne out by the fact that the five times daily prayers (*ṣalāh*) and particularly the Friday prayer (*ṣalāt al-Jumuʿah*) are to be performed in congregation with the whole community. Neither the Friday prayer nor the Eid prayer can be offered individually. The voluntary night-time prayer (*tahajjud*) is the only exception to this rule. Even prayer and supplication in moments of privacy are made with a sense of belonging to the community. In all individual prayers, one prays for Allah's mercy and blessings not only upon the Prophet's soul, but upon one's parents, members of one's family and even upon all believers who are living and those have passed away. Therefore prayer (*ṣalāh*) and supplication (*duʿā'*) are not simply a matter of individual salvation. Both involve pleading for the whole community of believers in seeking Allah's blessings, guidance and forgiveness.

In prayer, each bodily action represents an aspect of humbling oneself in the living presence of Allah Most Glorified and Exalted. In its essence, prayer is entering into a dialogue with Allah Most Glorified and Exalted. This dialogue begins with the purification of intention (*niyyah*), the purification of the body through ablutions (*wuḍū'*) and turning towards the Kaaba in Makkah, culminating in the raising one's hands up to the earlobes and declaring that Allah is Greatest (*Allāhu akbar*). This is followed by the Opening (*al-Fātiḥah*), an earnest prayer, glorifying Allah for His Compassion and Care and seeking His help and pleasure in living an ethical and moral life in this world in order to succeed in the Hereafter. This opening chapter of the Qur'an, recited with a spirit of conscious verbal supplication, is repeated in every cycle (*rakʿah*) of the prayer with mental concentration. Each bodily posture in the rest of the prayer – whether bowing (*rukūʿ*), prostrating (*sujūd*), standing (*qiyām*) or sitting (*qaʿdah*) – is coupled with conscious and meaningful dialogue with Allah, as if the believer is in front of Him or at least is being watched by Him.

The word *ʿibādah* has as its root *ʿabada*, meaning to become subservient, subdued or submissive. To be an *ʿabd* or servant (its plural form is *ʿibād*) entails a high degree of love of Allah, the Master of all creation, and, by extension, for His sincere servants. The expressions 'My servant' (*ʿibādī*) or 'Our servants' (*ʿibādunā*) are beautiful expressions overflowing with a sense of exclusiveness, intimacy, kindness, love, care and attachment of the Real Master towards His bondsmen. While *ʿibādah* literally means utter humbleness, humility and subservience on the part of a believer, it also connotes performing all acts of worship and devotion exclusively for Allah as the Sovereign, and obeying His commands unconditionally. *ʿUbūdiyyah* means to serve, while *al-ʿābid* (its plural is *ʿibād*) means bondsman of Allah.[7] Islam's real contribution lies in offering a holistic understanding of the concept of *ʿibādah*, generally translated as worship, but perhaps more correctly understood as serving Allah, One (Wāḥid) and Indivisible (Aḥad), in all walks of life.

Transcending the commonplace understanding of worship, the Qur'an challenges us: *Say: 'Surely my prayer and all my acts of devotion, and my living and my dying are only for Allah, the Lord of whole universe.'* (*al-Anʿām* 6: 162) In this supplication, the believer expresses his love, servitude and devotion to Allah. His spirituality is reflected in his *total commitment* to seek Allah's pleasure in all circumstances whether publicly or privately. *ʿIbādah* stands for this vision, commitment and unceasing effort to imbue it in all aspects of one's life and behaviour. To put it differently, it represents the realization of Allah's sovereignty in individual, social and collective life that reflects the model of life articulated in the Qur'an. The central issue is loyalty to Allah and living in His presence and rejection of all that invites His displeasure. This is what the prophets of Allah stood for. The Qur'an categorically states: *For We assuredly sent amongst every people a messenger (with the command): 'Serve Allah and eschew oppression.'* (*al-Naḥl* 16: 36)

When studied in the light of a similar statement in *Sūrah Yūsuf*, this verse of the Qur'an reaffirms that the realization of Allah's sovereignty includes its implementation in political, economic, social, legal and cultural realms:

> *Those whom you serve* (taʿbudūn) *beside Him are merely idle names that you and your forefathers have fabricated, without Allah sending down any sanction for them. All authority* (ḥukm) *to govern rests only with Allah. He has commanded that you serve none but Him. This is the right way of life* (dhālika al-dīn al-qayyim).
>
> (*Yūsuf* 12: 40)

Here *ʿibādah* of Allah Most Glorified and Exalted, as explained by Sayyid Abul Aʿlā Mawdūdī (1903–79), refers specifically to the recognition of His authority not merely in personal life, but in all realms of life, including the political, spiritual and the legal realms. This dimension of *ʿibādah* has raised eyebrows among a certain group of scholars who felt this constituted a virtual

[7] See '*ʿibādah*' in Sayyid Abul Aʿlā Mawdūdī, *Four Key Concepts of the Qur'ān*, trans. and ed. Tarik Jan (Markfield: The Islamic Foundation, 2006), pp. 122–44.

departure from the alleged conventional understanding of *dīn*, as acts of worship, spirituality, devotion, sacrifice and ceremony. Some have gone to the extent of reading into it some kind of extremism (*ghuluww*) and the 'politicization' of the Qur'anic term *ʿibādah*.[8] The Qur'an, however, is very clear on this issue. Allah's remembrance (*dhikr*) and seeking conformity with His Will in matters social, economic and financial are not two separate domains:

> *Believers, when the call for prayer is made on Friday, hasten to the remembrance of Allah and give up all trading. That is better for you, if you only knew. But when the prayer is ended, disperse in the land and seek Allah's bounty and remember Allah much* (wadhkur Allāh kathīr) *so that you may prosper.*
>
> (*al-Jumuʿah* 62: 9)

It is important to note that Allah's *dhikr* is the focal point in this verse. When the call for Friday prayer is made, the believers are directed to hasten to Allah's *dhikr*. And when *ṣalāh* is over to disperse in order to seek economic benefits while excelling in the *dhikr* of Allah Most Glorified and Exalted. In other words, Allah's remembrance (*dhikr*) should not be confined to the mosque but performed in the marketplaces, farms, factories, workplaces and every other place of human activity. This approach negates the allegedly traditional divide between sacred and secular space.[9] The entire earth is a mosque, as one hadith affirms (Tirmidhī and Nasāʾī). The domain of *ʿibādah* is not limited to the privacy of the home or the precincts of the mosque. A business transaction or any other activity in any realm of life made in accordance with the boundaries of what is halal or haram is an act of virtue and piety no less than an act of devotion.

A deeper understanding of the Qur'an establishes the notion that *ʿibādah* is not confined to certain rituals only. Each and every act of *ʿibādah* is an end in itself, but it is also a means to a wider end of living a life of virtue, piety, servitude and felicity, or a life of *taqwā*. The Qur'an categorically states that *prayer keeps one away from obscenity and evil* (*al-ʿAnkabūt* 29: 45) and that fasting has been enjoined so that one may achieve *taqwā* (*al-Baqarah* 2: 183). The message is very clear: *ʿibādah* means total commitment to serve Allah alone: *Believers enter wholly into the fold of Islam* (*al-Baqarah* 2: 208).

---

[8] Sayyid Abul Hasan Ali Nadwi, *ʿAṣr-i ḥāḍir men dīn kī tafhīm wa tashrīḥ* (Lucknow: Majlis-i taḥiqīqāt wa nashriyyāt-I islām, 1980), pp. 66, 75.

[9] See Mircea Eliade, *The Sacred and the Profane: The Nature of Religion* (New York: Harvest, 1959), pp. 20–115.

Elsewhere, Sayyid Mawdūdī writes at length about the comprehensive meaning of the four key terminologies of the Qur'an. His pioneering effort to analyse basic Qur'anic terms has been widely appreciated in academic circles.[10]

In the light of the aforementioned analysis, *ʿibādah* means to dedicate all devotion and servitude to Allah Most Glorified and Exalted: *Say: 'I am but a man like yourselves, (but) the revelation has come to me that your God is One God: whoever expects to meet his Lord, let him work righteously, and, in the worship of his Lord, admit no one as partner.'* (*al-Kahf* 18: 110) This and other verses in the Qur'an (e.g. *Maryam* 19: 64–65, *Hūd* 11: 123 and *Yūnus* 10: 104) make reference to this meaning of the term in an inclusive way. That is why the Qur'an, when referring to mandatory rituals like prayer (*ṣalāh*), fasting (*ṣawm*), *zakāh* or hajj, links their inalienable relationship with the performance of good deeds or ethical conduct in social, economic and political matters with serving Allah.

It would be useful to reflect at this point by looking again at the above-mentioned verse: *Say: 'Surely my prayer and all my acts of devotion and my living and my dying are only for Allah the Lord of the whole universe.'* (*al-Anʿām* 6: 162) Here the Qur'an invites us to discover the link between *ṣalāh,* in its ostensive sense of the five times daily prayers, and *duʿā'* (supplication, to seek Allah's help and favour for all actions that one intends to perform) to the whole exercise of human life and death. That is why this verse of the Qur'an further underscores two vital aspects, namely, what should be the ultimate objective of man's living in this world, and what should be the cause for which he may even sacrifice his life? This shows that *ʿibādah* is a comprehensive term. It transcends the formal meaning of devotions at specific times and in a prescribed manner. It equally stands for dedication of all human actions, thinking processes, feelings, reasoned decisions, and all forms of activity; in brief, it stands for all conceivable forms of human activities to seek Allah's pleasure.

Consequently, what is considered allegedly worldly and non-spiritual in some religious traditions, such as living a married life, is declared by the Prophet as his Sunnah or practice and in another hadith as an act that leads to the completion of faith (*īmān*), and so marriage is not just a worldly or merely sensual activity. He further underscores that if a person consciously denies living a married life, such a person does not belong to the Prophet's *ummah.*[11]

---

[10] Mawdūdī, *Four Key Concepts.* In a personal conversation with this writer, Professor Muhammad Qutb, the well-known Egyptian scholar, expressed his appreciation for this pioneering approach of Sayyid Mawdūdī.

[11] See Muslim, *al-Jāmiʿ al-Ṣaḥīḥ*, trans. Abdul Hamid Siddiqi (Lahore: Ashraf, 1976), vol. 2, hadith nos. 3,231, 3,233, and particularly 3,236, p. 703.

The domains of *dīn* and *dunyā*, or the so-called realms of the 'religious' and the 'secular' are fused together in an unambiguous manner by the Qur'an and the Prophetic Sunnah. This gelling together and forming of life into one single whole is a direct implication of monotheism (*tawḥīd*). Consequently, in Islam, all forms of worship converge towards and aim at the realization of *tawḥīd*.

If we reflect on the *ṣalāh*, it begins with a conscious pronouncement that Allah is Great (*Akbar*), and it is followed by a synchronized manifestation of Allah being the Highest, the Magnificent and Omnipotent, which is not only pronounced verbally but confirmed by bodily postures. Similarly, the essence of *zakāh* lies in the realization that wealth is a trust and an endowment from Allah, and is not merely the result of human effort. While we have every right to acquire wealth within the parameters of ethical living, and have a right to our wealth, others have a right on it also. Real pleasure is experienced when hard-earned wealth is given to the needy, the poor, orphans, the indebted, or for the liberation of prisoners of war. An elevation of the spirit is realized by liberating oneself from the love of wealth by making solely an instrument of what is good and just. The essence of hajj lies in the realization of Allah's love by renouncing the love of soil, tribe, country or any other attachments. Therefore, the pilgrim leaves his home, his family, his country and even his dress in order to adopt the colour of Allah (*ṣibghat Allāh*), leaving behind one's own likes or dislikes, to gather in Makkah to manifest a unique spectacle of human equality. Obedience to Allah thus means doing business or being political with a sense of deep commitment to Allah while scrupulously adhering to what is halal in doing so.

In the traditional religious teaching, worship or *ʿibādah* remains a devotional activity within a given space and time. On the other hand, the holistic understanding of *ʿibādah* means that in serving Allah Most Glorified and Exalted as the Only Authority, a believer is expected to fulfil his obligations toward those whom Allah wants to be taken care of, such as the orphans, the needy, those in debt, those taken as war captives, travellers in need of support or those who ask for help (*al-Tawbah* 9: 60). Such acts are not merely regarded as 'charity' in Islam but as a social obligation. If one fails to observe these obligations, then he will be held accountable on the Day of Judgment. *Zakāh*, one of the pillars of faith, is essentially an act of *ʿibādah*, mentioned around seventy times with prayer (*ṣalāh*) in the Qur'an. The purpose of this *ʿibādah* is Allah's remembrance in matters of money and the liberation of one's mind and soul from the love of wealth. At the same time, it represents the social dimension of *ʿibādah*. According to the Qur'an, *zakāh* is meant for the poor and needy, to free those in bondage, to help those burdened with debt, for the wayfarers, for those in the way of Allah, and for those who administrate its distribution. Social uplift, self-reliance, the eradication of poverty and the building of economic capacity are the measurable goals of *zakāh* (*al-Tawbah* 9: 60; *al-Naḥl* 16: 90). This is why one who consciously abandons prayer (*ṣalāh*) or *zakāh* loses faith.

In departing from the traditional *fiqhī* treatment of the subject, Sayyid Mawdūdī looks on *ʿibādah* in general and prayer (*ṣalāh*) and fasting (*ṣawm*) in the light of the message of the Qur'an and the Prophet's life and Sunnah, the lives and teachings of his Companions and the ethos of the Islamic *ummah*, even if it may apparently look somewhat dissimilar to the conservative, traditional narrative. He tries to discover through *ʿibādah* the inner link between humanity and its Creator and the ethical role that the human being is to play as Allah's deputy (*khalīfah*). To begin with, Sayyid Mawdūdī affirms that humanity has been given the capacity to distinguish between right and wrong in order to implement the directives of his Creator. After all, the Creator did not leave humanity without providing guidance and showing the right path to success. To enable humans to fulfil that mission, a comprehensive training system was provided by the Messengers of Allah in the form of *ʿibādah* and guiding principles for social, economic and cultural matters. The system of *ʿibādah* trains believers to be Allah's deputies (*khulafāʾ*). Believing men and women thus learn how to become carriers of the message of *tawḥīd* to humanity.

The Prophet of Islam embodies the model of desired spirituality. The first essential is faith in Allah Most Glorified and Exalted and complete devotion to Him. Hence prayer in solitude is a manifestation of spirituality as performed in the night prayer (*tahajjad*): *Surely getting up at night is the best means of subduing the self and is more suitable for uprightness in speech.* (*al-Muzzammil* 73: 6). However, even this voluntary *ṣalāh* (*tahajjud*) is to be performed with moderation and balance: *Stand up in prayer of night, all but a small part of it, half of it, or reduce it a bit and recite the Qur'an slowly and distinctly.* (*al-Muzzammil* 73:2–4).

The prophetic model of spirituality includes long prayers late at night as well as voluntary fasting on Mondays and Thursdays each week or on the thirteenth, fourteenth and fifteenth days of the lunar calendar. Fasting either three or eight days in a month also shows moderation, balance, and giving due importance to other areas of purification, enhancement and growth (*tazkiyah*). Voluntary fasting and prayers are essential means to acquire the consciousness of Allah (*taqwā*). Both help in promoting godliness, an ever-present feeling of being in front of Allah Most Glorified and Exalted. *Zakāh* and hajj are also acts of *tazkiyah* because believers purify their property and wealth as well as their hearts and souls when *zakāh* is distributed among the deserving and the needy or when they gladly bear the monetary and physical costs of hajj. The pilgrim is motivated to excel further in godliness and to reject consciously all temptations of wealth and pleasure.

Islamic spirituality creates a new relationship between the human being and the One Who, although totally unlike His creation, cares, loves and helps His servants when they are in need and dwells in their hearts. Islamic spirituality does not lead to a communion in which part and whole fuse together. As Allah Most Glorified and Exalted is Transcendent, Powerful and Unique, He is far beyond the fusion or association of any created thing with His Person. However, when a believer holds fast to Allah alone (*iʿtiṣām bi Allāh*), a hadith tells us His (grace) enters the eyes, ears, heart and the mind of a believer, not in a physical sense but in the sense that the servant watches only what the Lord wants him to watch and listens to only what makes his Rabb pleased with him.

The Prophet Muhammad – may Allah bless him and give him peace – said:

> O Allah! Place light in my heart, light in my tongue, light in my hearing, light in my sight, light above me, light below me, light on my right, light on my left, light in front of me, light behind me, place light in my soul, and make light abundant for me.
>
> (Muslim)

Islamic spirituality motivates a person to play the role of Allah's deputy (*khalīfah*) in the world. He tries his utmost to establish good (*maʿrūf*) in his own life, in that of his family, and his society. As Allah's deputy, a believer strives to ensure that no customs or traditions that conflict with the Prophet's shining example are observed by his family or his society.

Islamic spirituality creates a deep sense of accountability in front of Allah Most Glorified and Exalted throughout one's life, which will ultimately be realized on the Day of Judgement when we all will be held accountable. The Hereafter (*al-Ākhirah*) is no longer just a creedal matter of 'faith' but becomes the only motivating force behind each ethical, just, equitable and responsible act one makes in respect of one's family and society. All of a believer's activities, and even his thoughts, revolve around his concern for reward in the Hereafter. It no longer remains an abstract theological notion. Instead, it becomes the transformative motiving force in the believer's personality, moulding his character and behaviour in seeking Allah's pleasure.

To recapture the holistic vision of *ʿibādah*, we can summarize the whole discussion in five levels of spirituality. First and foremost is remembering Allah (*dhikr*) perpetually. *ʿIbādah* begins with praising and glorifying Allah, recounting His favours, His beautiful names, remembering Him, seeking His guidance at all times and for all our acts and decisions. When one interacts economically, socially, politically and culturally, and keeps Allah's pleasure in view and avoids His displeasure, it indicates his consciousness of Allah or *taqwā*.

Remembering Allah (*dhikr*) ritually as well as in social transactions is reflective of *taqwā*, which goes to make up the second important dimension of *ʿibādah*. *Taqwā* is commonly associated with certain outward manifestations that reflect the fear of Allah or offering of extra *nawāfil*. Of course, these are important but *taqwā* goes beyond them. *Taqwā* is the constant search for total conformity with Allah's Will, always acting with an ever-present feeling that Allah is watching us. Consequently, our attitudes and behaviour should be guided by the consciousness of Allah in every act or decision, whether small or big.

The third important dimension of *ʿibādah* is the inculcation of an attitude of *iḥtisāb* or self-evaluation, self-criticism and personal accountability. *ʿIbādah* institutes the habit of an on-going evaluation of our own behaviour and attitudes, as has been very well put by the second caliph ʿUmar ibn al-Khaṭṭāb, 'Bring yourselves to account before you are taken to account (*ḥāsibū anfusakum qabla an tuḥāsabū*)'. Without fail, *ʿibādah* should make people evaluate and measure their own behaviour in economy, society and governance, and not once a month or once a week but five times a day during and after the obligatory prayer. The Prophet, may Allah bless him and give him peace, has promised Heaven to those whose *ʿibādah* is performed with faith (*īmān*) and self-reflection and personal accountability (*iḥtisāb*).

The fourth important dimension of *ʿibādah* is the infusion of an attitude of balance, moderation, fairness, proportion and prioritization or, in the Qur'anic terminology, of *ʿadl*. It is the Prophetic Sunnah to observe *ʿadl* in all matters, including in all acts of *ʿibādah*. Therefore *ʿibādah* brings harmony and proportion (*taʿdīl*) in human attitudes and behaviour. Excessiveness and exaggeration (*ghuluww*) are disapproved in both the Qur'an and the Prophetic Sunnah. The proper observance of *ʿibādah* that captures its spirit makes a person moderate, balanced and fair in his relation with his Rabb as well as in all his dealings with others. One's speech, kind attitude, humbleness, punctuality, fulfilment of promises, avoidance of harshness, etc. are directly linked with one's concept of *ʿibādah*.

The final element of *ʿibādah* is to experience nearness to Allah Most Glorified and Exalted while involved in worship. A desire to be near (*qurb*) Allah persuades a person to develop attitudes and qualities that are liked by Allah (*ṣifāt maḥmūdah*) and to avoid actions that annoy Him (*ṣifāt mardūdah*). It is an on-going process in which a desire to excel in doing good that makes a person a friend (*waliyy*) of Allah. Thus, he avoids even those seemingly minor and insignificant things that are generally not taken seriously. In aligning one's self with what Allah likes, all these five important dimensions lead to self-affirmation and not to self-mortification and self-denial, which is often considered to be the culmination of spirituality and purity in several religions. In its fullest conception, *ʿibādah* thus becomes an expression of thankfulness to Allah for His favours and bounties, and concurrently an on-going remembrance (*dhikr*) of Allah while discharging one's personal, social, economic, political and cultural responsibilities. It also calls for solving new issues and problems through *ijtihād* in all walks of life.

There are three distinct features in Sayyid Mawdūdī's outstanding contribution to modern Islamic thought. Firstly, without breaking away from the tradition, he presents the message of the Qur'an and the Sunnah in a language that can be easily understood and grasped by an educated readership. Urdu religious literature in the twentieth century was full of Arabic and Persian phrases. Among so many others, Mawlānā Shiblī Nuʿmānī (1857–1914), Mawlānā Ashraf ʿAlī Thānawī (1863–1943) and Mawlānā Abul Kalām Āzād (1888–1958) were representative of this trend. Sayyid Mawdūdī departed from this literary tradition and developed his own style that could appeal to a new western-educated readership. His straightforward, logical and concise prose style made his writings absorbing and transformative, and he became a trendsetter in Urdu literature.

Secondly, Sayyid Mawdūdī avoids using the technical terminology of Islamic philosophical theology (*kalām*) and instead chooses examples from daily life to elaborate upon philosophical concepts. His immediate predecessors such as Mawlānā Shiblī and others addressed theological issues in this technical language and, as such, only the learned elite could easily follow and appreciate their writings. To the contrary, Sayyid Mawdūdī, addressed issues such as *tawḥīd*, *nabuwwah*, *al-Ākhirah*, *akhlāq* and *muʿāmalāt* in a simple language that an educated readership whom had not been exposed to the full *dār al-ʿulūm* curriculum could understand. This is perhaps one reason why his writings have been instrumental in inspiring a global Islamic reawakening from Indonesia to Tunis and from South Africa to North America.

Thirdly, Sayyid Mawdūdī's elaboration of the social dimension of *ʿibādah*, which has been discussed above, represents a departure from the traditional approach found in the jurisprudence of worship (*fiqh al-ʿibādah*), with its focus upon ritual or confining the significance of *ʿibādah* to self-purification only. Of course there is no doubt that *ʿibādah* is the encounter between the believer and his Lord. When performing the prayer (*ṣalāh*), the believer whispers and opens his or her heart to Allah Most Glorified and Exalted, supplicates and seeks forgiveness. Nevertheless, the transformative role of *ʿibādah* is also expressed in social life. Alongside the spiritual, moral and personal effects of *ʿibādah* upon a Muslim's life, Sayyid Mawdūdī highlights the social, economic and political dimensions of Islam. In so doing, he presents a holistic view of the Islamic system (*niẓām*) and a complete way of life with the full capacity to resolve emergent issues and problems that humankind encounters today and in the future.

Worship in Islam is a unique study of the dynamics of worship and spirituality in Islam. It is yet another outstanding publication as part of the well-received multivolume Essential Mawdūdī series of the Islamic Foundation, based in Leicestershire in the United Kingdom. Brother Ahmad Imam Shafaq Hashemi, himself a seasoned researcher, linguist and writer of standing, has done a commendable job by bringing together in an ably-translated and edited collection, Sayyid Mawdūdī's different writings on the true nature and significance of *ʿibādah* with special reference to *ṣalāh* and *ṣawm*. The material has been so selected and adapted by Brother Shafaq in consultation with Professor Khurshid Ahmad and myself. Part One of the book is based on the material selected and adapted from some of Sayyid Mawdūdī's important speeches: his address at the Karachi public meeting of Jamāʿat-i Islāmī on 13 November 1951, subsequently published as *Hidāyāt*, his concluding address at the Jamāʿat's last session in Pathankot, India on 21 April 1945, and relevant parts of his radio talk of 16 March 1948. The sources used for Part Two include: *Islāmī ʿIbādāt per ek Taḥqīqī Naẓar* and selections from *Towards Understanding Islam* (the English translation of the author's *Risālah Dīnīyāt*), *Let Us Be Muslims* (the English translation of *Khuṭbāt*), and *Tafhīm Aḥkām al-Qur'ān*, a compendium of the author's writings on the statutes and precepts of the holy Qur'an. Part Three is based on the material drawn from *Tafhīmāt* (vol. 2) and *Nashrī Taqrīren*, two popular collections of the author's articles and radio talks on different aspects of worship in Islam.

We are grateful to the Islamic Foundation, Markfield, Leicestershire, UK, the Institute of Policy Studies, Islamabad, the World of Islam Trust, Islamabad, and the Madina Trust, Peterborough, for their editorial, logistic and financial support for the Essential Mawdūdī series, which is expected to total either fifteen or sixteen volumes once it is completed, *inshā'Allāh*.

Wa ma tawfiqī illa bi'llāh, wa Allāhu aʿlamu bi al-thawāb

PART ONE

SPIRITUALITY AND THE ISLAMIC WAY OF LIFE

1 Islam and Man

Islam is *dīn* – a way of life and a complete code of conduct, unlike so many other religions. A religion is generally defined as the belief in the existence of God or gods and the activities that are connected with the worship of them. The sets of beliefs, rites and rituals that distinguish one religion from another have hardly any concern with man's worldly affairs and his life on the planet called Earth. Even the concepts related to the metaphysical world are virtually of no practical worth, and are much beyond the realm of reason and can lead to the traditional conflict between science and religion.

Islam is not a 'religion' in its conventional sense, but it is *the* religion. It is the religion of truth that upholds and promotes everything true and right and rejects and prevents everything false and wrong. It is *dīn al-fiṭrah*, the religion of nature that is in no conflict with the world of nature or science and offers guidance in all walks of life. It is the science that helps man understand his relationship with his Creator, his assigned role in this physical world of nature and the reward or punishment waiting for him in the Afterlife that he earns by the way he performs his role here. It is the religion to which each and every baby is born. Every newborn is thus a Muslim by birth until such time his parents and guardians convert him to Judaism, Christianity or idol-worship. The holy Prophet, may Allah bless him and give him peace, said:

عَن أبِي هُرَيره ﷺ عَنِ النَّبِيِّ ﷺ أنَّهُ قَال: كُلُّ مَولُودٍ يولَدُ عَلى الفِطرَةِ، أَبَوَاهُ يُهَوِّدَانِهِ أَوْيُنَصِّرانِهِ أو يُمَجِّسَانِهِ، كَمَثَلِ البَهِيمَةِ تُنتِجُ البَهِيمَةِ ، هَل تَرَىٰ فِيها جَدعَاء؟

> Abū Hurayrah narrated that the holy Prophet, may Allah bless him and give him peace, said: 'Every newborn child is born on the religion of nature [Islam]. His parents [and the environment around him] then turn him into a Jew, a Christian or a Magian [adherent of Mazdaism or Zoroastrianism], like the animal that always gives birth to an animal. Do you ever see his newborn offspring physically mutilated?
>
> (Bukhārī and Muslim)

1.1. Man's Relationship with God

Islam impresses upon humans the importance of their relationship with their Creator and how they must take due care of this relationship, because on its strength or weakness depends the success or failure of their life in this world and in the Hereafter. Islam does not deal with man in isolation but as a bondsman and slave (*ʿabd*) of his Lord, the Master, Creator, Sustainer and Dispenser of his destiny. It tells him that Allah Most Exalted alone is worthy of his worship (*ʿibādah*) and He is the sole authority to determine how His bondsman is to worship Him.

Islam is thus the way of life approved by the Lord. Any attempt to turn away from it is a rebellion against Allah, the Most Exalted and Glorified. It is a rebellion against our master and guide the Messenger of Allah as well, because it is only through him that humanity has rediscovered the lost way of happiness and bliss everlasting. No other way of life is now worthy of approval by the Lord:

وَمَن يَبْتَغِ غَيْرَ ٱلْإِسْلَـٰمِ دِينًا فَلَن يُقْبَلَ مِنْهُ وَهُوَ فِى ٱلْـَٔاخِرَةِ مِنَ ٱلْخَـٰسِرِينَ ﴿٨٥﴾

> *And whoever seeks a way other than this way of submission – Islam – will find that it will not be accepted from him and he will be among the losers in the Life to Come.*
>
> (*Āl ʿImrān* 3: 85)

Etymologically, the term 'Islam' comes from the root *s–l–m*. The root word *al-silm*, which is synonymous to Islam, means submission, peace, and safety. Islam may thus be defined as the religion that requires the human being to submit his entire self to the Will of God and thereby to ensure for himself a life of peace and safety in this world as well as in the Hereafter.

Islam is no doctrine or faith that emerged with a particular race, tribe or person. It is the religion, which was revealed by Allah Most Glorified and Exalted to all His Prophets from our master Adam to our master Muhammad, Allah's blessings and mercy be upon them all. Its sole objective has been to help mankind know right from wrong and virtue from vice and to facilitate everyone coming within its benign embrace to tread the path of true servitude to Allah Most High and thereby attain the happiness of this world and the eternal bliss of the Hereafter. Since no Prophet was to come after our master, the Messenger of Allah, the teachings and injunctions of Islam were meticulously preserved in the form of the holy Qur'an and its commentary the Tradition of the holy Prophet (Sunnah). Under Divine dispensation, humanity can follow so easily the religion of truth for all of its spiritual, moral, and material needs. Islam offers the Muslim man and woman, and society and state guidance in all spheres of life. Practical models of this guidance are available to mankind in the forms of Islamic social order, polity, governance and economy. These are all scientifically preserved and documented in the books of Qur'anic exegesis (*tafsīr*) Prophetic traditions (hadiths), biography and expeditions of the Messenger of Allah (Sīrah and *maghāzī*), and Islamic law and jurisprudence (*fiqh*).

Man has often been called a 'social animal'. Islam, however, elevates him to the status of a moral being so much distinct and different from all other creatures including the animals. The quality of being 'social' is not exclusive with man, for every living being is a social being that evolves its own social pattern, as may be seen even in the tiniest creatures like ants and bees. Man is viewed by Islam as the caliph of the Lord on earth and to be worthy of that exalted position he has to free himself first from all other bonds in favour of the true bondsmanship of the One and Only God,

1.2. Two Dimensions of Man's Personality

There are two dimensions of man's personality. These are different from each other and at the same time also interlinked. On the one hand, he has a physical and animal side of his existence, which is governed by the same physical laws of nature that govern the entire physical and animal world. The functioning of man's physical and animal existence is dependent, like other objects of nature, on material resources and the laws of nature, and is affected in its functioning adversely or favourably by the corresponding circumstances of the physical world.

The second dimension of man's personality is his moral side.[1] He is not just a physical being but a moral being too. Far from being dependent on the physical

---

[1] It is the moral aspect that distinguishes man from all other beings. Allah Most Exalted has instinctively endowed him with the capacity to differentiate between right and wrong, and between virtue and vice. This fundamental truth has been stated by the holy Qur'an thus:

وَنَفْسٍ وَمَا سَوَّىٰهَا ۝٧ فَأَلْهَمَهَا فُجُورَهَا وَتَقْوَىٰهَا ۝٨ قَدْ أَفْلَحَ مَن زَكَّىٰهَا ۝٩ وَقَدْ خَابَ مَن دَسَّىٰهَا ۝١٠

And by the soul and by Him Who perfectly proportioned it and imbued it with [the consciousness of] its evil and its piety. [The tendencies and inclinations towards good and evil are imbedded in man's nature and his subconscious is impregnated with the basic notions of good and evil.] He who purifies it [by consciously acting upon the dictates of his instinct] will prosper, and he who suppresses it [by siding with the forces of evil] will be ruined. (*al-Shams* 91: 7–10) — Editor.

laws of nature, the moral side of man's existence has the power to control and put to better use the physical side of his own personality and the world of nature in general. His basic tools in this respect are the moral and ethical faculties endowed upon him by the Almighty Lord.

Both physical and moral dimensions are at work within the personality of the human being, and his success or failure and rise or fall in life depend on both material as well as moral forces. As both these forces are at work in the human world, he cannot escape the consequences of his losing grip on one or both of them. In practical terms, however, the moral aspect of his personality plays a decisive role in his life much more than the material side.

1.3. Basic Human Ethics

The moral dimension of man also has two distinct parts: one of basic human ethics and the other of Islamic manners and morals. Basic human ethics mean the moral dimension that serves as the foundation for man's moral existence. Some essentials of basic human ethics are strength of willpower and the qualities of patience, forbearance, fortitude, courage, confidence, consistency, hard work, devotion to life objectives, correct vision, deep insight, sense of responsibility, the ability to make the right judgement at the right time, taking effective measures for the implementation of plans, keeping sentiments and emotions in check, and winning over the hearts of others.

Whoever is gifted with these basic human traits and attributes will reap the dividends regardless of whether he is a believer or an infidel, a Muslim or a Christian, cruel and tyrannical or a kind and courteous person.[2] A nation or society endowed with these qualities is similarly rich in human resources and is duly qualified to rise in the comity of nations by properly using its human assets. It is this aspect of basic human ethics to which the Messenger of Allah, may Allah bless him and give him peace, referred to when he told his Companions:

---

[2] Human history is witness to the fact that often too much cruelty and tyranny leads a suffering people towards an instinctive sense of revulsion and thereafter to revolt in search of a better life. The poet laureate of the world of Islam, Muhammad Iqbal, beautifully referred to this when he wrote:

Hay ʿayān fitnae Tātār ke afsāne se
Pāṣbān milgae Kaʿbah ko ṣanamkhāne se.

Evident from tales of strife of the Tatars and Mongols,
Is how caretakers rose for the Kaaba from the House of Idols. — Editor.

خِيارُهُم فِى الجَاهِلِيَّةِ خِيارُهُم فِى الإسلَام.

> The best of them during the pre-Islamic Days of Ignorance (*Jāhiliyyah*) is the best in [the glorious days of] Islam.
>
> (Bukhārī)

1.4. Basic Islamic ethics

Let us now turn to basic Islamic ethics. Islamic ethics are nothing apart from the essentials of human ethics but are their complementary and corrective side. What Islam has done is to give a correct focus and direction to basic human ethics. By virtue of that, all good human traits and attributes become absolutely beneficial to humanity and are not left merely as abstract moral qualities but become catalysts for virtue and moral uprightness. Human faculties are like a double-edged sword. The sword, whether in the hands of a robber or a righteous person, knows only how to cut the other side to pieces. Yet, when backed by moral force, the same sword acquires a distinct character. Thus, we see that the sword in the hands of a *mujāhid* and fighter against anti-human forces is quite different from its counterpart in the hands of a tyrant or a bandit.

For human resources to become the means of goodness it is essential that these are used in the way of good. The natural demand of Islam's message of *tawḥīd* is that the sole objective of all human efforts and endeavours in this worldly life is the attainment of Allah's pleasure. This is the commitment that a Muslim makes earnestly in all his prayers and supplications before the Lord. In *ṣalāt al-witr*, the last prayer before he goes to bed, he reaffirms this commitment thus:

اللّٰهُمَّ إيَّاكَ نَعبُدُ وَلَكَ نُصَلِّى وَ نَسجُدُ ، وَإلَيكِ نَسعٰى وَنَحفِدُ، وَ نَرجُورَحمَتَكَ، وَنَخشٰى عَذَابَكَ.

> O my Lord, You alone we worship; Only to You do we offer Prayer; before You alone we lie prostrate; You alone are the goal of all our quests and endeavours; we hope to receive Your mercy, and greatly dread Your punishment!

The second thing that Islam does in respect of human morals is to strengthen them and provide enlarged frontiers for their application. For example, let us take the attribute of patience and forbearance (*al-ṣabr*). Generally, even the most patient and forbearing person is unable to go beyond a certain level of patience, even if his material benefits are at stake. Yet when a believer has to face hardships and difficulties in the way of Allah and for the sake of His pleasure, he hardly gives in even in the most trying of times. We find, therefore, that a non-Muslim's patience is of limited nature, but the spiritual strength that Islam lends to a Muslim makes it a virtue encompassing all spheres of his life. It enables him to remain steadfast not only in the face of all kinds of dangers, problems and difficulties but it also helps him to hold his head high against all temptations, fears and dangers. For him, the gains of the Hereafter become the sole objective and it feels easier to him to lead a life of virtue and shun vice in all its forms.

Thirdly, Islam builds the superstructure of higher moral values on the foundations of basic human ethics such that a person can easily reach the heights of moral glory, personal respect and honour. It purifies his self of the dirt of selfishness, sycophancy, oppression, tyranny, immodesty, lewdness, profligacy and libertinism.

1.5. The Concept of Spirituality in Islam

Islam is the only way towards human emancipation and well-being, materially and spiritually. It not only transcends the dualism of matter and spirit, but is also the nucleus of an integrated and unified concept of life. In context of Islam's concept of spirituality, let us first note to what position it has elevated man.

1.5.1. Man as God's Deputy on Earth

Islam treats man as Allah's deputy on earth (*khalīfat Allāh fī al-arḍ*). To have a deeper insight into the concept of spirituality in Islam we need to have a correct understanding of this exalted position of man. As caliph or deputy of the Lord, man cannot take himself as an independent entity responsible to none but himself or his superiors and seniors in life. He is the caliph of Allah Most Glorified and Exalted and is as such answerable to Him for all his actions. Man is duty-bound to use all the powers vested in him and all the means placed at his disposal strictly in accordance with the Divine injunctions. For the sake of Allah's pleasure, he has to utilize to the fullest extent the faculties and potentials bestowed upon him. In his interactions with fellow humans he has to follow the path approved by the Lord. As a member of a social order, man is required to direct all his efforts and energies towards regulating its affairs in the way He would like them to be regulated.

The more admirably man performs his assigned role as Allah's deputy, the nearer he will be to Him. He always has to be motivated with a sense of responsibility, obedience, humility and allegiance, and with the objective of seeking His

Pleasure under all circumstances. Conversely, if he is motivated in his actions by self-interest, transgresses the right path, and is slothful and disobedient, he can never achieve nearness to the Lord, the Most-Beneficent, the Most-Merciful. Man's spiritual development in Islam means his nearness to God and his spiritual decline and decay signifies his distance from Him. This subject has been dealt with in greater detail in the next chapter.

1.5.2. *Body–Soul Conflict*

That the body and the soul are mutually antagonistic and in conflict with each other has traditionally remained a predominant concept in philosophy and metaphysics. The notion generally adopted by the 'spiritualists' has been that the body and soul cannot go together in life, and one can develop only at the cost of the other. The confines of the body and matter are viewed as the prison-house of the soul and the mundane activities of worldly life as the shackles with which the soul is kept in bondage and its growth is arrested. The concept has inevitably led to the well-known classification of the universe into the 'spiritual' and the 'secular'.

At the very outset, those who chose the secular path were convinced that the demands of spirituality could not be complied with and thus went headlong to an extremely narrow attitude to life marked by stark materialism and hedonism. Consequently, all spheres of worldly activity, be they social, political, economic, or cultural, were deprived of the light of spirituality and the world became full of injustice and tyranny.

On the other hand, those who wanted to tread the path of spiritual excellence invented exclusive ways and devices for the development and elevation of the spirit. This approach turned them virtually into a bunch of 'noble outcasts' in the world. They believed that it was impossible to find a normal process for spiritual growth in worldly life, and so deemed physical self-denial and mortification of the flesh necessary for developing and perfecting the spirit. The spiritual exercises and ascetic practices invented by them were intended to kill physical desires and render the body senseless, and even useless. In their view, forests, mountains and similar solitary places were ideal locations for spiritual development because in such hideouts the hustle and bustle of civilization would not interfere with their spiritual forays and navel-gazing meditations. They could not think of any better means of spiritual development other than withdrawal from the world and its affairs and severing all contacts with society and civilization.

This avowed conflict of body and soul resulted in the evolution of two different ideals for the perfection of man. One was the ideal of material perfection, which meant that man should have all the material comforts and bounties of the world and enjoy life as a 'social animal'. The result was that he did excel physically and materially, but the real 'man' in him could have no avenues for its flowering. Man learned to fly like birds, swim like crocodiles, run like horses and even terrorize and destroy those of his own species even worse than wolves and beasts. He could not learn, however, to live like a noble human being because he had no training to explore his moral worth or spiritual value.

The other ideal was of the perfection of spiritual life to an extent that the senses were not only subdued and conquered but supra-sensory powers were awakened in an attempt to do away with the limitations of the sensory world. With these forays into the realm of spirituality, the self-anointed 'saint' claimed to catch distant voices like a powerful wireless set, see remote objects as one does with the telescope, and develop powers through which he could heal the unhealed by the mere touch of his hand or the focus of his gaze.

1.5.3. *The Middle Road of Islam*

Between these two extremes, Islam leads us to the middle road of material progress as well as spiritual advancement. Islam elevates man as the caliph of Allah in the universe. He has vested man with certain authority, and has laid upon him certain responsibilities and obligations for the fulfillment of which God has endowed him with the best and most suitable physical frame, power and potential. The body has been created with the sole objective of enabling the soul to make use of it in the exercise of its authority and the fulfillment of its duties and responsibilities. Hence, the body is not a prison for the soul but its workshop, factory and power house. And if there is any possibility for the growth and development of the soul, it is only through the use of that power house and its essential tools and instruments. Hence, the physical world of nature is not a place of punishment for the human soul. Instead, it is a realm that God has put at man's disposal to display his worth as His true and sincere deputy and discharge the duty assigned to him by his Lord the Creator.

The immense potentialities and possibilities of this wide, vast world and the universe as a whole have been placed at man's disposal to discharge the obligations of his caliphate and deputyship of his Lord. His natural urge to grow and develop physically and materially has given rise to civilization, culture and society. Avenues have also been provided to him for his spiritual development. For this the Lord made special arrangements and deputed His chosen ones, the Prophets and Messengers, to guide humanity according to the message and mission revealed to them. Thus God has made the world a place of test and trial for man in which he is expected to give the best account of himself in all walks of life. Man is on trial here as an individual, as head of a family, as a neighbour, as a member of the society, as a worker at the factory, school, office, law courts or police stations, and as holder of the position of power and authority in parliament, the presidency, at a peace conference or on the battlefield. If he fails to attempt the exam questions given to him, or leaves part or most of the answer sheet blank, he is bound to fail in the examination. His success and failure in life depend entirely on how he performs in his test and in the way he attempts to answer the questions before him.

Islam does not approve of the way the ascetic lifestyle rejects the secular and materialistic approach. It has laid down a set of modes and processes for the spiritual development of man, not away from this world but very much within it. Everyone has to pass through the rough and tumble of life. According to Islam, the real place for the growth and elevation of the human spirit lies right in the midstream of life, with its ups and downs, and not in solitary places of spiritual hibernation.[3]

[3] Instead of encouraging asceticism and monasticism, Islam has forbidden such modes of life as these are neither of use to the individual human being nor to humanity in general. Islam does not approve of the institutions of papacy and theocracy as it does not divide religion and state. Individually and collectively, every Muslim is duty-bound to acquire knowledge of the basics of his religion and Islamic manners and morals. He is accountable before his Lord for his role as a true Muslim and as an effective member of the Islamic social order. — Editor.

2 The Spiritual System of Islam

The cornerstone of spirituality in Islam is proximity to the One and Only God, the Lord who is our Creator, Sustainer and Dispenser of our destinies. This proximity can be achieved only by our firm faith in oneness and uniqueness of God (*tawḥīd*) and and the finality of the prophethood of our guide and master the Messenger of Allah (*risālah*). This is the first of the five pillars (*arkān*; its singular is *rukn*) of Islam's grand structure. The remaining four are the obligatory prayer (*ṣalāh*), obligatory fasting (*ṣawm*); obligatory charity (*zakāh*); and pilgrimage to the House of God (hajj). These five fundamentals of Islam are then to be translated into action by the believer's active participation in the Islamic system of worship (*ʿibādah*), the details of which are dealt with below.

No worship worthy of its name in Islam is without sincere devotion to God. No ethics and morality are worth anything unless backed by fear of Allah. And no social activity is truly blessed unless conducted with His pleasure in view. The reason is obvious. Whatever one does, whether it concerns worldly affairs or religion, the motivating force behind that is always the objective one has in mind. The more one is keen and sincere about one's objective, the more one is concerned and active to achieve that. A person moved to work exclusively in his own self-interest will naturally be selfish and devoted entirely to the dictates of his self. The intensity of self-love determines the intensity of his craze for self-gratification. We often notice that those passionately in love with their children often cross all limits of ethics and decency for their sake. They sacrifice their comforts and peace of mind and do not bother even to barter away the everlasting bliss of the Hereafter for few temporary gains. Motivated by patriotic spirit, a person may similarly not consider any sacrifice too great for his country and nation.

By the same analogy, we can easily understand how important it is in matters of faith to keep our ties with Allah Most Exalted not only intact but extremely firm and strong. We must always be impelled by the urge to keep our ties with the Lord as strong as possible and let no earthly or mundane considerations weaken it. It is imperative, therefore, to clearly understand what it means to be close to Allah and how to achieve that cherished goal.

2.1. The Meaning of Being Close to God

The Most Glorified Lord has explained to us how can we achieve nearness to Him. The Qur'an says:

قُلْ إِنَّ صَلَاتِى وَنُسُكِى وَمَحْيَاىَ وَمَمَاتِى لِلَّهِ رَبِّ ٱلْعَٰلَمِينَ ﴿١٦٢﴾ لَا شَرِيكَ لَهُۥ ۖ وَبِذَٰلِكَ أُمِرْتُ وَأَنَا۠
أَوَّلُ ٱلْمُسْلِمِينَ ﴿١٦٣﴾

Say: 'Surely my Prayer, my service of sacrifice and all worship rituals, and my living and my dying are only for Allah, the Lord of the whole Universe. He has no associate. Thus have I been bidden, and I am the foremost of those who submit themselves [to Allah].'

(*al-An'ām* 6: 162–163)

Through the Prophet, may Allah bless him and give him peace, all followers of the religion of truth have been practically guided on how to be true Muslims. We have been told that all our acts of worship must transform our way of life and nothing should be as important to us as our total submission to the dictates of the Almighty. God has no associates or partners in His domain and hence whatever we do as Muslims from the age of adolescence until our death must necessarily be in conformity with His injunctions. This is a way of life of which our master the Messenger of Allah, may Allah bless him and give him peace, is the perfect practical example, and his illustrious Companions stand out as glorious models. Accordingly, we are required to devote our entire lives in service of the Lord and live the way He has asked us to live. This is the right path that He has always commanded human beings to follow:

وَمَآ أُمِرُوٓا۟ إِلَّا لِيَعْبُدُوا۟ ٱللَّهَ مُخْلِصِينَ لَهُ ٱلدِّينَ حُنَفَآءَ وَيُقِيمُوا۟ ٱلصَّلَوٰةَ وَيُؤْتُوا۟ ٱلزَّكَوٰةَ ۚ وَذَٰلِكَ دِينُ ٱلْقَيِّمَةِ ﴿٥﴾

And they have been commanded no more than this: to worship Allah, devoting themselves exclusively to Him; to establish regular Prayer; and to practice regular Charity. That is the Right Faith.

(*al-Bayyinah* 98: 5)

The holy Prophet, may Allah bless him and give him peace, explained so elaborately through his words and actions the meaning of being close to Allah Most Exalted. From the teachings of the Qur'an and the Sunnah, it is quite easy to understand properly the import of man's ties with his Creator and the need to devote his entire life to Him and live the way He has asked him to live. A Muslim is required to seek Allah's pleasure under all circumstances, even by displeasing everyone else. He should love others for Allah's sake and hate others for His sake; he should give to others to the best of his capability as desired by Him; and withhold from giving where he has been forbidden to be generous. This is exactly what the , may Allah bless him and give him peace, told us in the well-known hadith:

عَن أبِى أُمَامَة البَاهِلِى ﷺ عَن رَسُولِ الله ﷺ أنَّهُ قَالَ: مَن أَحَبَّ لله وَأبغَضَ لله وَأعطىٰ لله وَ مَنَعَ لله فَقَدِ استَكمَلَ الا يمَانَ.

Abū Umāmah al-Bāhilī narrated that the Messenger of Allah said: 'He who loved for Allah's sake, displayed hatred for Allah's sake, gave something [to others] for Allah's sake, and withheld for Allah's sake, he has definitely perfected his faith (*īmān*).'

(Abū Dāwūd)

2.2. Strengthening of One's Bond with God

Every Muslim is first and foremost a bondsman and slave (*ʿabd*) of his Lord and Master.[1] As His slaves, our primary concern must always be to know how to take Him in all earnestness and with the inner core of our hearts as our Master, the Lord of the Universe, the only Deity worthy of *ʿibādah*, and the Supreme Authority to Whom belongs the ultimate power and dispensation of everything that we have or may have in future. We are also to be firm in our belief that none is a partner or associate in His attributes or authority.

A person can achieve strength of ties with his Lord in two ways: firstly, through correct understanding of his status as Allah's slave and then secondly by practically acting upon the teachings of the Qur'an and the Sunnah. In order to have proper insight into this relationship with our Lord, we need to have the correct understanding of the injunctions of the Book of God and the Tradition of our master the Messenger of God. For this, we must carefully and constantly study the Qur'an and the Sunnah and in light of their teachings evaluate our status and see how far we qualify for proximity to our Lord and what are the shortcomings we must overcome to come up to the desired level.[2]

---

[1] From the same root *ʿ–b–d* we have the word *ʿibādah*. — Editor.

[2] It is imperative for us to have basic knowledge of the Qur'an and the Sunnah, for if we do not we will remain Muslims in name only with no direct access to the teachings of our religion. The Lord has made the Qur'an easy to understand. It has been made easier through the hadiths to follow and practise the teachings of Islam. We are not expected to be scholars of the Islamic sciences, but only to be in constant touch with the Book of God and the Prophetic Traditions for our proper guidance. This can be done easily either directly through standard translations or by way of regular contact with well-known and reputed religious scholars (*ʿulamāʾ*). — Editor.

To elaborate this further, let us see the various dimensions of our relationship with our Most Glorious Lord. First and foremost is the relationship that we have with Him as His slaves and He as our Master and Only Deity. Secondly, as His deputies on earth He has bestowed on us so many bounties, which include the qualities of head and heart, physical powers and potentials, and immense human and material resources. Thirdly, by pronouncing our faith and fealty to Him we have executed a deal with our Lord, Master and Sustainer, and have accordingly sold out our lives and worldly gains to Him in return for the promised reward of eternal bliss of the Hereafter. The fourth aspect of our relationship with the Lord is that we are answerable to Him for all our deeds and misdeeds. He has the complete record of our lives, even of our motivations and emotions. There are other dimensions too of our ties with Him and we always have to be mindful and keen not only to keep them firm but to strengthen them further.

2.3. The Practical Way to Achieve Nearness to God

The quality of close proximity to Allah Most Glorified and Exalted is not something that can be achieved easily. While drawing sustenance from faith, our relationship with the Lord needs reaffirmation and support through some practical means which the Most-Beneficent Lord has Himself taught His bondsmen. Let us make a brief overview of that.

Īmān: From the root word *al-amn*, which means safety, security and protection, *īmān* literally means security and protection from everything repugnant to faith. As a Qur'anic term, *īmān* signifies firm faith in the oneness and uniqueness of God (*tawḥīd*) and the finality of the prophethood of our master the Messenger of Allah (*risālah*). The firmness of our *īmān* is the starting point of our journey to nearness to Allah (*taqarrub ilā Allāh*). It requires us to have the unshakable belief that we are bondsmen of Allah and members of the nation of Islam (*ummah*), raised by our master the Messenger of Allah, and as such we must sincerely and honestly obey the dictates of the Qur'an and the Sunnah and do as our Lord has directed us to do and shun everything He has asked us not to do. To sincerely obey Him means to faithfully discharge the duties enjoined by Him, not because of any material or worldly considerations, but solely in obedience to His command. Whatever we do must be done for His pleasure alone, and always keeping His displeasure in mind we must also stop doing, both openly and secretively, everything that has been disapproved of by the Lord.

Islām: Islām is the practical manifestation of *īmān*. It represents the outward physical and moral contours of a Muslim, while *īmān* gives it the spiritual depth that serves as its foundation. The strength or weakness of this foundation actually signifies a believer's capacity of being safe and well-guarded against unbelief and everything liable to cause Allah's displeasure. The term *muslim* (plural, *muslimūn*) is the active participle from *islām*, while, *mu'min* (plural, *mu'minūn*) is the active participle from *īmān*, meaning the believer, the faithful one.

The relationship between *īmān* and *islām* can also be explained by the analogy of the seed and the tree. *Īmān* is like the seed and *islām* the tree. The quality of the seed determines the physical growth of a tree. Just as no plant can grow without a seed, similarly it is not possible for a seed sown in fertile soil not to bloom in the form of a tree. *Īmān* and *islām* are similarly integral to each other. The heart that throbs with *īmān* will naturally result in its physical manifestation in the shape of a Muslim's way of life, his manners and morals, his social relationships, his devotion to everything Islamic, and his distance from everything repugnant to Islam and the Islamic way of life. It is virtually impossible for *īmān* to be rooted firmly within the self of a believer yet its impact not be manifest externally.

Taqwā: The firmness of *īmān* and strength of *islām* leads a believer to the next stage of *taqwā*. From the root word *al-waqy* meaning protection and safeguard, the Qur'anic term *taqwā* literally means the protection of the self from the temptations of vice. As a term, it denotes qualities of immense piety, uprightness and virtue. *Taqwā* is the state when a believer becomes the embodiment of love and fear of his Lord, when all his actions are motivated by his sense of bondsmanship, when he is always mindful of his accountability to the Almighty, and is conscious of the fact that he is on trial in this world for all his acts and deeds and that his success depends entirely on the way he discharges his obligations and uses his God-given potentials and capabilities in a manner approved of by the Lord. A true *muttaqī* (the active participle from *taqwā*) is he who is inspired also to use his potential in service of Allah's subjects, those in his responsibility, and in furtherance of the cause of right and virtue and in prevention of everything wrong and un-Islamic.

Iḥsān: From *taqwā*, a believer can move forward on the road of spiritual progress to the next stage of *iḥsān*. From the root *ḥ–s–n*, the noun *ḥusn* means beauty, loveliness and excellence. The Qur'anic term *iḥsān* stands for the sublime quality of one's selfless and sincere devotion and dedication to every right cause. To achieve the noble position of *iḥsān*, one is to stand steadfast in the way of Allah and never to be found lagging behind in jihad against the forces of evil. A *muḥsin* (or one endowed with the quality of *iḥsān*) never feels self-elated because he is engaged in something extraordinary or obliging someone by his noble acts. Instead, he always feels grateful to the Lord for granting him the courage, capability and opportunity to bear the hardships of this struggle.

Such a noble person is always ready for the greatest of sacrifice required of him in the way of Allah.

The qualities of *taqwā* and *iḥsān* are virtually the apex of *īmān* and *islām*. Nonetheless, it may be added that these sublime qualities do not absolve us of our responsibility to demonstrate practically their vitality by observing regularly the duties enjoined on us as Muslims. The Most Beneficent Lord has Himself taught us, therefore, some practical means that inculcate within us the qualities of allegiance and devotion to His cause, His love and fear, and the firmness to stand upright in His way through thick and thin. Prescribed to demonstrate our firmness as *mu'min* and *muslim*, these practical means may be summed up in paragraphs that follow.

2.3.1. *Prayer* (Ṣalāh)

The regular prayers are mandatory (*farḍ*) for every Muslim, which he has to offer five times a day. The best way to keep our ties with the Lord intact and promote them further is to observe not only the obligatory prayers but also the supplementary ones (*sunan*), those offered regularly by our master the Messenger of Allah, and also the supererogatory (*nawāfil*, singular *nafl*) prayers, which the Prophet, may Allah bless him and give him peace, also offered. All the three categories of prayer, namely the obligatory, supplementary and supererogatory ones, are the best way to seek Allah's pleasure and be close to Him. The only difference in how to offer these prayers is that while the obligatory prayer is offered with the congregation in its appointed time, it is better for the supplementary and supererogatory ones to be offered at home to avoid the aspect of showing off and also to attain an air of devotion and perfect peace of mind in an isolated corner of one's residence.

At the end of the day and before we go to bed, we have to perform *ṣalāt al-witr* after the obligatory prayer of 'Ishā'. The last of the three-cycle *witr* prayer (called *witr* because of the odd number of cycles or *rak'āt*) has a supplication that the one offering prayer (*muṣallī*) is to submit in all humility to his Lord.[3] This is called the supplication of subservience (*du'ā' al-qunūt*), and is a covenant reaffirming our humility, devotion and bondsmanship to Allah Most Glorified and Exalted. Let us go carefully through this covenant and ponder over its meanings:

---

[3] From the root *r–k–'*, meaning to bend and bow, the term *al-rak'ah* (plural, *rak'āt*) denotes the act of bending the torso (*rukū'*) by the one offering prayer from the upright position (*al-qiyām*), followed by two prostrations (*al-sajdatayn*, singular *al-sajdah*, plural *sujūd*). — Editor.

اَللّٰهُمَّ اَنَّا نستَعِينُكَ، وَنَستَغفِرُكَ، وَنَستَهدِيكَ، وَنُوءمِنُ بِكَ، وَنَتَوَكَّلُ عَلَيكَ، وَنُثنِى عَلَيكَ الخَيرَ كُلّه، وَنَشكُرُكَ، وَلَانَكفُرُكَ، وَنَخلَعُ وَنَترُكُ مَن يفجُرُك. اَللّٰهُمَّ اَياكَ نَعبُدُ وَلَكَ نُصَلِّى وَنَسجُدُ، وَاِلَيكَ نَسعٰى وَنَحفِدُ، وَنَرجُو رَحمَتَكَ، وَنَخشٰى عَذَابَكَ. اِنَّ عَذَابَكَ الجِدَّ بِالكُفَّارِ مُلحِقّ.

O my Lord, we seek help from You. We seek pardon for our sins, and we seek Your guidance. We have faith in You, we put our trust in You, and we lavish the best of praise on You. We are grateful to You, and we will never be ungrateful to You. We sever all ties and leave everyone who disobeys You. My Lord, we worship You alone: we pray only to You, and we prostrate before You alone. You alone are the goal of all our quests and endeavours: we hope to receive Your mercy, and dread very much Your punishment! Without doubt, Your great punishment will engulf those who are unbelievers.

Of all the supererogatory prayers, the night prayer (*ṣalāt al-tahajjud*) that one offers before rising for the obligatory pre-dawn prayer (*ṣalāt al-fajr*), is the most auspicious one for nearness to Allah Most Exalted. The holy Prophet, may Allah bless him and give him peace, never missed the night prayer and ever since it has remained the most coveted supererogatory prayer for the believers. The spirit of deep devotion and subservience to the Lord that is reflected in the supplication that our master the Messenger of Allah used to recite while preparing for the night prayer is quite similar to what we just saw in the *du'ā' al-qunūt*:

اَللُهمَّ لَكَ أسلَمتُ وَبِكَ اٰمَنتُ وَعَلَيكَ تَوَكَّلتُ وَإلَيكَ أَنبتُ وَبِكَ خَاصَمتُ وَإلَيكَ حَاكَمتُ.

O my Lord, I submit in all humility to You. I have absolute faith in You, and in You I repose my confidence. I turn to You for reprieve: I have quarreled only for Your Cause; and I always submit my case (for justice) to Your Lordship.

2.3.2. *Remembrance of God* (Dhikr Allāh)

Literally meaning the remembrance of Allah, informally *dhikr Allāh* is the act of constantly keeping our heart, mind and tongue engaged in the remembrance of our Lord, the Most Beneficent, the Most Merciful. Formally, however, the best way of His *dhikr* is by way of supplication, conducted by invoking His sacred name and attributes and offering prayers, as taught to us by our master the Messenger of Allah, may Allah bless him and give him peace. That is another way of rejuvenating our ties with the Lord. Islam does not want us to leave aside the world and our duties towards Allah's subjects and engage ourselves exclusively in a certain mode, which the mystics (or Sufis) evolved later on. The best course is to remember Allah Most Exalted by His name and attributes and sincerely pray for His blessings. If one has learnt by heart the supplications offered by the holy Prophet, may Allah bless him and give him peace, and is aware of their meanings, these are definitely the best way of invoking His mercy. Otherwise, one can supplicate in his native tongue as well. The state of *dhikr* also means absolute devotion, dedication and peace of mind and heart in order to make one's invocation more effective.

2.3.3. *Fasting* (Ṣawm)

Fasting in the month of Ramadan is obligatory for every adult Muslim. During the whole month, he has to reorganize his daily schedule in a manner so as to prioritize his acts of sincere devotion to his Lord over and above everything else. In addition to the obligatory prayers, after 'Ishā' he has to offer *ṣalāt al-tarāwīḥ* in congregation, which is the additional prayer devoted to the complete recitation of the holy Qur'an in a phased manner. From dawn to dusk, his daily routine is so reorganized that it offers him the best roadmap for self-restraint, piety, remembrance of his Lord, and inculcating within himself the spirit of *taqwā* and *iḥsān.*

In addition to the obligatory fast, we have also been taught to observe the supererogatory fasts as many times as we can, drawing inspiration from the way practised by our beloved Prophet, may Allah bless him and give him peace. There can be nothing more effective as a means of strengthening our ties with our Lord the Creator than fasting, both obligatory and supererogatory.

2.3.4. *Obligatory and Voluntary Charity (*Zakāh *and* Ṣadaqāt*)*

To spend whatever one can afford in the Way of Allah is the best form of monetary worship (*'ibādah*). In the Islamic lexicon, this monetary form of worship is called spending in the way of Allah (*infāq fī sabīl Allāh*). While *infāq* is generally voluntary spending, a particular amount of obligatory charity that the believer has to pay once a year is called *zakāh.* It is the third obligatory duty, after *ṣalāh* and *ṣawm,* and the fourth pillar (*rukn*) of Islam. For *zakāh,* a believer's assets must be above a certain specified limit. Additionally, he is also encouraged to spend in the way of Allah any amount he can easily afford to promote His cause. These donations are called *ṣadaqāt* and are voluntary acts of financial charity. The money that a bondsman of Allah contributes thus towards the welfare needs of society, such as feeding the needy even at the cost of his personal necessities, or providing financial help to the deserving even by curtailing his own expenses, becomes yet another source of Allah's pleasure, His mercy and blessings.

2.3.5. *Pilgrimage to the House of God (Hajj)*

Hajj is the fifth pillar of Islam and is obligatory once in a lifetime for the believer who is financially and physically able to undertake the journey. In a way, it is the biggest of all acts of worship because none can embark on such an arduous journey and spend so much unless he really loves Allah and is eager to reach the closest point of his proximity to Him.

These are the prescribed means to bring one closer to God. By observing them, we can achieve nearness to Allah Most Exalted without undergoing any arduous regime of ascetic exercises or monastic practices. That is how we can gain proximity and further strengthen our ties of bondsmanship with our Lord even while leading a normal social life, discharging our obligations towards our family, friends, society and the state, and performing our daily chores undisturbed.

2.4. Accountability in the Hereafter

The last and the most vital aspect of a believer's quest for nearness to the All-Merciful Lord is his belief in the Day of Reckoning and accountability in the Hereafter. The concept that each one of us is to account for whatever good or bad we may have done in his worldly life is an essential part of our faith as Muslims. It must always be the guiding force of our lives as individuals as well as members of the Islamic community and the nation of Islam; this is the concept that must determine the course of all our actions.

The Book of God repeatedly tells us that this world of ours is a temporary abode and we are here on trial to prove our worth physically, materially and spiritually, whereas the place of eternal bliss is the Hereafter. It has warned us also against losing sight of this crucial fact:

بَلْ تُؤْثِرُونَ ٱلْحَيَوٰةَ ٱلدُّنْيَا ۝ وَٱلْـَٔاخِرَةُ خَيْرٌ وَأَبْقَىٰٓ ۝

No, but you prefer the life of this world, whereas the Hereafter is better and everlasting.

(*al-Aʿlā* 87: 16–17)

The limited powers, resources and time at our disposal in this world are only to test as to whom amongst us will prove worthy of these gifts from God and how we use them to make ourselves and our nearest and dearest ones eligible for the eternal life of Paradise. We are on trial here not to show our expertise in the field of agriculture, our potential in the realms of trade and industry, science and technology, governance and empire-building, or progress in the sphere of civilization and culture.[4] We are on trial here solely to prove our worth as deputies to our Lord, the Creator, Who has entrusted us with immense capabilities as His caliphs in the land and would like us to show how fit and trustworthy we have been in discharging our assigned role and responsibilities in that capacity.

Each one of us is thus required to prove practically whether we have led our lives independently of our obligations to our Lord, the Master of the Day of Judgement, and remained wayward in our actions and attitudes to life, or been subservient to His authority and perfect in obedience and allegiance to Him. Have we fulfilled His Will and did what we were directed to do, or continued to treat as supreme the will and dictates of the self and those of our worldly masters? Did we try to make this world of our Lord develop and flourish according to the standards and parameters set by Him, or mishandled and mutilated its inherent beauty and charm by our willful actions in the interests of the self and our earthly lords? Did we remain firm and unwavering in the unending conflict with satanic forces or succumb to the temptations of temporary worldly gain?

These are some of the crucial questions in light of which those to be selected from the human world for eternal bliss in the Hereafter are to undergo a series of tests and trials. Hence, it hardly matters if the one on trial has been tested under a royal canopy seated on a gorgeous throne or is strung up by the hangman's noose. Nor is it of the least significance if someone has been tried by entrusting him with the rule of a big empire or by confining his life needs to a small hut. If the time passed in this house of trial was good and the circumstances favourable, it does not lead necessarily to success and well-being in the Eternal Abode. Neither the hardships nor failures of this life are in any measure indicators of failure and loss in the Life Hereafter.

[4] It would be too naïve and simplistic to misconstrue the author as negating here the importance of material progress, academic excellence, and scientific and technological advancement. He is actually explaining the need for our material growth and advancement not to be at the cost of our spiritual development. Our priorities must be well-defined in accordance with the dictates of our Lord to help us achieve happiness in this world and in the eternal bliss of the Hereafter. — Editor.

What is needed of us as bondsmen of Allah Most Glorified and Exalted is to carry out wholeheartedly and sincerely whatever task has been entrusted to us here and in whatever capacity as His true and loyal subjects. This is a quality that is not easy to attain and needs conscious effort, both individually and collectively, to keep our ties with our Supreme Lord strong and to keep ourselves engaged in welfare of society and the state.

2.5. Measuring the Strength of Spiritual Ties with God

Finally, let us see how we can measure this extremely crucial relationship of ours with our Lord, the Master, Creator and Sustainer, and how we can know if this relationship is getting stronger or weaker. Do we need any extraneous means for this, like the blessing of a saint, glad tidings in the form of a dream, or an extraordinary mystical experience? Let us be reassured that we need none of these artificial means, since the Lord has very kindly placed a barometer within ourselves in the form of our conscience. We can assess and check daily where we stand in our relationship with the Almighty. For this, we have to review constantly our daily routines, efforts, passions and emotions. This process of self-evaluation and personal accountability will always tell us whether we have progressed or faltered. We can easily check if we have been true to the deal we have made with our supreme Lord, and how much of our time, energy, resources and potential have been consumed in matters concerning Him and how much has been expended in furthering our own ends.

Through such a process of self-appraisal we can easily measure our feelings of satisfaction and happiness over everything we may have done to strengthen our spiritual bonds, and cultivate a sense of anger and revolt over actions that invite Allah's displeasure and wrath. This is the essence of our faith in *tawḥīd* and *risālah* and that is how we can reassure ourselves of the strength of our ties with our Lord and the firmness of *īmān* in our Lord, His Last Prophet, may Allah bless him and give him peace, His Angels, the Books He revealed to His prophets for humanity's guidance, of which the holy Qur'an is the final revelation, and the Day of Reckoning.

This is the way to prepare ourselves to live successful lives as true Muslims, eligible for Allah's blessings and mercy in this world and the Hereafter. There can be no glad tidings greater for a believer than the assurance given to him by the All-Merciful Lord of his being entitled to the reward of Paradise for being steadfast in the way of Allah:

إِنَّ ٱلَّذِينَ قَالُوا۟ رَبُّنَا ٱللَّهُ ثُمَّ ٱسْتَقَـٰمُوا۟ تَتَنَزَّلُ عَلَيْهِمُ ٱلْمَلَـٰٓئِكَةُ أَلَّا تَخَافُوا۟ وَلَا تَحْزَنُوا۟ وَأَبْشِرُوا۟ بِٱلْجَنَّةِ ٱلَّتِى
كُنتُمْ تُوعَدُونَ ﴿٣٠﴾ نَحْنُ أَوْلِيَآؤُكُمْ فِى ٱلْحَيَوٰةِ ٱلدُّنْيَا وَفِى ٱلْـَٔاخِرَةِ ۖ وَلَكُمْ فِيهَا مَا تَشْتَهِىٓ أَنفُسُكُمْ
وَلَكُمْ فِيهَا مَا تَدَّعُونَ ﴿٣١﴾ نُزُلًا مِّنْ غَفُورٍ رَّحِيمٍ ﴿٣٢﴾

Those who say 'Allah is our Lord' and then remain steadfast, upon them descend angels (and say): 'Do not fear nor grieve, and receive good tidings of Paradise which you were promised. We are your companions in this world and in the Hereafter. There you shall have all that you desire and all what you will ask for. This is by way of hospitality from Him Who is Most Forgiving, Most Merciful.'

(*Ḥā Mīm al-Sajdah* 41: 30–32)

3 Islamic Social Order – The Catalyst for a New World System

Today the world is caught in a quagmire of civilizational and moral crisis. Human civilization, culture, economy and politics are in absolute disruption and decline. Oppression and tyranny are ruling the roost, while human manners and morals are generally in total disarray. The achievements of scientific and technological progress are being used increasingly not for the welfare of man but for his destruction and doom. When we examine the situation carefully, the main reason for this sad state of affairs becomes crystal clear. We come to the conclusion that though there is no dearth of honest, sincere and morally upright people, the world's material resources, governance and leadership are concentrated entirely in the hands of those who are morally bankrupt and spiritually impoverished. Materially, they may be prosperous but morally they are very poor. They may not be atheists and infidels but their relationship with God is just a formality. They keep the Church and the priesthood financially and politically satisfied, but have neither the insight nor the capability or concern to see the writ of the Lord made supreme in human affairs.

How to tackle this general disorder? This is the biggest and most crucial question facing individuals, societies and states today. The answer may not be quite so simple but the objective of global change is not too difficult to achieve either. Let us now explore this in the following paragraphs.

3.1. Human Society and Its Leadership

Human society's all-round progress and well-being depend on two most crucial factors: (1) the principles that govern its affairs; and (2) the quality of its leadership, especially from moral and spiritual standpoints. If the principles that govern the affairs of a community and nation are materialistically oriented, and its leadership is similarly least concerned with man's moral and spiritual well-being, then the result is bound to be the same as we are witnessing today all over the world. Unless and until there is proper care taken, and arrangements made to see good prosper and evil perish and to spread virtue and curb vice, no human society can be strong and welfare-oriented, no matter how prosperous and flourishing it might appear to be materially.

On the other hand, a morally strong community cannot retain its moral strength both unless and until it has entrusted its leadership to those who are morally upright and spiritually strong. The social order that evolves under the leadership of God-fearing and upright personalities will naturally promote good and eliminate evil. Even those who are morally not so good will be encouraged and inspired to follow the path of virtue and shun vice. Conversely, if the leadership of a community that is otherwise good slips into the hands of the rebels against God, the profligate and the libertines, then the moral and spiritual goodness found in that community or nation will gradually evaporate, giving way to moral corruption and social disorder. A nation led by a morally corrupt and practically godless individual or group will be a bastion for vice and a barricade to virtue. It will be very easy for a person in such a society and community to follow the course of vice and extremely difficult to tread the right course.

3.2. Islamic Social Order and Its Leadership

It is evident from our discussion so far that Islam enables a total change in an individual's lifestyle and mindset. When a Muslim attains the position of *iḥsān*, his every act becomes an act of worship. Even in a lesser degree he is expected to be fearful of Allah Most Exalted and love Him so much that the spirit of *taqwā* never lets him go astray. The qualities of *īmān*, *islām*, *taqwā* and *iḥsān* change the Muslim both from within and from without.

There are, however, some most crucial questions that arise here. How can such an upright Muslim save himself from the impact of his not-so-healthy surroundings? Can he remain untainted by the filth of immorality around him? Should he rest content with his personal virtue and the efforts he also makes to keep his household an abode of virtue? The obvious answer is that his piety and righteousness cannot remain unaffected by the environment he lives in. Hence, it follows that he cannot tread the path of *taqwā* and *iḥsān* unless he goes further, to join hands with the forces of virtue in the society of which he is a member. But how can he do that? Let us examine this in the following paragraphs.

3.2.1. *The Party of Islam and the Struggle for Islamic Social Order*

In his capacity as the deputy and bondsman of his Lord, a believer cannot afford to live an isolated life away from his social environment. First and foremost among his social obligations is to be good himself and a true slave of his All-Merciful Lord, to raise his family according to the life-pattern enjoined by the Qur'an and the Sunnah, and to then join hands with everyone good and upright like him in society to form a group of the true bondsmen of Allah. Such a group of well-meaning righteous people are needed to weave themselves into a larger social set-up of spiritually-motivated men and women, young and old, to emerge as the party of Islam (*al-jamāʿah al-islāmiyyah*). Only through such an effective arrangement can they keep Muslim society on the right track.

When moral values permeate the personal, private and public lives of individuals, the community throbs with noble souls dedicated to the cause of right, and its collective conscience helps in promoting virtue and preventing vice. By joining hands and forming an organizational force of collective goodness in the shape of the party of Islam, the forces of virtue emerge as the community's core group and as standard bearers of spirituality and moral uprightness. The party soon becomes the bulwark against forces of evil, both within and outside of society. It provides an effective platform for the propagation of the message and mission of Islam and practically makes the writ of religion supreme in all walks of life. Howsoever meager its moral and human resources might be, such an organized force eventually succeeds, with the guidance of its dedicated and dynamic leadership, in its struggle to establish an Islamic social order and makes the Divine law of the Sharīʿah the law of the land.

The leadership of the party of Islam essentially has to be in the hands of an outstanding personality who is duly qualified morally, spiritually and intellectually to be the leader (imam) of an organized force of goodness and virtue. The revolutionary change Islam seeks to bring in society and the nation to create a sublime social order based on the injunctions of the Qur'an and the Sunnah is not possible unless such a party is firmly established under the leadership of the most upright and sagacious leader, who is elected by the votes of its members for a fixed term. The imam of the party of Islam is thus required to be a leader who is endowed with the qualities of *taqwā* and *iḥsān*: he should have an impeccable character, be trustworthy and truthful, and be intellectually farsighted.

Under its dynamic leadership, the party of Islam is also required to keep itself equipped with the necessary material resources, in addition to both drawing upon and strengthening the moral resources of society and the state. Only such an organized force and leadership can stand up as the guardian of Islamic manners and morals and as a strong bulwark against the forces of social disruption and moral decay. Duly led by such a force, no Muslim society and state can ever lose their grip on the currents and crosscurrents of events: they are bound to emerge naturally with dignity in all moments of trial and tribulation.

The Divine pattern (*Sunnat Allāh*) has always been to make the morally upright, physically fit and materially strong nation of believers in Allah supreme in all spheres of life, provided that it is solid as a rock under the banner of Islam and the party of Islam. These are the fortunate ones the Supreme Lord has raised as His deputies in the land for the leadership and guidance of its people. History bears witness to the fact that the nation of Islam, both as society and state, had always been victorious against overwhelming odds so long as it was governed and guided by morally upright and spiritually strong leaders. Conversely, when it became morally weak and leaderless and the party of Islam became directionless, it lost its strength, even in the bastions of its political power and prestige and despite all its material strength.

Therefore, the institution of leadership or imamate is of crucial importance to the Islamic polity and Islamic social order. The basic objective of an Islamic leadership is to free human beings from being slaves of the slaves of Allah and to bring them back into the fold of Allah's slavery and bondsmanship. It is essential, therefore, for the party of Islam and the nation of Islam to have a leader who is duly qualified to rule the land and keep the writ of the Lord supreme in every walk of life.[1]

---

[1] The nation of Islam has been described by Allah Most Exalted as 'the community of the middle way' (*ummah wasaṭ*), see *al-Baqarah* 2: 143. It is required to tread the middle road in every field of human activity and to avoid the course of extremism. The Lord has reminded it repeatedly that to enjoin good and forbid evil is its collective obligation. This is the reason why the nation of Islam has been elevated to the rank of 'the best nation' (*khayr ummah*):

كُنتُمْ خَيْرَ أُمَّةٍ أُخْرِجَتْ لِلنَّاسِ تَأْمُرُونَ بِالْمَعْرُوفِ وَتَنْهَوْنَ عَنِ الْمُنكَرِ وَتُؤْمِنُونَ بِاللَّهِ ... ﴿١١٠﴾

> *You are now the best nation brought forth for mankind. You enjoin what is right and forbid what is wrong and believe in Allah.*
>
> (*Āl ʿImrān* 3: 110)

To establish an Islamic social order remains the principal duty of the party and the nation of Islam, which unless strictly observed, the consequences become suicidal both for the Muslim community and the state, as is evident from our sad present-day plight:

الَّذِينَ إِن مَّكَّنَّاهُمْ فِي الْأَرْضِ أَقَامُوا الصَّلَاةَ وَآتَوُا الزَّكَاةَ وَأَمَرُوا بِالْمَعْرُوفِ وَنَهَوْا عَنِ الْمُنكَرِ ۗ وَلِلَّهِ
عَاقِبَةُ الْأُمُورِ ﴿٤١﴾

> *Those [will certainly get Divine support] who, were We to bestow authority on them in the land, will establish prayers, render* zakāh, *enjoin good and forbid evil. The end of all matters rests with Allah.*
>
> (*al-Ḥajj* 22: 41) — Editor.

3.2.2. *Essentials of the Islamic System of Governance*
Our discussion of the Islamic polity and Islamic social order will remain inconclusive unless we have an overview of the basic norms of the Islamic system of governance and the qualities most desirable for Islamic leadership and the community, of the ruler and the ruled. The essentials of the Islamic system of governance have been dealt with conclusively in chapters devoted to the topic in the compendiums of the Prophetic traditions. Let us briefly make mention here a few of the best-known hadiths in this respect.

In a letter addressed to the Christians of Najrān, our master the Messenger of Allah impressed upon them the need to stop scheming against the Islamic state and its leadership and to cooperate in matters of moral and spiritual significance. The basic point he stressed in context of the obligations the citizens and the state had towards each other is as important today for the rulers and the ruled as it was during his sacred times:

إنَّ رَسُولَ الله ﷺ كَتَبَ ألى أهلِ نَجرَانَ كِتَاباً وَّفِيه ... أمَّا بَعد فَإنى أدعُوكُم إلى عِبَادَةِ الله مِن عَبَادَةِ العَبَادِ، وَ اَدعُوكُم إلى وِلَا يةِ الله مِن وِلَايةِ العِبَاد.

The Messenger of Allah, may Allah bless him and give him peace, addressed a letter to the people of Najrān in which he said: '[...] After praising the Lord, I would like to invite you to the slavery of Allah and the freedom from the slavery of Allah's slaves. I also invite you to the overlordship of Allah and freedom from the overlordship of His subjects.

(Ibn Qayyim al-Jawziyyah, *Al-Bidāyah wa al-Nihāyah*, vol. 5, p. 66)

The following are some highly significant Traditions on this matter, which are especially important for members of the Islamic community and nation, for citizens and rulers both:

عَنْ أبِى هُرَيرَة ﷺ عَنِ النَّبِّى ﷺ قَال: إنَّكُم سَتَحرِصُونَ عَلَى الإمَارَةِ ، وَسَتكُونُ نَدَامةً يومَ القِيامةِ.

Abū Hurayrah narrated that the Holy Prophet, may Allah bless him and give him peace, said: 'You people will be keen to have the authority of government, but it will be a thing of regret on the Day of Resurrection.'

(Bukhārī)

عَن مَعقَل بنِ يسَارٍ ﷺ قَالَ:سَمِعتُ رَسُولَ الله ﷺ يقُول: مَا مِن عَبدٍ استَرعَاهُ اللهُ رَعِيةً فَلَمَ يَحُطهَا بِنُصحِهِ، إلاَّ لَم يجِد رَائِحةَ الجَنّةِ.

Ma ʿqal bin Yasār narrated: 'I heard the Messenger of Allah, may Allah bless him and give him peace, saying: "A bondsman of Allah whom the Almighty granted the authority to rule a people but did not care for proper governance would not get even the scent of Paradise."'

(Bukhārī)

عَن جُندُبٍ ﷺ قَالَ: سَمِعتُ رَسُولَ الله ﷺ يقُول: مَن سَمَّعَ سَمَّعَ اللهُ به يَومَ القِيامةِ، وَمَن يشَاقِق يَشقُق اللهُ عَليهِ يومَ القِيَامَه.

Ṭarīf Abū Tamīmah Jundub narrated: 'I heard the Messenger of Allah, may Allah bless him and give him peace, saying: "Whoever [and especially among the rulers] does a good deed in order to show off, Allah will expose his intentions on the Day of Reckoning, and whoever puts the people into difficulties, Allah will subject him to hardships on the Day of Accounting."'

(Bukhārī)

عَن ابنِ عُمر ﷺ عن النَّبىّ ﷺ قَالَ: السّمعُ وَ الطَّاعةُ حَقٌّ مَالَم يُؤمَر بِالمَعصِيَّةِ، فَإِذَا أُمِرَ بِمَعصِّيةٍ فَلاَ سَمعٌ وَلاَ طَاعةٌ.

ʿAbdullāh bin ʿUmar narrated that the Holy Prophet, may Allah bless him and give him peace, said: 'It is obligatory [for the subjects] to listen to and obey [those in authority] so long as they are not ordered to disobey the Lord. But in case of the orders involving disobedience [of the Lord], the subjects are not bound to listen to and obey [their rulers].'

(Bukhārī)

عن أبي أُمَامه البَاهِلى ﷺ أنَّ رُجُلاً سَألَ النَّبِىَّ ﷺ اَىُّ الجِهَادِ أفضَلُ يارَسُولَ الله؟ قَال: أفضَلُ الجهادِ كَلِمةُ حَقٍّ عِندَ سُلطَانٍ جَائرٍ.

Abū Umāmah al-Bāhilī narrated that a man asked the Holy Prophet, [...] 'Which jihad is the best, O Messenger of Allah?' The Holy Prophet, may Allah bless him and give him peace, replied: 'The best jihad [i.e. individual and collective struggle in the way of Allah] is to raise the voice of truth [and the people's rights] before an oppressive authority.'

(Bayhaqī, *Shuʿab al-Īmān* and Ṭabarānī, *Al-Muʿjam al-Kabīr*)

عَن عَبدِ الله بِنِ مَسعُودٍ ﷺ عَن النَّبِي ﷺ أَنَّهُ قَالَ: كَيفَ بِكَ يا عَبدَ الله إذَا كَانَ عَلَيكُم أُمَرَاءُ يُضَيِّعُونَ السُّنَّةَ وَ يُؤَخِّرُونَ الصَّلاَةَ عَن مِيقَاتِها؟ قَالَ: كَيفَ تَأمُرُنِى يَارَسُولَ الله؟ قَــالَ ﷺ : تَسـأَلُنِى إبنَ أُمِّ عَبـد، كَـيفَ تَفعَـلُ؟ لَاطَاعَةَ لِـمَخلُوقٍ فِى مَعصِيَّةِ الله عَزَّ وَجَل.

ʿAbdullāh bin Masʿūd (also by ʿAlī ibn Abī Ṭālib and ʿImrān ibn Ḥusayn) narrated that the Messenger of Allah said: 'What would be your circumstance, O ʿAbdullāh, when you are governed by rulers who take the Sunnah lightly and delay the obligatory prayer beyond its prescribed time?' ʿAbdullāh bin Masʿūd then asked: 'What would you order me to do then, O Messenger of Allah?' The Holy Prophet, may Allah bless him and give him peace, replied: 'So you ask me, Ibn Masʿūd, what to do then? There is no obedience to any being in matters of disobedience to Allah the Almighty, the Most-Glorious.'[2]

(Aḥmad and Muḥammad Nāṣir al-Dīn al-Albānī, *Silsilat al-Ḥadīth al-Ṣaḥīḥah*)

[2] Note the general principle stated here. — Editor.

4 Addendum

From the discussion that preceded we naturally come to the conclusion that for an individual to retain his Islamic moorings, and remain a vibrant and dynamic Muslim, it is necessary that he should work for a collective Islamic social order and be an active and effective member of Muslim society; and for a Muslim society to be Islamic and distinct from other societies it is essential to be unified under the banner of the party of Islam, the party with the sole agenda of making the writ of God Supreme and the dictates of the Shariah (the Divine Law) effective in the land. As discussed earlier, such a party will obviously have to be led by a leader and guide who is himself a devoted bondsman of Allah Most Glorified and Exalted and enjoys a good reputation for his Islamic knowledge, virtuous character and qualities of spirituality and leadership.[1] Only under a dispensation like this it is possible to firmly establish an Islamic social order that can fight effectively against social, moral and material disorder not only locally within the Islamic state but also globally.

This is the social order that can eventually emerge and certainly act as the catalyst for a sublime new global system. Theoretically, what may appear as a distinct possibility today was practically a living reality only a few centuries ago. The Islamic state of Madinah and its successor the Islamic state of the Arabian Peninsula stand out in human history as practical models of glorious Islamic social order and dynamic Islamic spiritual leadership.

It is also evident from the discourse we are about to conclude that, as a true bondsman of Allah and follower of the teachings of our master the Messenger of Allah, may Allah bless him and give him peace, every Muslim is always required to be conscious of his obligations towards the rights of Allah (*ḥuqūq Allāh*)

[1] While an effective role for the party of Islam is essential to keep society and state on the right track, it does not mean a single-party system or the oligarchy of the chosen few. Similarly, the leader responsible for making the writ of the Qur'an and the Sunnah supreme in the land is not to be an autocrat or theocrat, as Islam is absolutely against both autocracy and theocracy. The role the *majlis al-shūrā* is designed to play and the freedom and justice available to the common man in a truly Islamic state, with his basic rights fully guaranteed, can be found nowhere in any other polity or system of governance, neither in the past nor today. For greater details on the subject, see Sayyid Mawdūdī's book *Islāmī Riyāsat* (English version: *Islamic Law and Constitution*). — Editor.

and the rights of His subjects (*ḥuqūq al-ʿibād*). He is always to be mindful of the consequences of his disobedience to his Lord and his accountability in the Hereafter. His devotion to the right cause and his dedication to seek Allah's pleasure should keep him restless to do more than he is normally required to do. He should see no sacrifice as too great to please his Lord. A believer is expected to be good not only in all his personal deeds but to be engaged continuously in the struggle to see the good prosper and be supreme. Similarly, he cannot rest content with keeping himself and his family away from everything bad, but instead he should earnestly and sincerely try to the best of his capabilities and potential to keep the bad at bay. To promote the right and prevent the wrong is to remain his mission. He must not be found lagging behind in an organized struggle against the forces of evil or in promoting the causes of virtue in society. He must aspire to be imbued with the quality of *iḥsān* that virtually raises the bondsman of Allah to the pedestal where whatever he does becomes an act of worship (*ʿibādah*). The overpowering sense of his being in the presence of his Lord and always being watched in all his actions and deeds helps him to keep strong his ties of bondsmanship (*ʿubūdiyyah*). He will thus never be tempted to deviate from the right path.

This is exactly the meaning and import of the highly significant hadith of Jibrīl in which our master the Messenger of Allah's responses to the queries of the Archangel Gabriel help us have an insight into the dynamics of spirituality in Islam and the system of *ʿibādah* that has been devised to promote our ties with Allah Most Glorified and Exalted:

عَن أبِى هُرَيرَة ﷺ قَالَ: كَانَ رَسُولُ الله ﷺ بَارِزاً يوماً لِلنَّاسِ، فَاَتَاهُ رَجُلٌ فقَال: مَاالإيمَانُ؟ قَالَ: الإيمَانُ أن تُؤمِنَ بِالله وَ مَلاَئِكَتهِ وَ بِلِقَاءِهِ وَ رُسُلهِ وَتُؤمِنَ بِالبَعث. قَالَ: مَا الإسلاَمُ؟ قَالَ: أن تَعبُدَ اللهَ وَلَاتُشرِكَ بهِ، وَتُقِيمَ الصَّلاَةَ ، وَ تُؤَدِّىَ الزَّ كوٰةَ، وَتَصُومَ رَمَضَان. قَالَ: مَا الإحسَانُ؟ قَال: أن تَعبُدَ اللهَ كَاَنَّكَ تَراهُ، فإن لَم تَكُن تَرَاهُ فَإنّهُ يرَاكَ قَالَ: مَتَى السَّاعة؟ قَال: مَا اَلـمسؤُولُ عَنَها بِأعلَمَ مِنَ السَّائل، وَ سَاُخبِرُكَ عَن أشرَاطِهَا: إذَاوَلَدَتِ الأمةُ رَبّها، وَإذَا تَطَاوَلَ رُعَاةُ الإبِلِ البُهم فِى البُنيان، فِى خَمسٍ لَايعلَمهُنَّ إلّا الله. ثُمَّ تَلا النَّبِىّ ﷺ: (إنَّ اللهَ عِندَهُ عِلمُ السَّاعَةِ...) إلَى آخِرِالآيه، ثُمَّ أدبَرَ فقَالَ: «رُدُّوهُ». فَلَم يرَوا شَيئاً فقَال: هٰذَا جِبرِيلُ جَاءَ يُعلِّمُ النَّاسَ دِينهُم.

Abū Hurayrah narrated that while the Messenger of Allah, may Allah bless him and give him peace, was among the people [responding to their queries], a man came and asked: 'What is faith (*īmān*)?' The Messenger of Allah, may Allah bless him and give him peace, replied: '*Īmān* is to believe in Allah, His angels, in meeting Him, in His Messengers, and to believe in the Day of Resurrection'.[2] Then, the newcomer asked: 'What is *islām*?' Allah's Messenger replied: '*Islām* is that you worship Allah alone and associate no partner unto Him; properly perform regular prayers, pay the *zakāh*; and observe the fast of Ramadan.'[3] The man asked: 'What is *iḥsān*?' The Prophet answered: '[*Iḥsān* is that] you worship Allah with devotion as if you see Him, for if you cannot see Him, He is definitely watching you'. His next [and last] question was: 'When is the [Final] Hour?' The Messenger of Allah replied: 'The one answering has no better knowledge than the one who is asking. I will inform you, however, of its portents: when the bondmaid will give birth to her master; and when the shepherds of jet-black camels start competing [with others] in constructing tall buildings. These are the two of the five [hidden facts] that nobody else knows except Allah.' The Holy Prophet then recited the relevant verse[4] in this context [*Luqmān* 31: 34]. The man then left. The Holy Prophet asked [his Companions] to call him back, but they found no trace of him. The Prophet, may Allah bless him and give him peace, then told them: 'That was Gabriel who came to teach the people their religion [through the answers the Prophet gave to his queries].'

(Bukhārī; also narrated by 'Umar in Muslim and
by Ibn 'Umar in Tirmidhī)

---

[2] In another narration, the holy Prophet mentioned two more items of faith: belief in His Books, and in Divine predestination (*al-qadr*). — Editor.

[3] Of the five pillars (*arkān*) of Islam, the fifth one of hajj is not mentioned in this narration, although ones from 'Umar and Ibn 'Umar do. — Editor.

[4] This verse informs us of the World of the Unseen (*'ālam al-ghayb*), including the appointed Hour of Resurrection, which no one else knows but Allah Most Glorified and Exalted:

إِنَّ ٱللَّهَ عِندَهُۥ عِلْمُ ٱلسَّاعَةِ وَيُنَزِّلُ ٱلْغَيْثَ وَيَعْلَمُ مَا فِى ٱلْأَرْحَامِ ۖ وَمَا تَدْرِى نَفْسٌ مَّاذَا تَكْسِبُ غَدًا ۖ وَمَا تَدْرِى
نَفْسٌۢ بِأَىِّ أَرْضٍ تَمُوتُ ۚ إِنَّ ٱللَّهَ عَلِيمٌ خَبِيرٌ ﴿٣٤﴾

Surely Allah alone has the knowledge of the Hour. It is He Who sends down the rain, and He Who knows what is in the wombs. Nor does anyone know what it is that he will earn tomorrow: nor does he know in what land he will die. Indeed, Allah is All-Knowing, All-Aware.

(*Luqmān* 31: 34) — Editor.

PART TWO

ʿ*IBĀDAH*: ITS SIGNIFICANCE IN THE ISLAMIC SOCIAL ORDER

5 ʿ*Ibādah:* Its Meaning and Significance

According to the holy Qur'an, ʿ*ibādah* is the grand purpose for which man has been created:

وَمَا خَلَقْتُ ٱلْجِنَّ وَٱلْإِنسَ إِلَّا لِيَعْبُدُونِ ﴿٥٦﴾

I created the jinn and human beings for nothing else but that they may serve Me.

(*al-Dhāriyāt* 51: 56)

The purpose for which the Prophets were sent was also nothing other than to invite human beings to Allah's ʿ*ibādah*:

وَلَقَدْ بَعَثْنَا فِى كُلِّ أُمَّةٍ رَّسُولًا أَنِ ٱعْبُدُوا۟ ٱللَّهَ وَٱجْتَنِبُوا۟ ٱلطَّـٰغُوتَ ... ﴿٣٦﴾

We raised a Messenger in every community [to tell them], 'Serve Allah, and shun the evil one.'

(*al-Naḥl* 16: 36)

It is, therefore, necessary for us to understand what is meant by ʿ*ibādah* and what the real significance is of the tenets prescribed by Islam for the worship of God. If we remain unaware of this we, then will be unable to fulfil the very purpose for which we have been created.

5.1. The Spirit of ʿ*Ibādah*

The term ʿ*ibādah* is derived from ʿ*abd*, which means a slave and bondsman. Literally translated, it means worship, submission and devotion. Allah is our Master and we are His slaves and whatever a slave does in obedience to and for the pleasure of his Master is ʿ*ibādah*. The Islamic concept of ʿ*ibādah* is very broad. If we free our speech from filth, falsehood, malice and abuse, speak the truth, talk goodly things, and do all this only because Allah has so ordained, this constitutes ʿ*ibādah*, howsoever secular those acts may appear to be. If we obey the injunctions of Allah Most Glorified and Exalted in letter and spirit in our day-to-day affairs, and abide by them in our dealings with our parents, relatives, friends and everyone who comes into contact with us, then all these activities become *ʿibādah.* If we help the poor and the destitute, feed the hungry, serve the afflicted and do all this not for any personal gain but only to seek our Lord's Pleasure, then it is *ʿibādah.* Even our economic activities – the activities we undertake to earn our living and to feed our dependents – are *ʿibādah* provided we do everything honestly and truthfully according to the Divine commands.

In short, all our activities are *ʿibādah* if these are in accordance with the precepts decreed by Allah and His Messenger. A believer's ultimate objective in life is to seek the All-Merciful Lord's pleasure and to shun evil and everything that displeases his Lord. In other words, this is the true spirit of *ʿibādah,* which is total submission to the will of God and shaping one's entire life to the Islamic model in a way that not even the most insignificant detail is left out.

To help achieve this objective, Islam has drawn up a formal system of *ʿibādah* as a course of training and education for the believers. The more assiduously we follow the training, the better equipped we are to harmonize ideals and practices. The Islamic acts of worship are thus the pillars on which the edifice of the religion rests.

5.1.1. ʿIbādah *in the Age of Ignorance (Jāhiliyyah)*

ʿIbādah in Islam is more than worship. It means prayer, service, adoration, devotion and bondsmanship. *ʿIbādah* in the sense of worship only is actually a concept of the Age of Ignorance (al-Jāhiliyyah). Ignorant nations always compare their deities with human beings: They think that these deities expect from human beings exactly the same level of sycophancy, offerings and show of humility as do their feudal lords, chiefs and kings, who are pleased with flattery, offerings, supplications with folded hands, and similar shows of humility, which remain the only way of seeking favours from them. Based on this notion, pagan religions allocated certain times for the performance of certain rituals and termed them as *ʿibādah* or worship.

5.1.2. *The Ascetic Concept of Worship*

Islam does not believe in a system of worship whereby a person is required to renounce his worldly life in order to seek proximity to God. Those who follow this path are called upon to develop their inner faculties and achieve miraculous powers through meditation, self-renunciation, self-torture and occult practices. That is how they hope to attain salvation in the Hereafter, for which they also abdicate from all their worldly responsibilities. This concept of *ʿibādah* is found in religions based on an ascetic view of life, which considers religiosity and worldliness as opposed to each other. Such a system seeks salvation beyond worldly life and its responsibilities and relationships, and demands material regression or dissociation from anything material as a prerequisite for the human being's spiritual growth and development.

5.2. The Islamic Concept of *ʿIbādah*

The Islamic concept of *ʿibādah* is entirely different and much more meaningful. Islam views the human being as the bondsman of the One and Only God. Allah, the Lord of the worlds, the Creator, Sustainer, Master and Supreme Sovereign, has appointed man as His deputy on earth. He has delegated some powers to him and bestowed upon him certain responsibilities and obligations. He has also granted him some authority over a part of His kingdom and subjects. Thus, man's task is to fulfil his Lord's mission, to understand and discharge his responsibilities, to carry out the duties assigned to him by his Master, to use the powers and authority delegated to him at the Supreme Sovereign's pleasure, and [to obey] the dictates of His law. The more active and efficient man is in discharging his assigned duties on earth, and the more loyal and dutiful his observance of his Lord's rules and regulations while exercising the powers and authority bestowed on him, the more successful he will be as his Lord's bondsman. His future well-being depends on how he fares on the Day of Reckoning and whether his life-record affirms his being a dutiful, loyal and obedient bondsman in his lifetime, and not a negligent, unwilling, disloyal and rebellious subject.

Therefore, from the Islamic perspective, the ignorant (*jāhilī*) and ascetic concepts of worship discussed earlier are totally flawed. Someone who allocates a little of his time to worshipping God and performing certain rituals on the assumption that he has done his duty by his Lord and Master and is now free to handle the rest of his affairs in the way he likes is not doing his duty as a true worshipper. According to Islam, such a person is exactly like the servant in your full-time employ who was paid and sustained at your expense but in return showed up only in the mornings and evenings to salute you in all humbleness and was busy thereafter whiling away his time or working for so many other masters. Similarly, there is a person who leaves the world and its affairs aside and confines himself to a corner, spending his time in isolation offering prayers, fasting, reciting the holy Qur'an and counting the beads of his rosary. Such a person is exactly like the man you employ to keep your garden, but who left the garden and his duty aside and prefers to stand before you with folded hands, constantly invoking your pleasure and reciting with full-throated ease the instructions you gave him for the upkeep of your garden, but not doing the actual work assigned to him. Islam's view of such a devotee is no different from the opinion one may form of such an employee. Allah Most Exalted will treat such self-deluded worshippers the way an employer would treat such an employee.

According to the Islamic concept of *ʿibādah,* we are to spend the whole of our lives in service of our Lord and Master. We are to consider ourselves full-time servants and no single moment of our life is to be free from *ʿibādah.* Whatever we do in this world should accord with the Shariah, the Divine law of Islam. Asleep or awake, eating or drinking, moving or stationary, all our acts should conform to the injunctions of the Shariah.[1] We should keep firm the bonds we have been bound with by our Lord; we should tie the knots of our human relationships and untie or break them the way He has directed us to do. The responsibilities or duties enjoined by Him in our worldly lives must be undertaken willingly and discharged the way we have been guided to do by His Prophets. We should always consider ourselves answerable to Him and guided by the spirit of accountability for whatever we do here. Whether we are dealing with our wives and children at home, with people in our neighbourhoods, our friends and associates in our social lives, or interacting with colleagues at our places of work, we must be mindful of the limits prescribed by our Lord for each and every occasion. In the dead of night, when we are in a position to commit acts of transgression unnoticed by anyone else, we keep a check on ourselves because we know we are in the watchful presence of the Almighty. We

---

[1] These days, a gentleman has raised an unnecessary controversy by declaring that God's worship means obedience of His physical law, which may or may not conform to His moral law. Thus, according to him, those engaged under the physical law (or law of nature) in society's welfare through their organizational skill or scientific discoveries, etc. are also worshipping God and are His deputies and true believers, and they may or may not abide by His moral law. This is a blunder that virtually turns unbelief (*kufr*) into Islam, rebellion into submission and disobedience into obedience. Such a view is tantamount to distorting the very spirit of Islam's mission and message. This gentleman perhaps does not know that Islam's basic objective is to teach mankind how to use the physical law in service of the moral law. Had man's task been only to act according to the dictates of the physical law, then there would have been no need for Prophets or the Book, and the animal instinct of man would have been enough to guide him. Had man's duty been only to follow the law of nature, there would have been no difference between him and an animal. Just as the wolf tears apart the sheep, as it is the law of nature for him, similarly, if a man who is more powerful tears apart the one less powerful, he would only be following the dictates of the physical law. A nation capable of producing more fighter planes and bombs would thus be justified in subduing by force another nation under the same law. Such a theory reduces man to the level of a beast. Islam is too benign a religion to permit such a degradation of humanity and such bestiality in man in the name of God's worship. — Author.

are in a thick forest and can do anything wrong and unlawful as there is none to catch us or be a witness against us, but our fear of our Lord prevents us from committing a crime. We are free to accumulate wealth through deceit, treachery and tyranny, unchecked by any worldly authority, but avoid it out of fear that it will invite His wrath. We know that to be truthful and honest may cause us immense harm, but we prefer to bear the loss only because we care more for Allah's pleasure.

ʿIbādah or worship in Islam, therefore, does not mean renunciation of worldly life so that one can pray to God in isolation like a hermit. Instead, it means obeying His commands while engaged in worldly commitments and discharging all the responsibilities of day-to-day life. Remembrance of Allah does not mean just the movement of one's tongue to repeat His holy name. It actually means our involvement in worldly matters without being unmindful of our Lord. In this life, there are many occasions for violating the Divine law, but we are to remember Him and obediently follow the dictates of His law. We may occupy the government's chair of authority, but we should keep on reminding ourselves that we are not the lord and master of His subjects but like everyone else are subjects of our Lord and Master. In our capacity as judges, we may be capable of committing injustice, but are held back by the very thought that we are under obligation to God to do justice. We may have within our custody the resources of the land, but we should remind ourselves that we are not the masters of these resources, but only custodians and will have to account for each and every penny before the Lord, Who is actually the Master of the land and all its resources. When we command a regiment, fear of Allah should stop us from committing any transgressions. When we conduct trade and commerce, business and finance, we need to keep a watch on the permissible and the impermissible, the lawful and the unlawful, and then go on exploring avenues of success. Something forbidden (haram) by the Lord may seductively lure us at each step, but our progress should remain unfaltering. We may have all avenues open to us for committing oppression, fraud, treachery, corruption and immorality, and worldly gains and material attractions may raise their heads adorned with glittering crowns, but our fear of the Almighty and accountability in the Hereafter should keep us on right track. There may be thousands of difficulties in observing the limit (*ḥadd*), set by our Lord, and establishing His order, but we must remain steadfast, firm and unshakable in our commitment to His Shariah.

This is what is meant by *ʿibādah* or worship in Islam. This is what is meant by invocation of Allah's name, and it is this *dhikr* that the holy Qur'an alludes to in the following verse:

فَإِذَا قُضِيَتِ ٱلصَّلَوٰةُ فَٱنتَشِرُواْ فِى ٱلْأَرْضِ وَٱبْتَغُواْ مِن فَضْلِ ٱللَّهِ وَٱذْكُرُواْ ٱللَّهَ كَثِيرًا لَّعَلَّكُمْ تُفْلِحُونَ ﴿١٠﴾

But when the prayer is ended, disperse in the land and seek Allah's bounty, and remember Allah much so that you may prosper.

(*al-Jumu'ah* 62: 10)

5.2.1. *The Pathway to Allah*

Islam teaches us that the way to spiritual progress and communion with our Lord does not require reclusion and retirement to woods or caves. Instead, the human being can reach up to his Creator while interacting with his fellow human beings and in the midst of his day-to-day engagements. The person who resolutely faces the temptations of the forbidden, the lure of the unjust and attractions of the immoral and remains steadfast, definitely succeeds in getting closer to his Lord. He is thus almost in His benign presence at every moment. He could not otherwise have moved so safely away from that perilous precipice. Whether at home enjoying moments of leisure, or in midst of his daily routine, whoever does his job with the conviction that Allah Most Exalted is not far away from him will find that his Lord is close, indeed so very close to him. He who successfully acquits himself in the trying moments of life and its aspects like politics, governance, finance, trade, industry, war and peace and refrains from deviation and Satanic seductions for apparent worldly success, he alone is an upright Muslim and a true believer. No one else can succeed in being close to their Lord better than him. If such a person is not a friend (*waliyy*) of Allah, then who else can claim such an elevated position?

From the Islamic perspective, this is the way to spiritual progress and development. Spiritual emancipation does not mean that you increase your will power through certain exercises like a wrestler or a gymnast or that you start displaying spell-binding tricks. What spiritual emancipation actually means is the capacity to exercise self-restraint, to keep every temptation in check and to use correctly all faculties given to man by the Lord. If a person succeeds in his worldly life, where he is on trial at each step, and moves forward, avoiding animal desires and devilish temptations and remains firmly committed and steadfast on the path lit by Divine guidance, the level of his humanity is bound to rise higher and higher. That is how he will be closer to Allah Most Glorified and Exalted with each passing day. There is nothing that one may call this other than spiritual emancipation.

6 Islamic Acts of Worship

Islam demands that no moment of our life should be without Allah's worship. The very proclamation of the first article of our faith, 'There is no god but Allah and Muhammad (peace be upon him) is His Messenger', makes it binding upon us to live as His bondsmen once we have acknowledged Allah as our only Deity. The attribute of being an *ʿabd* or bondsman of God is called *ʿibādah.* It may be simple and easy to utter as words, but certainly not as simple and easy to turn one's entire life in all its facets into an act of worship. One needs rigorous training for this. Therefore, it is essential first to train our minds, develop strong character, shape our behaviour and traits into a particular pattern, and not be contented with our character-building as individuals. Instead, every one of us must try collectively to establish a social order capable of preparing individuals for the basic objective of *ʿibādah* on a wider scale, a social order wherein an individual should have community backing and support to reform his weaknesses. This is the goal for which Islam has prescribed the tenets of obligatory prayer (*ṣalāh*), obligatory fasting (*ṣawm*), obligatory charity (*zakāh*) and the obligatory pilgrimage (hajj) and yet another vital pillar of Islam, jihad or an organized struggle against the forces of evil.

These tenets are *ʿibādah* in the sense that they prepare the believer for Allah's worship in its true essence and spirit. Hence, they form part of a compulsory training course. It is through these that a particular frame of mind is nurtured, a special kind of character is built, a definite pattern of group behaviour takes shape, and the foundations of a social order are laid without which human life cannot become imbued with Divine worship. There is no means other than these tenets through which that goal can be achieved. This is why Islam terms these obligatory acts of worship as its pillars (*arkān*). It means that these are the pillars on which the edifice of a Muslim's life is raised and by which that edifice remains intact. Let us now see how each of these pillars contribute in raising the grand edifice of the Islamic social order and how as discussed above this prepares the individual for the ultimate goal of *ʿibādah* in a wider sense.

6.1. Obligatory Prayer (*Ṣalāh*)

Ṣalāh is the most fundamental and important of the obligatory duties enjoined in Islam. *Ṣalāh,* or the regular prayer, is to be performed five times a day in order to refresh and reaffirm our faith as believers.

We get up early in the morning, purify ourselves through ablution and then present ourselves before the Lord in prayer. Our various postures during the prayer embody the spirit of submission. Each and every word we recite during the *ṣalāh* reminds us of our commitment to our Lord. We seek His guidance and beg Him again and again to enable us to avoid His wrath and follow His chosen path. We recite from the Book of God, bear witness to the truth of His teachings conveyed by His Prophets, renew our belief in the Day of Judgement and enliven in our memory the fact that we have to appear before Him and give an account of our whole life. This is how we start our day. After a period of time, when the appointed moment comes, the muezzin calls us to the prayers and we respond to the call to prayer and refresh our covenant with the Lord. We dissociate ourselves from worldly engagements for a few moments and seek communion with Him. This keeps on refreshing in our minds our actual role in life. After this rededication, we revert to our other preoccupations before presenting ourselves to our Lord again a few hours later. *Ṣalāh* also serves as a reminder whereby we refocus our attention repeatedly on the essential requirements of our faith. When the sun sets and the darkness of the night begins to overtake us, we submit ourselves to our Lord to remind us practically of our duties and obligations in the midst of the approaching shadows of night. We appear again before our Lord a few hours later for our last prayer of the day. Thus, before going to bed we once again refresh our faith and prostrate ourselves humbly before our Lord. This is how we complete the task of our daily communion with Allah Most Glorified and Exalted. The frequency and timings of the prayers never let us lose sight of the objective and mission of our lives in the midst of our worldly activities.

It is easy to understand how the daily prayers strengthen the foundations of our faith, and prepare us for the observance of a life of virtue and obedience to Allah and refresh our commitment to His cause. Through this highly important practice, the fountains of courage, sincerity of purpose, purity of heart, emancipation of the soul and moral enrichment spring forth.

Let us now see how this is achieved. We perform our ablutions the way the holy Prophet, may Allah bless him and give him peace, practically demonstrated. Then we say our prayers as instructed by him. Why do we do that? We follow in the footsteps of our master the Messenger of Allah, may Allah bless him and give him peace, because he is our most respected and loved guide and we sincerely believe in his prophethood and deem it to be our binding duty to follow him correctly in the true spirit of followership.

Similarly, we dare not intentionally recite the holy Qur'an incorrectly. This is because we believe the Book to be the Word of God and consider it a sin to deviate from it even by a letter. In our prayers we recite many things quietly. There is, of course, no one to stop us if we do not recite them, or if we add to them something of our own, but we never do that except by mistake or due to a lapse in memory. Why? It is because we believe that God is ever watchful, listens to all that we recite, and is aware of things both open and hidden. What makes us say our prayers in places where there is no one to ask us or even see us offering them? Is it not because of our belief that we are being observed by our Lord? What impels us to leave our other important engagements and hurry towards the mosque for prayer? What makes us break our sweet sleep in the early hours of morning, come to the mosque in the midday heat, or leave our evening pastimes for the timely observance of prayer? Is there anything else other than our sense of duty that impels to fulfill our responsibility to our Lord come what may? And why are we so careful to avoid any mistake in our prayers? It is because our heart is definitely filled with the fear of God and we know that we will appear before Him and account for our deeds on the Day of Judgement.

Keeping the above factors in mind, can we think of a better course of moral and spiritual training for a believer than *ṣalāh*? It is this system of training that makes a person a perfect Muslim. This reminds him of his covenant with the Lord, refreshes his faith in Him, and keeps his belief in the Day of Reckoning alive and fresh in his mind. It enables him to follow the glorious path of the holy Prophet, may Allah bless him and give him peace, and correlate his actions with his ideals.

When a person is so conscious of his obligation towards his Lord the Creator that he prizes it above all worldly gains and keeps refreshing it through prayer, he is bound to be honest in all his dealings as he knows that he will otherwise be inviting His displeasure, something so dreadful that he has all along taken so much care to avoid. He will try his best to abide by the injunctions of the All-Merciful Lord in all spheres of his life in exactly the way he follows them in his five daily prayers. He will prove to be trustworthy in all walks of his life and try to avoid a sinful act the best he can. If even after such training a person disobeys the Divine command, it can only be because of some inherent weakness and waywardness of his self.

We are not left alone to observe our prayers in isolation, but instructed to do that in congregation, especially the Friday prayer. This intimate social interaction creates a bond of love and a sense of affiliation and fraternity among

Muslims. It fosters within them a feeling of unity and a spirit of harmony and national cohesion. The regular prayer is thus a symbol of the equality of the poor and the rich, the low and the high, the rulers and the ruled, the educated and the unlettered, black and white, as all of them stand in a row and prostrate themselves before their Lord and Master. *Ṣalāh* also inculcates a strong sense of discipline and allegiance to a common cause. In short, *ṣalāh* trains people in all those virtues that make possible the development of an extremely rich individual and collective life.

These are just a few of the myriad benefits that we can derive from our daily prayers. If we fail to avail of these for ourselves, we and we alone are to be blamed. Shirking the responsibility of the proper observance of our obligatory prayers would entail one of the following two cases: either that we do not acknowledge *ṣalāh* as our duty, or we do acknowledge it but refuse or fail to perform it. In the first case, our claim to faith in Allah (*īmān billāh*) becomes a shameless lie for if we are not willing to comply with His orders, then we actually are unwilling to acknowledge His authority. In the second case, we do recognize His authority but have the audacity to flout His commands and are thus the most unreliable of His creatures, for if we can do this to the highest Authority in the universe, there is no guarantee that we cannot do the same in dealings with our fellow human beings. And if the accursed trend of double-dealing dominates in a society, then it is bound to be afflicted with terrible discord.

6.2. Obligatory Fasting (*Ṣawm*)

What the obligatory prayers seek to do five times a day, the month-long fast of Ramadan, the ninth month of the lunar calendar, does once a year. During this period, we neither eat a morsel of food nor drink a drop of water from dawn to dusk, no matter how delicious the dish or how hungry or thirsty we are. What is it that makes us voluntarily undergo such rigours of self-control? It is surely nothing but a manifestation of our strong faith in Allah Most Exalted, and the fear of Him and the Day of Judgement. While fasting we take care to suppress our wayward thoughts and desires and by so doing proclaim the supremacy of the Divine command.

This month-long drill not only strengthens the bond of faith, but also inculcates within us a sense of discipline and purpose. We are thus brought face to face with the hard realities of life like hunger, thirst and the human need for food, while also becoming conscious of our moral obligation towards those without the basic necessities of life. It also helps us make our life during the rest of the year one of true subservience to the will of our Lord.

From yet another perspective, *ṣawm* has an immense collective impact. Every Muslim, regardless of his status in life, must fast during Ramadan, which helps to create an environment of compassion, fellow-feeling, love and brotherhood. Furthermore, during the holy month, the evil within and without withdraws meekly and the good comes to the fore and so the whole atmosphere is filled with an air of piety and purity.

This training in discipline and self-control has been imposed on us for our own benefit. Those who do not fulfill this primary duty cannot be relied on to discharge their other duties. Those who call themselves Muslims but do not hesitate to eat and drink in public during the holy month are the worst of their Lord's subjects. They profess to be among the believers but actually they are not. Their conduct shows that they do not care in the least for their obligation towards their Creator and Sustainer. They are disloyal to the community to which they belong and it can expect no good from them.

6.3. Obligatory Charity (*Zakāh*)

Zakāh is the third obligatory duty of a believer. Those Muslims whose assets are valued above a certain specified limit must give 2.5 per cent of their cash balance annually for the uplift of the poor, the needy, the wayfarers, those in debt, in the way of Allah, and to support those who have left everything to become a member of the Islamic community. This is the minimum for those who are well off. The more one contributes to the welfare of society the greater one's reward will be from the Lord.

The money we give as *zakāh* is not something that Allah needs or receives. He is above any want and desire. In His benign mercy, He promises us manifold rewards if we help our brethren. However, there is one basic condition for being thus rewarded: when we give in the name of Allah, we should neither expect nor demand any worldly gain from the beneficiaries nor should we seek acknowledgement as philanthropists and generous people.

Zakāh is as basic to Islam as other forms of *'ibādah*. Its fundamental importance lies in the fact that it fosters within us the quality of sacrifice and rids us of the evils of selfishness and plutocracy. Islam only accepts within its fold those who are ready to give away in the way of Allah some of their hard-earned wealth willingly and without seeking any temporal or personal gain. It has nothing to do with misers. When the call comes, a true Muslim willingly sacrifices whatever he has in the way of Allah for *zakāh* has trained him to do so.

Muslim society has much to gain from the institution of *zakāh*. It is the bounden duty of every well-to-do member of society to provide help and support to his lowly-placed poor brethren. His wealth is not to be spent solely for his own comfort and luxury. He knows that there are rightful claimants on his wealth like his community's widows and orphans, the poor and the invalided, those who have the ability but lack the means to get employment, and those who have the talent but not the money to acquire knowledge and become useful members of their society. He who does not recognize the right on his wealth of such members of his own community is indeed a cruel sinner. There definitely can be no greater cruelty than to fill up one's own coffers while others die of hunger or suffer the agonies of want and penury. Islam is the sworn enemy of anti-social tendencies like selfishness, greed and acquisitiveness. One can expect an unbeliever to be devoid of the noble feelings of love and brotherhood, only knowing how to preserve his wealth and adding to it by lending it out usuriously. Islam's teachings are the antithesis of this attitude. Here one shares one's wealth with others and thereby helps them stand on their own feet and become productive members of society.

6.4. Pilgrimage to the House of God (Hajj)

Hajj, or the pilgrimage to the House of God, is the fourth pillar of Islam's grand edifice of *ʿibādah*. The holy Kaaba is a simple but awe-inspiring structure that Prophet Abraham, may Allah's peace and blessings be upon him, built and dedicated to the worship of Allah. Allah rewarded him by calling it His own House and by making it the centre towards which every believer must face when offering prayer. He also made it obligatory on those who are able physically as well as financially to visit the place at least once in a lifetime. This visit is not a courtesy call but an act of duty. When we undertake the pilgrimage, we are required to fulfil certain terms and conditions and make ourselves worthy of the task ahead. It is a journey to seek Allah's pleasure and hence we are to shun all worldly temptations, cravings for material gain, name and fame, and be pure in our words and deeds and filled with the spirit of love and fear of Allah.

In a way hajj is the biggest of all acts of worship, for unless a man really loves Allah he can never undertake such a long journey at such an exorbitant cost, leaving his near and dear ones behind. The pilgrimage to the House of God is very much unlike any other journey. A person's thoughts are focused entirely on his Lord, Creator and Sustainer. His very being vibrates with the spirit of intense devotion. When he reaches the holy place, he finds the atmosphere filled with piety and godliness, he visits places which bear witness to the glory of Islam, and all this leaves an indelible impression on his mind and soul, which he is expected to carry to his last breath.

As with other acts of *ʿibādah*, there are so many benefits that a Muslim can derive from the pilgrimage. The holy city of Makkah where the Kaaba is situated is the centre towards which those among the believers who can afford it converge once a year: they perform the prescribed rites, meet fellow Muslims and discuss topics of common interest. The visit helps to create and generate within them the belief that all bondsmen of Allah are equal and deserving of mutual love and sympathy, regardless of their geographical or cultural origins. Thus, the hajj helps to unite the Muslims of the world into a single global fraternity.

6.5. Collective struggle against the forces of evil (Jihad)

Although jihad is not a formal tenet, its need and importance have been repeatedly emphasized in the Qur'an and the Sunnah of the holy Prophet, may Allah bless him and give him peace. In essence, it is a test of our sincerity and truthfulness as believers. If we fail to defend Islamic causes and are solely guided in our actions by selfish motives, or if we have no urge to remain steadfast when tested or when facing forces inimical to Islam and Muslims, we cannot claim to be sincere and worthy believers. Similarly, if we profess faith in Islam it becomes our bounden duty to guard it jealously and to uphold its prestige and honour.

Jihad is an integral part of the Islamic system of *ʿibādah* and is intended for the overall defence of Islam and its social order. Lexically, jihad means to struggle to the utmost of one's capacity. It stands for a concerted and organized struggle against the forces of evil. A person who exerts himself physically, materially or financially in the way of Allah is indeed engaged in jihad. In the language of the Shariah, the term is used particularly for a war that is waged solely in the name of Allah against the forces that are hostile to Islam and Muslims.

Jihad is a supreme sacrifice that devolves upon all Muslims. If only a section of the Muslim society offers itself for this, the community as a whole is absolved of its responsibility. Conversely, if none comes forward, then everybody is negligent. However, this concession is withdrawn in the event of an Islamic State being attacked by a non-Muslim power. In such a situation, everybody is duty-bound to come forward to join the jihad. If the state under attack does not have enough strength to fight back, then it is the religious duty of neighbouring Muslim countries to come to its aid. If they fail to rise to the occasion, then Muslims around the world are to join the fight against the common enemy. As such, jihad is among the primary duties of Muslims similar to other basic tenets of Islam. Anyone who shirks it is a sinner and his claim to being a Muslim becomes doubtful.

With this brief overview of *ʿibādah* in Islam, let us now discuss in detail the basic features of *ṣalāh* and *ṣawm*.[1]

---

[1] Those interested in learning more about the Islamic tenets of *zakāh*, hajj and jihad may supplement their reading with a study of the author's *Khuṭubāt* (*Let us be Muslims*). — Editor.

7 Obligatory Prayer (*Ṣalāh*)

7.1. A Reminder

In order for an individual's life to be considered *ʿibādah*, the thing most needed is that he always keeps alive, fresh and vibrant the awareness that he is a slave and bondsman of Allah Most Exalted and that whatever he has to do in this world must be done as His bondsman. To refresh this awareness is necessary because the Lord is out of our sight and beyond our senses. On the other hand, the devil within coaxes us all the time to believe that we are his slaves. We are invited by millions of devils the world over to be their associates, servants and slaves. The devils may be out of our sight, but we feel their presence as every minute we encounter more and more of their machinations. Therefore, to keep our conviction alive and active that we are bondsmen of Allah and not of Satan and his disciples it is not enough to only verbally reaffirm the supremacy of One God or to understand this fact just as some kind of scientific formula. Rather, it is imperative that this perception is repeatedly invoked and kept ever fresh. *Ṣalāh* does the same thing. It reminds us of this fundamental truth before everything else as we rise from our bed early in the morning. Twice during the day, when we are busy with the humdrum of daily routine, it takes us away for brief intervals to refresh our sense of commitment to our Lord. Then, in the evening when it may be time for leisure and other personal engagements, it reminds us that we are His bondsmen and not servants of our own selves. Then comes the night, the time for which the devil within and the devils without have been waiting throughout the day to darken us with the gloom of disobedience, yet *ṣalāh* is there again much to their chagrin to take care of us and remind us of our duty towards our Lord.

This is the first advantage of *ṣalāh*. This is why the Qur'an also calls it *dhikr*, which means a reminder and remembrance. Even if there had been no other advantage to regular prayer, then this important aspect would have been enough to make it a pillar (*rukn*) of Islam. The more we look into the significance of this aspect of *ṣalāh*, the more we are convinced that it would have been difficult for the believers to live as bondsmen of their Lord without such an effective reminder.

7.2. The Obligation of Duty

As we are required to obey our Lord throughout our lives in this world and to perform the duties enjoined upon us, it is essential for us to be trained in the discipline of dutifulness in such a way that it becomes part of our character. Anyone unaware of his duty and its meaning and significance can obviously never be in a position to discharge it. Similarly, a person well aware of the duty he is required to perform and its significance but who has inadequate training for its proper discharge can hardly be expected to fulfil it in the way it should be done. Therefore, it is imperative for each and every servant of the Lord to be adequately trained in the discipline and art of devotion to duty. The advantage of such training is not restricted to the preparation of a trained cadre alone, but also serves as the criterion to distinguish between the useful and useless individuals of the supreme Lord's kingdom. In every active service, as we know, individuals are routinely required to pass through tests to distinguish and differentiate the competent ones from incompetents.

Let us see how the armed forces of a country pass through an elaborate process of rigorous training to achieve the excellence and competence to discharge their duties properly. The bugle is sounded many times during the day and night and the men are asked to fall in line at a particular place, where they have to do the drill routine. Why do they do this? Firstly, because the servicemen need to be groomed to obey orders. They are required to be a disciplined force capable of performing their duties in an orderly and trained manner. The second obligation is to test them daily to know who is fit and who is unfit for the job for which they have been recruited. If anyone sits back listlessly and does not rush to the parade ground at the sound of the bugle he is singled out. He is too unreliable to be trusted for any future call of duty.

Care is taken and drills are arranged for the manpower, which is only used as and when the need arises for its deployment. As for the workforce that Islam recruits, all times are its times of duty. This is the manpower that is always engaged in the discharge of its assignments. Its every moment is the moment of battle against the forces of evil. It has to defend the boundary lines drawn by Allah and execute His commands. Islam is not just a set of rituals. It stands for full-time duty, wherein there are no holidays, no leave or times to relax. We are on duty around the clock. Let us keep the analogy of armed forces in mind and then ponder how much more must be needed by way of strict discipline, rigorous training and intensive trials to execute such a difficult and tough assignment! Can the mere pronouncement of a solemn declaration be enough for a recruit who is to perform such an important duty? The declaration of one's faith is only an expression of one's interest in being a candidate for recruitment.

Following this, it is imperative that one passes through the drill as the member of a disciplined force. It is only within this discipline that an individual becomes worthy of his mission as a Muslim. If he is unwilling to be part of that discipline and respond to the call of duty and obey the instructions, then he is of no use to Islam. Allah Most Glorified and Exalted and His *dīn* – Islam as the way of life – are in no need of such a worthless person.

These are the twin objectives for which *ṣalāh* has been made obligatory five times a day. The bugle (of the call to prayer) is sounded five times a day so that the soldiers of Allah rush to the call and prove that they are dutiful and subservient to His supreme authority and are always ready to carry out His orders. On the one hand, this helps in training these soldiers and on the other in distinguishing believers from hypocrites: those who respond punctually to this call and are groomed in the qualities of devotion to duty, discipline and obedience; and, conversely, those who are unmoved by this call. They prove by their inaction that they are either unaware of their obligation, or they simply do not recognize the Authority that has made that duty obligatory for them, or it may be that their level of intelligence is so low as to keep them away from the first and foremost injunction of the Lord whom they have accepted as their Master and Sustainer. Even if such people claim to be among the believers, they are either untrue to their faith or they lack steadfastness. In the first case, they are not true Muslims and in the second they are not worthy of being part of the Muslim community.

This is why the holy Qur'an says about the *ṣalāh*: وَإِنَّهَا لَكَبِيرَةٌ إِلَّا عَلَى ٱلْخَٰشِعِينَ *Truly Prayer is burdensome for all except the devout* (*al-Baqarah* 2: 45). This means that the obligatory prayer is only hard for those who are reluctant to obey Allah's command and be His true bondsmen. In other words, those among the believers who find it hard to offer prayers demonstrate that they are unwilling to worship and obey the Lord. Therefore, the Qur'ān has declared:

فَإِن تَابُوا۟ وَأَقَامُوا۟ ٱلصَّلَوٰةَ وَءَاتَوُا۟ ٱلزَّكَوٰةَ فَإِخْوَٰنُكُمْ فِى ٱلدِّينِ ... ﴿١١﴾

But if they repent and establish prayer and give zakāh *they are your brothers in faith.*

(*al-Tawbah* 9: 11)

This obviously means that without prayer nobody can be a member of the community of Islam. The same is true with relation to other obligations. The holy Qur'an has been proclaimed, therefore, as being:

... هُدًى لِّلْمُتَّقِينَ ۝ ٱلَّذِينَ يُؤْمِنُونَ بِٱلْغَيْبِ وَيُقِيمُونَ ٱلصَّلَوٰةَ وَمِمَّا رَزَقْنَٰهُمْ يُنفِقُونَ ۝

It is a guidance for the pious, for those who believe in the existence of that which is beyond the reach of perception, who establish prayer and spend out of what We have provided them.

(*al-Baqarah* 2: 2–3)

On the other hand, the hypocrites are decried for having the following attributes:

... وَإِذَا قَامُوٓا۟ إِلَى ٱلصَّلَوٰةِ قَامُوا۟ كُسَالَىٰ ... ۝

When they rise to prayer they rise reluctantly.

(*al-Nisā'* 4: 142)

فَوَيْلٌ لِّلْمُصَلِّينَ ۝ ٱلَّذِينَ هُمْ عَن صَلَاتِهِمْ سَاهُونَ ۝

Woe, then, to those who pray, but are heedless in their prayers.

(*al-Mā'ūn* 107: 4–5)

This is the reason why it has been stated in a Prophetic tradition:

بَينَ العَبدِ وَ الكُفرِ تَركُ الصَّلوٰة

[The dividing line] between a bondsman [of the Lord] and an apostate is abandoning of Prayer.

(Muslim)

This tradition warns the believer that by wilfully abstaining from prayer one crosses the limits and moves on from the state of belief (*īmān*) to unbelief (*kufr*). This is why the holy Prophet, may Allah bless him and give him peace, whom history knows as 'mercy for all beings', sternly warned us: 'As for those who do not leave their homes even after listening to the *adhān*, I feel like going to their houses and setting them alight. He also declared:

العهدُ بَينَنَا وَبينهُم الصّلوٰةُ، فَمَن تَرَكَهَا فَقَد كَفَر

The bond linking us and the Bedouins is prayer. Whoever leaves it will be deemed to have disbelieved.

(Tirmidhī, Nasā'ī and Ibn Mājah)

Due to an inadequate knowledge of Islam, Muslims today are neither generally moved by the *adhān* nor care to know whom the muezzin is calling or for what. This is nothing but a sign of apathy and absence of commitment to Islam. When Islam was the leading light and a dynamic movement, the situation was entirely different and every believer bothered about the others and took those who lagged behind along with him on the right path. According to a tradition, the situation then regarding the observance of mandatory prayers was as follows:

كَانَ اَصحَابُ النَّبِيِّ ﷺ لَا يَرونَ شَيئاً مِنَ الاَعمَالِ تَركُهُ كُفرٌ غَيرَ الصَّلٰوةِ

> The Companions of the holy Prophet, may Allah bless him and give him peace, did not consider any act other than wilfully giving up *ṣalāh* as being akin to apostasy.
>
> (Tirmidhī)

7.3. Building Character

The third important aspect of prayer is that it builds one's character in a manner that is essential to leading an Islamic way of life. In other words, *ṣalāh* has been made mandatory to help the believer turn his whole life into an act of worship of Allah Most Glorified and Exalted.

As we all know, every state, nation or organization in the world tries to devise a system of training for its manpower in furtherance of its objectives. For example, the purpose of a civil service is to run a country's administration faithfully. Therefore, the main thrust in training its workforce is inculcating allegiance to the government in power and the ability to administer the system. The qualities of piety and purity do not constitute an essential part of that training. In his private life, a person may have many flaws of character, but there is no bar to check him from entering the civil service and rising in office to the highest level. That is because the government does not have on the agenda of its training programme for civil servants adherence to moral principles like righteousness, uprightness and truthfulness, nor does it make ethics the basis of its politics.

Similarly, the purpose of military training is to boost defence capability and preparedness for war. Soldiers are trained, therefore, to be constantly on a war footing. They parade routinely to teach them the disciplined way of doing things, are taught how to handle arms and ammunition, and are groomed to obey commands unhesitatingly so that they do anything the authority demands of them. With no higher moral objective in the agenda of their training, there is no particular concern to inculcate the spirit of *taqwā* or love and fear of God in a soldier's personal life. So long as he is disciplined, it fulfils the state's purpose. Beyond that it hardly matters if he is adulterous, alcoholic, tells lies, or is cruel or dishonest.

To the contrary, Islam seeks to develop a community whose principal objective is to establish virtue and eliminate vice. It is a community where permanent moral values prevail in every walk of life, be it politics, justice, trade, industry, war or peace, domestic affairs or international relations. Its mission is to enforce Shariah law on God's earth. Therefore, it grooms its functionaries, soldiers and officers under a different system of training in order to build within them the type of character suited to the special nature of their service. The essentials of the Islamic faith provide the foundations for this character: fear of the Lord, seeking His love, approval and pleasure as life's only goal, total allegiance to His supreme authority, and belief in being answerable to Him on the Day of Reckoning. A Muslim cannot move forward on the Islamic path without a firm belief that he is being observed at every moment, everywhere, and in all circumstances, and that God is aware of each and every action that he makes. He is being watched in darkness and daylight by his Lord Who is aware of the intentions that churn within his heart in his solitude and the ideas and thoughts which rage within his mind – neither is secret to Him. A man can escape punishment in this world, but not the penalty of the Hereafter. The good one does here may appear to bear no fruit in this world. One may even get a bad return for his good deeds [from people]. However, that is not possible before God.

The bounties of this world are limited but the blessings of the Lord are infinite. The gains and losses of this world are temporary and ephemeral; the gains and losses of the world beyond are permanent and everlasting. It is this firm belief that helps a person obey his Lord's commands and follow the dictates of His law. Inspired by the strength of his faith, a believer is always eager to abide by the norms and parameters of the lawful (halal) and the forbidden (haram), which Allah Most Exalted has set for the daily conduct of his life. It is this consideration that prevents him from surrendering to personal whims, the temptations of unlawful gains and lust for leisure and pleasure. It is this strength of faith that keeps a man on the right track of justice, truth, righteousness and the nobility of conduct. It is this that inspires him to stand up for the most difficult task of humanity's reformation, a task so immense that no unbeliever could ever think of shouldering such an onerous and enormous responsibility.

Ṣalāh is the discipline that keeps on refreshing these notions and planting them firmly within our minds and hearts. When we look deeper, we notice that the very intention to offer prayer sets in motion a process of character-building.

We notice that each and every movement, action and spoken word concerning *ṣalāh* has been so arranged that a believer's conduct and behaviour are automatically moulded into an Islamic frame.

7.4. Self-Control

In addition to building character, *ṣalāh* also rejuvenates an individual's power of self-control, without which the very purpose of human character remains unfulfilled. The objective of self-control is that it grooms the human ego and makes it more cultured. If this well-groomed ego does not have full control over the body's physical and psychological potential, which are like tools for it, then the very purpose of its training, i.e. correct behaviour and right conduct, cannot be achieved. Let us take for example the analogy of a motor car and its driver and think for a while that an individual is a combination of a car and its driver. Can we imagine this combination will work properly without the driver having full control over all parts of the vehicle and its mechanisms? Obviously not. Unless both the driver and his vehicle are in perfect harmony and the one in the driving seat has complete command of the system, the combination cannot function. Furthermore, the driver must be equipped with driving skills and know the route he has to follow. If the driver is fully trained, but does not have proper control over the steering, brakes and accelerator, then he will not drive the vehicle. Instead, the vehicle will drive him. Since the car only knows how to run but lacks eyesight, judgement or road sense, when in motion it will unwittingly take its driver through any obstacle that comes its way.

According to this analogy, the physical potential of man, his psychological stimuli and intellectual prowess make the vehicle, while his ego or personal self represents the driver. This human motor car is as ignorant a machine as its counterpart in steel: the only difference being while the former is full of life the latter is lifeless. This vehicle has desires, feelings and motives and is always keen not to allow the driver to do his job, but be the driver itself. The teachings of all the Prophets of God aim at training this driver in such a way that the vehicle does not override him. Instead, he should ride over the car according to his own discretion, taking the right road to his destination.

The prescribed supplications and phrases in praise of the Lord (*tasbīḥāt*), the observance of punctuality of time, cleanliness (*ṭahārah*), etc. have been included as prerequisites for the proper performance of prayer. These have the express purpose of keeping the driver in firm control and making him an expert in the art of driving. That is how the waywardness of the car is checked five times a day: its brakes are tightened, and the accelerator and steering are kept in perfect order.

An individual is lulled into sound sleep by the early morning breeze and his leisure-loving psyche tells him to stay in bed; but the time for prayer comes and it calls him to rise up from his bed, have a bath if the need be or perform ablution, even if he does not have hot water on a freezing winter morning. He then has to walk to the nearest mosque braving the early morning chill. These are two opposing demands. If he submits to his psyche's dictates, it means he has let the car ride over him. Yet if the call for *ṣalāh* is answered, he succeeds in keeping his vehicle under his firm control.

We may similarly have so many excuses of preoccupations, gains and losses, rest and relaxation, and other exigencies to prevent us from our Ẓuhr, ʿAṣr, Maghrib and 'Ishā' prayers. Our inner self is always on the lookout for an opportunity to exploit our weaknesses and ride over us, but the prayer is there to reawaken our will power and tell us to tighten our belts for a perfect ride. This is a daily battle that we face at different times, circumstances and ways. At times of rest, during business or leisure hours, in times of joy and sorrow, during summer or winter, at home or while traveling, we are always in a state of constant strife between our inner selves and the call of duty from our Lord. It is a test of our self-control. If we surrender to the dictates of our whims, we lose the battle. The servant then becomes the master and we are left at the mercy of a blind and ignorant force, one that drags us uncontrollably through all the ups and downs. Conversely, if we fulfil the demands of *ṣalāh*, we are in a position to crush the might of this rebellious force and use it according to our knowledge and expertise.

This is why the holy Qur'an cautions us regarding the immediate and inevitable result of one's disregard for prayer, according to which one is turned into a blind follower of one's temptations and desires, is lost in alleyways and back alleys, and strays away from the right path:

فَخَلَفَ مِنۢ بَعۡدِهِمۡ خَلۡفٌ أَضَاعُواْ ٱلصَّلَوٰةَ وَٱتَّبَعُواْ ٱلشَّهَوَٰتِۖ فَسَوۡفَ يَلۡقَوۡنَ غَيًّا ﴿٥٩﴾

They were succeeded by a people who neglected the prayers and pursued their lusts. They shall soon meet with their doom.

(*Maryam* 19: 59)

7.5. A Training Programme

The discourse so far has covered just one aspect of the benefits and advantages we draw from *ṣalāh*, namely how *ṣalāh* prepares a person as an upright individual. Before we proceed further, let us have an overview of the individual's training programme through *ṣalāh*. The five-part programme is designed to do the following: (1) create awareness that no individual is a sovereign entity but a subject of the Supreme Lord of all the worlds and in that capacity he has to do his part here; (2) make every individual dutiful as a subject and inculcate within him the quality of devotion to duty; (3) cultivate the ability to distinguish between obedience and disobedience, and right and wrong; (4) instil deep into the human mind a whole system of thought and action such that it becomes part of one's character; and (5) empower a person ethically so effectively that it is convenient for him to act correctly according to his faith, knowledge and insight and make the best use of the potential of his body and soul.

The social order that Islam creates helps in the character-building of each and every believer through its unique system of prayer. *Ṣalāh* becomes mandatory for every Muslim boy and girl when he or she nears adulthood. It is a duty a Muslim has to perform under all circumstances, except when incapacitated or insensible or – in case of a woman – during menstruation or childbirth. It is obligatory even when sick, while traveling, or on the battlefront. If a person cannot stand up, he is to perform the prayer while sitting. If he can't sit up, he can discharge this duty reclining or lying down. If one cannot even move one's limbs, then one may nod one's head. If water is unavailable for ablution or bathing, then one can use the clean soil for *tayammum*.[1] If one is unaware of the direction of the *qiblah*, then one can use his discretion to face the most likely direction. In short, there is no excuse for a Muslim not to perform this fundamental obligation, which becomes due the moment the time for prayer comes in.

We may say without any fear of contradiction that there is no social order in the world other than Islam that has devised such a comprehensive programme to train society's constituent parts – each and every individual – so thoroughly. The main thrust of the world's social systems is on strengthening the respective community's structural set-up and tying individuals together through external bolts and screws. Generally, little effort has been made to synergize each component from within and mould individuals according to the aims and objectives of a particular community. The community is like a wall made from bricks in the form of its members. Unless each and every brick is held firmly in place, the wall as a whole remains weak. Similarly, if there is weakness in the character of individuals, if their perceptions do not conform to the community's social

[1] *Tayammum* is the act of rubbing both hands on a clean hard surface and then moving them across the face as in ablution and then for a second time wiping one's hands from fingertips up to the elbow. This has a symbolic significance as substitute for *wuḍū'* in exegencies when water is unavailable. — Editor.

norms and if they display anti-community trends, then no external checks can keep its social order intact for long. Eventually, a revolt from within is bound to rise up and shatter the system to bits.

7.6. Building Community

Let us now look at another aspect of *ṣalāh*. Even individuals of sterling character cannot have a desirable impact unless the collective character of the community is receptive. How can an individual attain his noble objectives without the active cooperation and support of those among whom he lives? A person, however correctly motivated, can hardly practise the principles which he believes in unless and until the entire life of the community is based on them too. No one is born in isolation in this world, nor can one do anything singlehandedly. The whole fabric of life is interwoven with thousands of strands, including family, friends, associates, superiors and subordinates, etc. Man has been commissioned on earth by Allah Most Exalted to enforce Divine law in his individual as well as collective capacities. *ʿIbādah* in practical terms is nothing but to act upon this law and to enact it in letter and spirit. If a person is surrounded by people who do not believe in the Divine law, are given as a whole to rebellion or in their social interaction are unwilling to cooperate with each other for its implementation, then it will be naturally difficult for him to enforce it even in his personal life, let alone achieve its enforcement in the community as a whole.

Moreover, life for a Muslim in this world is a battlefront. He is confronted with a complex struggle and perpetual strife and conflict. At each and every step, he has to encounter strong bands of rebels against God who are busy enforcing their own self-made laws. On the other hand, the believers have been assigned by their Lord with the onerous responsibility of spreading His message and enforcing the dictates of His Shariah in all walks of life. No Muslim can undertake such a difficult task alone. Even if millions of believers launch their individual efforts independently, they would still not succeed against the organized collective strength of the rebel force. It is therefore imperative that all bondsmen of Allah Most Exalted, who wish sincerely to worship Him and turn their individual and collective life into *ʿibādah* should become a single team, support one another, and stand hand in hand to achieve their cherished goal collectively.

To materialize their objective needs, Muslims should get together on the correct lines. What is needed is not just any social order, but a lofty social order in which each and every tie between Muslims are exactly those desired by Islam. These ties are to be marked by a strong sense of love, equality, fraternity, solidarity, and unity in thought and action. Allah's love and fear are to be the driving force of community life. The spirit of cooperation and goodwill must be the hallmark of their collective action. Each of them should be aware of their position and responsibility in society: their duties towards their fellow men and women; the parameters of their allegiance to a person entrusted with the community's leadership, and the duty of the leader towards the community and its collective well-being.

7.7. The Congregational Prayer (*Ṣalāt al-Jamāʿah*)

In addition to facilitating the building of character both individually and collectively, regular prayer also helps to raise the entire structure of the Islamic social order, sustaining it and reactivating it five times a day. It keeps it vibrant like a well-oiled machine. Therefore, our Lord has made it obligatory for us to offer regular prayers in congregation. According to the Islamic Shariah, the offering of prayer individually is only permissible when there is a genuine excuse that prevents it from being offered collectively in a mosque. If someone does so wilfully and without any sanction from Divine law, he will be committing a sin. This emphasis on congregational prayer in the mosque assembly helps to keep alive the dynamism of Islam's community life. Getting together five times a day in a mosque lays the foundation stone for Muslim community life. The strength of the community's structure depends on the strength of this foundation. Once this foundation becomes weak, the whole edifice crumbles.

The purpose of *adhān* is to assemble the believers together in a mosque. The very act of getting together has many advantages. We know that each of us is assembling there in his capacity of being bondsmen of the One and Only God, the follower of one Prophet, the believer in one Book, and sharing the same objective in life. We assemble there bearing in mind the obligation of this oneness. We are expected to have the same spirit of unity and oneness outside the mosque. Such a collective sense automatically generates within us the feeling that we are all a single nation, the soldiers of a single army, and brothers and comrades in arms of one another. We develop the feeling that we share common goals and objectives, common stakes for gains and losses in this world, and that we have so much in common with each other that if we rise we rise together and if we fall we fall together.

Moved by this notion, when we see each other in the mosque we keep our eyes and our hearts wide open. This is not like seeing the enemy, but as one friend looks at another and a brother at his brother. When we face each other from this perspective and find that a brother of ours is in tatters, another looks disturbed and worried, the signs of hunger are writ large on someone else's face, or that a person is physically handicapped, lame or blind, then we naturally feel sympathy for them.[2] The affluent among us automatically feel compassionate towards those who are poor and in need. Those in distress have easy access to the rich to apprise them of their plight. If someone is missing from the congregation, his brothers from the mosque visit him to enquire about his welfare and, in case of death, his comrades from the mosque attend his funeral, visit his home and console his bereaved family and friends. These are some added advantages of the mosque assembly. The assembly thus becomes directly responsible for promoting mutual trust, love and affection and bringing the people together and infusing within them the spirit of cooperation and compassion.

The factor responsible for bringing us together in the mosque has nothing to do with worldly gains, pastimes, entertainment, gambling, drinking or carnal desire. Our intentions and motives are free from the impurities of heart and mind that characterize the gatherings of the self-seekers of this world. The mosque assembly is one of Allah's bondsmen who flock together in His House in utter humility. Most of them are humbled with a sense of guilt as they are conscious of their sins. In the event of a chance encounter in the mosque with someone against whom we might have done some wrong, it adds to our feelings of remorse and guilt and may well provide us with an opportunity for reconciliation and redress of the wrong done. Furthermore, many among the congregation know how best to use the qualities of good counsel, sympathy and affection to reform such a situation. The mosque assembly, therefore, is of great significance. It has the potential to reform society and forge the whole congregation into a tight-knit group of well-meaning and God-fearing people.

7.8. The Call to Prayer (*Adhān*)

Let us now briefly examine various aspects of our regular prayers. We may take the *adhān* first. Let us see how we are called to prayers five times a day:

Allah is the Greatest, Allah is the Greatest!	اَللّٰهُ اَكبَر، اَللّٰهُ اَكبَر
I bear witness that there is no God but Allah [None is fit for worship but He].	اَشْهَدُ اَن لَّا اِلٰهَ اِلَّا اللّٰه

[2] With this sense of the Islamic bond, care and compassion for the less privileged and the afflicted has been demonstrated time and again in our community. In times of emergencies and natural disasters, like earthquakes, floods, droughts, epidemics, etc., we have seen how our philanthropists have moved forward, individually and collectively, to provide the affected persons with the maximum possible succour. Even non-Muslim communities are offered help purely for Allah's pleasure without any personal, political or missionary considerations. In fact, we are second to none in the world in philanthropy and it has been acknowledge even by world figures and the free press. — Editor.

I bear witness that Muhammad is the Messenger of Allah.	اَشْهَدُ اَنَّ مُحَمَّداً رَّسُولُ الله
Come to Prayer!	حَيَّ عَلَى الصَّلٰوة
Come to His Blessing!	حَيَّ عَلَى الفَلَاح
Allah is the Greatest! Allah is the Greatest!	اَللهُ اَكبَر، اَللهُ اَكبَر
There is no God but Allah.	لَآ اِلٰهَ اِلَّا اَللهُ

The following line is added in the call for the pre-dawn prayer (*adhān al-Fajr*):

Prayer is better than sleep.	اَلصَّلٰوةُ خَيرٌ مِّنَ النَّوم

See, what a forceful call this is? We are reminded five times every day that all the false deities of this world, all those claiming godhood, are shams. Greatness is just for the One and Only God and He alone is worthy of worship. Come and worship Him, for in His worship lies our well-being, both in this world and the Hereafter! Who would not be moved by such a call? Is it possible for anyone with faith in his heart not to respond to such a forceful invitation and hasten to bow his head in humility before his Lord and Master?

We have been directed to respond to the call to prayer, to leave everything else and make a beeline towards the mosque. A Muslim's scramble at this call towards a focal point has almost the same connotations we notice with the scrambling of men in uniform. Soldiers rush to the appointed place at the sounding of the bugle. Every one of them is moved by the same thought of obeying the command and leaves aside all other work to assemble at one place. Why has this been prescribed for those in the armed forces? It is firstly done to inculcate in each and every soldier the habit of obedience to the call of duty and his ever-readiness to respond to that call. Secondly, its purpose is to mould the soldiers into a tight-knit group and team that is well-motivated and disciplined, to scramble at the beck and call of the commanding officer so that as and when the need arises they can be quickly reassembled for an expedition or the task ahead. In this way, the group of individual soldiers is ready for deployment as a single unit. In military terminology, this is called rapid mobility and it is the driving force of military life. Should an army lose this capability and the soldiers become ill-disciplined, it would be unable to carry out any manoeuver or operation effectively, although it may be composed of soldiers, whom, in their individual capacity, might be full of the spirit of bravado and chivalry. A single, well-disciplined platoon of enemy troops can exterminate a thousand such 'brave' but disorganized soldiers.

It is exactly for the same community interest that it has been enjoined upon each and every Muslim to rush to their nearest mosque on hearing the *adhān*. The drill takes place five times a day, because as soldiers of the Divine force the task before the believers is much more difficult than the one before normal soldiers. As stated earlier, soldiers in uniform have to take part in important missions once in a while for which they are kept battle-ready through a series of drills. Muslim men and women, who are soldiers of Allah on His earth, are faced all the time with an expedition against the forces of evil. It is only natural for them to be drilled into battle-readiness for which they are required to assemble at least five times a day at the sounding of the *adhān*'s 'bugle'.

7.9. How to Proceed for Prayer

As we intend to offer prayer, we first ascertain if we are in a state of cleanliness and purity (*ṭahārah*). Are our clothes clean, soiled or dirty? Have we performed *wuḍū*'? Let us reflect for a moment about this concern for *ṭahārah*. Had we offered our prayer in a state of uncleanliness or without ablution, who would have known this and caught or punished us? What is the reason for our being so conscious about this prerequisite for prayer? Obviously, there is no reason other than our fear of our Lord, our Master and Sustainer.

7.9.1. *Ablution* (Wuḍū')

On hearing the call to prayer, we leave our other activities and go and perform our ablutions in the prescribed manner. What does this show? It makes us realize that to have an audience with our Lord is different from everything else that we do. Unless we are physically clean, our clothes are unsoiled, and we have performed *wuḍū*', we are unworthy of being in His presence. During the course of *wuḍū*', while washing our limbs, we constantly remember Allah. After ablution, we recite the following supplication taught to us by our master the Messenger of Allah, may Allah bless him and give him peace:

اَشْهَدُ اَنْ لاَ اِلٰهَ اِلاَّاللهُ، وَحْدَهُ، لاَ شَرِيكَ لَهُ، وَاَشْهَدُ اَنَّ مُحَمَّداً عَبْدُهُ وَرَسُولُهُ.
اَللّٰهُمَّ اجْعَلْنِى مِنَ التَّوَّابِينَ وَاجْعَلْنِى مِنَ الْمُتَطَهِّرِين

> I bear witness that there is no god but Allah: He alone is God, and none is His partner. I also bear witness that Muhammad is Allah's servant and His messenger. O God! Make me among those who repent and keep themselves pure.

Now, we are bodily clean and spiritually fit to line up for *ṣalāh* with due solemnity, as though we are in the very presence of Allah Most Glorified and Exalted. We face the *qiblah*, signifying the focal point of our attention. Now we do our best to perform each and every act of prayer and recite the verses from the holy Qur'an, and the supplications and salutations exactly the way these have been prescribed. Why is there this strict adherence to the prescribed text? Some recitations are not done aloud and one can easily skip them, or replace them with something of one's own choosing. There is nobody to hold one responsible, but we do not do that and observe the prescribed way strictly. Whom do we fear knowing of our transgression? I am sure the answer is obvious to each of us.

7.9.2. *Lining Up for Prayer* (Taswīyat al-Ṣufūf)
Every Muslim in the mosque enjoys an equal status. A cobbler will occupy the first row if he comes first; a millionaire will stand in the back-row if he is late. No matter how eminent or powerful, no one has the right to reserve a place. Nobody is entitled to stop someone from occupying a place, or to ask him to vacate his place for someone else. No one has the right to disturb the order by pushing past others to reach the front rows. Everyone has to fall into one line, standing shoulder to shoulder with his fellow Muslims to offer prayer. There is neither big nor small here, neither high nor low. No one becomes 'impure' if touched by someone else or is dishonoured by rubbing shoulders with somebody less privileged. A sweeper or scavenger may sit next to or stand beside a governor or president and nobody has any right to object.

This is the type of social democracy that Islam alone has established successfully on God's earth. It is here in the mosque that the society's 'privileged' and 'unprivileged' stand equally five times daily: the egos of the privileged are purged of self-conceit and arrogance and the sense of lowliness is removed from the minds of the socially deprived. Each one of us is reminded of the fact that we are all equal before the Lord.

This process of lining up for prayer (*taswīyat al-ṣufūf*) not only removes feelings of class distinction, but also helps to eliminate ethnic, tribal, national and racial prejudices. No mosque discriminates in favour of a particular group that occupies a distinct position in life. Every believer lining up for prayer enjoys the same status. He may be white, black, brown or yellow, Asian or European, Semitic or Aryan, or speak whatever language or dialect, but he is first and foremost a Muslim. An assembly of this type five times a day is an effective means of uprooting the prejudices that generally flourish in human societies. It promotes the spirit of human unity, strengthens the roots of universal brotherhood, and deeply injects within our minds and hearts the thought that all differences on the basis of ethnicity, clan, caste and colour are meaningless. Every believer is a bondsman of Allah and those who unite in His *ʿibādah* make one *ummah*, a universal community.

When these worshippers stand together in one row, shoulder to shoulder and feet to feet, and perform *rukūʿ* and *sujūd* in unison, they are naturally in a position to develop within themselves the qualities of a collective manoeuvre, the development of which soldiers are made to assemble and march on the parade ground. This is the purpose behind such drills: to enable Muslims to forge the spirit of solidarity and unity of action and become like one body in their bondsmanship of Allah Most Glorified and Exalted.

7.9.3. *The Call for Commencement of Prayer* (Iqāmah)

The performance of *wuḍū'* means that we are ready for *ṣalāh*. The time then comes to rise up and join the lines of the congregation (*ṣufūf al-muṣallīn*). As we stand up in straight rows, the person behind the imam calls the *iqāmah*. The wordings of the *iqāmah* are the same as those for the *adhān*, except that the following announcement is repeated twice:

The prayer is about to commence.	قَد قَامَتِ الصَّلٰوٰة

7.9.4. *Collective Supplication*

The advantages accrued by this act of standing in a row for prayer are made doubly beneficial by the supplications made to the Almighty in *ṣalāh*. The congregation submits in unison to the Lord: *You alone do we worship and You alone do we turn for help* (إِيَّاكَ نَعْبُدُ وَإِيَّاكَ نَسْتَعِينُ), *Direct us on to the straight way* (اَهْدِنَا الصِّرَاطَ الْمُسْتَقِيمَ), and 'Peace be upon us and on all good bondsmen of Allah' (اَلسَّلَامُ عَلَيْنَا وَعَلَىٰ عِبَادِاللهِ الصَّالِحِينَ.). In these collective prayers and supplications, no singular pronoun or verb is ever used; these are always in a plural form.

Our collective action in the performance of *ṣalāh*, bowing down (*rukūʿ*) and prostration (*sujūd*), impresses upon every Muslim five times a day that he is not alone. He should not only aspire towards and desire things for himself; instead, his life is linked with his community. In the well-being of his community lies his own well-being. His own good lies in following the right path being taken by his community. He can have his share of the blessings and bounties of Allah Most Exalted only if his community is worthy of these. All this helps in purging the human mind of individualism and infusing the spirit of social cohesion within it. This is how the noble sentiments of compassion, love and fellow-feeling are promoted among members of the Muslim *ummah*.

7.9.5. Ṣalāh *from Beginning to End*

Now, let us go through the entire process of this most sublime exercise. From beginning to end, each and every syllable that we utter in *ṣalāh* reflects the basic concepts and spirit of Islam. As we repeat certain expressions, those basics of our faith are refreshed repeatedly in our minds upon which stands the whole edifice of Islamic character.

Firstly, we raise both our hands up to our earlobes, as if we are abdicating and renouncing all worldly things.[3] Then we say 'Allah is the Greatest' (اَللهُ أَكبَر), fold our hands together and stand in humility and respect before our supreme Sovereign.[4] And then we solemnly intone as follows:

إِنِّي وَجَّهْتُ وَجْهِيَ لِلَّذِي فَطَرَ السَّمَاوَاتِ وَالأَرْضَ حَنِيفًا وَمَا أَنَاْ مِنَ الْمُشْرِكِينَ .

> I have turned my face wholeheartedly towards Him Who has created the heavens and the earth, and I am not one of those who assign partners unto Him in His Kingdom.

We are now ready to proceed further. The actual act of *ṣalāh* begins with submissions and recitations from the holy Qur'an as indicated below:

7.9.5.1. Glorification of God (*Tasbīḥ*)

We glorify and praise the Lord with these words:

سبُحَانَكَ اللّٰهُمَّ وَبِحَمدِكَ وَ تَبَارَكَ اسمُكَ وَ تَعَالىٰ جَدُّكَ وَلاَ اِلٰهَ غَيرُكَ.

> How perfect You are, My Allah! All praise be to You! Most blessed is Your name and exalted is Your majesty! There is no god but You![5]

---

[3] The raising of one's hands symbolizes two things: the first is the act of surrender, i.e. abandoning resistance from within and without for total surrender to the will of the Lord. The second is abdication, or lifting one's hands away from everything that belongs to him. — Author.

[4] To stand before somebody with hands folded together is an expression of extreme respect, obedience and humble submission. Therefore, this has been a favoured act of humility that kings introduced to royal protocol. However, Islam restricted this act exclusively for appearing before the supreme Sovereign. — Author.

[5] Allah Most High is 'perfect' and far above any flaw, defect, or weakness. To Him belongs all praise, i.e. He alone is worthy of all good attributes. — Author.

7.9.5.2. Seeking Refuge and Protection with the Lord (*Ta ʿawwudh*)

اَعُوذُبِاللهِ مِنَ الشَّيطٰنِ الرَّجِيم.

I seek protection of the Lord from the mischief of Satan, the damned.

7.9.5.3. Invocation of His Name (*Tasmiyah*)

بِسْمِ ٱللَّهِ ٱلرَّحْمَـٰنِ ٱلرَّحِيمِ ۝

In the name of Allah, the Most Merciful, the Most Compassionate.

7.9.5.4. Praise and Supplication (*al-Ḥamd*)

As contained in *Sūrah al-Fātiḥah*, the opening chapter of the holy Qur'an:

ٱلْحَمْدُ لِلَّهِ رَبِّ ٱلْعَـٰلَمِينَ ۝ ٱلرَّحْمَـٰنِ ٱلرَّحِيمِ ۝ مَـٰلِكِ يَوْمِ ٱلدِّينِ ۝ إِيَّاكَ نَعْبُدُ وَإِيَّاكَ نَسْتَعِينُ ۝
ٱهْدِنَا ٱلصِّرَٰطَ ٱلْمُسْتَقِيمَ ۝ صِرَٰطَ ٱلَّذِينَ أَنْعَمْتَ عَلَيْهِمْ غَيْرِ ٱلْمَغْضُوبِ عَلَيْهِمْ وَلَا ٱلضَّآلِّينَ ۝ (آمين!)

Praise be to Allah, the Lord of the entire Universe, the Most Merciful, the Most Compassionate, the Master of the Day of Recompense. You alone do we worship and You alone do we turn to for help. Direct us on to the straight way; the way of those whom You have favoured, who did not incur Your wrath, who are not astray. (My Lord, Grant us our prayers!)

(*al-Fātiḥah* 1: 1–7)

7.9.5.5. Reciting Qur'anic Verses

Some selected verses frequently recited in *ṣalāh* are as follows:

وَٱلْعَصْرِ ۝ إِنَّ ٱلْإِنسَـٰنَ لَفِى خُسْرٍ ۝ إِلَّا ٱلَّذِينَ ءَامَنُوا۟ وَعَمِلُوا۟ ٱلصَّـٰلِحَـٰتِ وَتَوَاصَوْا۟ بِٱلْحَقِّ
وَتَوَاصَوْا۟ بِٱلصَّبْرِ ۝

By time! Surely, man is in a state of loss. Save those who have faith and do righteous deeds; and counsel each other to hold on to truth and counsel each other to be steadfast.

(*al-ʿAṣr* 103:1–3)

In these few uniquely brief but extraordinary verses, some universal truths have been brought home to man. He has been told that he cannot escape loss, failure and destruction until he follows the path of his Lord and does good deeds. Additionally, it is imperative for his well-being that the good he does should not be just through individual acts, but his entire social set-up must be such that the spirit of righteousness prevails in it. For this, he must form or join the group of the faithful, who strive together and help each other in remaining steadfast in the cause of truth. Time as the record-keeper of human history has been a witness to this fact throughout the ages.

أَرَءَيْتَ ٱلَّذِى يُكَذِّبُ بِٱلدِّينِ ﴿١﴾ فَذَٰلِكَ ٱلَّذِى يَدُعُّ ٱلْيَتِيمَ ﴿٢﴾ وَلَا يَحُضُّ عَلَىٰ طَعَامِ ٱلْمِسْكِينِ ﴿٣﴾ فَوَيْلٌ
لِّلْمُصَلِّينَ ﴿٤﴾ ٱلَّذِينَ هُمْ عَن صَلَاتِهِمْ سَاهُونَ ﴿٥﴾ ٱلَّذِينَ هُمْ يُرَآءُونَ ﴿٦﴾ وَيَمْنَعُونَ ٱلْمَاعُونَ ﴿٧﴾

Did you see him who gives the lie to the reward and punishment of the Hereafter? Such is one who repulses the orphans away; and urges not the feeding of the needy. Woe, then, to those who pray but are heedless in their prayers; those who do good (in order) to be seen; and deny people the articles of common necessity.

(*al-Mā'ūn* 107: 1–7)

In this seven-verse chapter, we are reminded of the impact that firm belief in the reckoning of the Hereafter has on man's moral conduct, and how its absence makes the individual's attitude and social behaviour devoid of sincerity and sympathy for his fellow human beings. It has been impressed upon us that faith that does not lead to a responsible and kindly sharing with others of the joys and sorrows of life is no faith at all.

وَيْلٌ لِّكُلِّ هُمَزَةٍ لُّمَزَةٍ ﴿١﴾ ٱلَّذِى جَمَعَ مَالًا وَعَدَّدَهُۥ ﴿٢﴾ يَحْسَبُ أَنَّ مَالَهُۥٓ أَخْلَدَهُۥ ﴿٣﴾ كَلَّا ۖ لَيُنۢبَذَنَّ فِى
ٱلْحُطَمَةِ ﴿٤﴾ وَمَآ أَدْرَىٰكَ مَا ٱلْحُطَمَةُ ﴿٥﴾ نَارُ ٱللَّهِ ٱلْمُوقَدَةُ ﴿٦﴾ ٱلَّتِى تَطَّلِعُ عَلَى ٱلْأَفْـِٔدَةِ ﴿٧﴾ إِنَّهَا
عَلَيْهِم مُّؤْصَدَةٌ ﴿٨﴾ فِى عَمَدٍ مُّمَدَّدَةٍۭ ﴿٩﴾

Woe to every fault-finding backbiter; who amasses wealth and counts it over and again. He thinks that his wealth will immortalize him forever. Nay, he shall surely be thrown into the Crusher. And do you know what the Crusher is? It is the Fire kindled by Allah, the Fire that shall rise to the hearts (of criminals). Verily it will close in upon them in outstretched columns.

(*al-Humazah* 104: 1–9)

Similarly, this chapter instructs us in important social attitudes. It censors those who engage in slandering others and spreading false reports. Love of worldly wealth is what leads them to treat others with contempt, but the wealth they accumulate they eventually leave behind, only to see it again as a fire raging within and around their hearts.

These are just a few references, which give us an idea as to why it has been made obligatory to recite some verses from the holy Qur'an in prayer. The definite purpose is to remind us repeatedly of God's injunctions, guidance and instructions. This world of ours is a place of labour where man has been sent to work. To run it smoothly, man needs to be called at intervals away from his routine to remind him of the code of conduct prescribed for him and the guidance necessary for him to lead a successful life. Whichever chapter or verses we recite in *ṣalāh* they enlighten us about the guidelines Allah Most Exalted has revealed for human beings to follow.

7.9.5.6. Bowing Down (*Rukūʿ*)

After reciting the Qur'anic verses, the devotee (*muṣallī*) says 'Allah is the Greatest' (اَللهُ اَكبَر) and bows down.[6] During this act of *rukūʿ* we keep our hands on our knees and repeat, 'Glory be to my Lord, the Magnificent' (سُبحَانَ رَبِّیَ العَظِیم). We then stand up and say, 'Allah listens to him who praises Him' (سَمِعَ اللهُ لِمَن حَمِدَه).

7.9.5.7. Prostration (*Sujūd*)

Now, he goes twice into the act of prostration (*sajdah*) while saying, 'God is the Greatest' (اَللهُ اَكبَر).[7] During this act of prostration he repeats thrice, 'Glory to my Lord, the Most High' (سُبحَانَ رَبِّیَ الاَعلٰی).

7.9.5.8. The Act of Bearing Witness (*Tashahhud*)

Then follows the sitting posture (*qaʿdah*). The devotee sits in all humility and recites the following as 'an act of bearing witness to and reaffirming his faith and allegiance to Allah Most Glorified and Exalted and His Prophet our master Muhammad, may Allah bless him and give him peace' (or *tashahhud*):

اَلتَحِيَّاتُ لله وَالصَّلَوَاتُ وَالطَّيِّبَاتُ، اَلسَّلاَمُ عَلَيكَ ايُّهَا النَّبِیُّ وَرَحمَةُ الله وَ بَرَكَاتُهُ،
اَلسَّلاَمُ عَلَينَا وَعَلٰی عِبَادِالله الصَّالِحِين. اَشـهَدُ اَن لاَّ اِلٰهَ اِلَّا اللهُ وُ اَشـهَدُ اَنَّ مُحَمداً
عَبدُهُ وَرَسُولُهُ.

[6] This act of bowing down (*rukūʿ*)is a progression of the same process of submission and surrender that started with the raising of the hands for *ṣalāh*. — Author.

[7] The act of falling prostrate (*sajdah*) complements the same process of submission and surrender. It signifies man's willing submission before his Lord by putting his forehead on the ground in an expression of self-negation and surrender of his ego. — Author.

> To God belongs all greetings of praise, and all prayers, and all good deeds. Peace be upon you, O Prophet, and the mercy of God and His blessings. Peace be upon us and on all true servants of God. I bear witness that there is no god but Allah and I bear witness that Muhammad is His servant and His Messenger.

During this act of witness (*shahādah*), he raises the index finger of his right hand. As this is the declaration of a Muslim's faith during the course of his *ṣalāh*, he is required to be more assertive when reciting these words.

7.9.5.9. Sending Blessings upon the Prophet (*Ṣalāt ʿalā al-Nabiyy*)

Next, he invokes Allah's benedictions upon the holy Prophet, may Allah bless him and give him peace, and his family and says:

اَللّٰهُمَّ صَلِّ عَلىٰ مُحَمَّدٍ وَعَلىٰ آلِ مُحَمَّدٍ كَمَا صَلَيتَ عَلىٰ اِبرَاهِيمَ وَ عَلىٰ آلِ اِبرَاهِيمَ، اِنَّكَ حَمِيدٌ مجِيد. اَللّٰهُمَّ بَارِك عَلىٰ مُحَمَّدٍ وَعَلىٰ آلِ مُحَمَّدٍ كَمَا بَارَكتَ عَلىٰ اِبرَاهِيمَ وَ عَلىٰ آلِ اِبرَاهِيمَ، اِنَّكَ حَمِيدٌ مجِيد.

> O, my Lord, let Your mercy be upon Muhammad and the family of Muhammad the way You were merciful upon Abraham and the family of Abraham. Indeed, You are the Most Praiseworthy and the Most Glorious. O, my Lord, let Your blessings be upon Muhammad and the family of Muhammad, the way You showered Your blessings on Abraham and his family. You are the Most Praiseworthy and the Most Glorious.

7.9.5.10. Seeking the Protection of the Lord

The whole *ṣalāh* is an act of prayer and supplication before the Lord, but towards the end we conclude with a special prayer seeking the protection of the Almighty from all kinds of evils that might afflict us.

اَللّٰهُمَّ اِنِىّ اَعُوذُ بِكَ مِن عَذَابِ جهنَّمَ، وَاَعُوذُ بِكَ مِن عَذَابِ القَبرِ، وَاَعُوذُ بِكَ مِن فِتنةِ المَسِيحِ الدَّجَّال، وَاَعُوذُ بِكَ مِن فِتنةِ المَحيا وَالمَمَات، وَاَعُوذُ بِكَ مِن المَأثَمِ وَالمَغرَم.

> O God! I seek Your protection from punishment in Hell, and I seek Your protection from punishment in the grave, and I seek Your

protection from the mischief of the Great Imposter (*al-masīḥ al-dajjāl*), and I seek Your protection from the trials of life and death, and I seek Your protection from sins and indebtedness'.

7.9.5.11. Greeting (*Salām*)

Following the recitation of *du'ā'*, our prayer is complete. Now we are to turn our faces from our audience with the Lord towards our right and left and pray for our safety and the Lord's blessings for all those present and not present from amongst the believers:

السَّلَامُ عَلَيْكُم وَرَحمَةُ الله

Peace be on all of you and the mercy of God.

The *salām* symbolizes the good tidings that the one offering prayer brings for himself and those around following his return from God's presence.

This is the prescribed way to offer *ṣalāh* five times a day. We begin our daily routine by offering the pre-dawn prayer. Just after midday, we present ourselves again before our Lord. In the afternoon, we again offer *ṣalāh* and then repeat it immediately after sunset. Finally, before going to bed, we present ourselves before the Almighty. The evening prayer (*ṣalāt al-'ishā'*) is immediately followed, however, by yet one more prayer called *ṣalāt al-witr*.

7.9.5.12. The Supplication of Subservience (*Du'ā' al-Qunūt*)

The process of 'Ishā' prayer concludes with *ṣalāt al-witr*, which is also the last prayer of the day. In its last prayer-cycle (*rak'ah*), which turns *ṣalāt al-witr* into the odd number of three-*rak'āt* and hence it is called *witr*, the devotee makes an important and comprehensive covenant with the Lord. This is called the 'supplication of subservience' (*du'ā' al-qunūt*). The meaning of *qunūt* is reaffirmation before God of our humility, subservience and bondsmanship. The person offering prayer is expected to ponder carefully over the words with which he makes his pledge to his Lord. (The text of the supplication and its meaning can be found in Section 2.3.1.)

The text of the *du'ā' al-qunūt* demonstrates amply how Islam trains each and every member of the Muslim society with their end in view and the qualities and traits that it seeks to develop and inculcate within them, both individually and collectively. Islam needs 'soldiers' and 'civil servants' who are endowed with the spirit of *taqwā*, discipline and dedication, or those are capable not just of offence and defence but who can change hearts and minds and mould characters, and who do not only administer the land but also know how to reform the people inhabiting it.

When we consider the obligatory and primary duty of *ṣalāh* from a larger perspective, we become convinced automatically that there is no training course better than *ṣalāh* for the fulfilment of Islam's cherished objective, the objective of turning the whole life of a believer into bondsmanship (*ʿibādah*) of Allah Most Glorified and Exalted. Only those who are properly trained in this system can faithfully shoulder the responsibilities entrusted to them in their different obligations and duties towards God and His subjects.

This is the reason why the holy Qur'an declares: *Surely Prayer forbids indecency and evil* (إِنَّ ٱلصَّلَوٰةَ تَنْهَىٰ عَنِ ٱلْفَحْشَآءِ وَٱلْمُنكَرِ) (*al-ʿAnkabūt* 29: 45). This is why *ṣalāh* as an individual and collective obligation has been an essential part of the Islamic way of life since time immemorial. The Shariah of all the messengers of God, sent down for mankind's guidance through the ages, had prayer as its first pillar. Islam's decline as message and mission has always been due mainly to disruptions in this 'training programme' of the believers – a fact the Lord Himself has pointed out in the holy Qur'an:

فَخَلَفَ مِنۢ بَعْدِهِمْ خَلْفٌ أَضَاعُوا۟ ٱلصَّلَوٰةَ وَٱتَّبَعُوا۟ ٱلشَّهَوَٰتِ ۖ فَسَوْفَ يَلْقَوْنَ غَيًّا ﴿٥٩﴾

They were succeeded by a people who neglected the Prayers and pursued their lusts. They shall soon meet with their doom.

(*Maryam* 19: 59)

7.10. Leading the Congregational Prayer (*Imāmat Ṣalāt al-Jamāʿah*)

Ṣalāh being a collective form of worship, it cannot be offered without the prayer leader (imam). Even if two people assemble to offer the obligatory prayer, one would have to lead it as the imam and the other would be his follower (*muqtadī*). It is not permissible to offer the obligatory prayer separately when the congregational *ṣalāh* is being performed. Those coming late have to join the congregation behind the imam. The position of imamate (*imāmah*) or the leadership of the prayer is not exclusive to any particular class, race or group. Nor does it require any particular academic degree or certificate. Any knowledgeable Muslim is in principle eligible to lead the prayer. Under the Shariah, however, certain qualifications have been recommended for the imam, as is discussed below.

Each and every aspect of the relationship established between the imam and his follower in the congregation is extremely significant. In fact, each and every Muslim has a comprehensive training in both leadership and followership imparted to them. He is acquainted with a system that the Muslim community ought to follow beyond the four walls of the mosque in the vaster and bigger mosque called Earth. The imam is trained about his status in the congregation – the community on a larger scale – about his rights and obligations and what his attitude and conduct as the leader of his congregation must be. On the other hand, the congregation is trained in the discipline to be followed, the exact meaning of followership and how it is to be observed. Should the prayer leader make a mistake, then how should the congregation react? How far can they go in following him in spite of his mistake? Are they entitled to stop him? Do they have the right to demand that he correct his mistake? And in what circumstances can they remove him from leadership (imamate)? Each and every follower knows the answer to all such questions that are likely to arise during the congregational prayer. In other words, this can be viewed as an exercise in statecraft conducted on a miniature scale in every small or large mosque five times a day.

Muslims have been directed to select as an imam to conduct the prayer only such a person who is God-fearing, has a good character, is well-versed in the injunctions of the Qur'ān and the Sunnah, and is mature in age. The Prophetic traditions have laid down these qualifications in order of priority. Thus we have been instructed about the essential prerequisites the Muslim community must keep in mind in selecting its leader and head of the nation. We have been ordered not to appoint a person as an imam who is not in the good books of the congregation. Minor differences may be overlooked, but should the majority opinion not favour allowing a person to take the position of leadership in prayer, their view would have to be upheld and such a person cannot perform the office of imam. The nation of Islam has thus been instructed in yet another principle about the selection of its leader. Somebody of dubious reputation, whom people do not like because of his questionable character and ill-repute, is unfit to become the emir or head of an Islamic state.

According to an injunction, in conducting the prayer the imam must be mindful of the weak and the aged in the congregation. He should not prolong his recitation, bowing down or prostration, thinking that the best part of the congregation consists of young, healthy and strong people. He should be equally mindful of those who are old, sick, physically weak or so busy that they are required to rush back to their work soon after the prayer ends. The holy Prophet, may Allah bless him and give him peace, has left us with an excellent example of compassion and mercy. According to authentic traditions, we know that whenever he heard a baby's cry in the midst of prayer, he shortened his recitation lest the baby's mother be disturbed. This is how he guided those at the helm of affairs holding positions of leadership to be mindful of the interests of their community.

If the imam is unable to conduct the prayer for some reason, he has been instructed by the Shariah to leave his place at once and depute someone from among those standing behind him in the congregation to lead the prayer instead. This instruction is equally applicable to the nation's leader. He too is duty-bound to vacate his position in favour of the next most eligible person on seeing himself unable to discharge his responsibilities as a leader. There is no room at all in an Islamic system of governance for any complacency, selfishness or self-preservation at the cost of the nation.

The Islamic Shariah also enjoins the follower to follow the imam strictly in all his actions. No movement is permissible before he moves. The observance of the imam's lead is so important that the holy Prophet, may Allah bless him and give him peace, warned that if somebody bowed down or prostrated before his imam did, he would be resurrected on the Day of Judgement as a donkey. The Muslim *ummah* has been thus taught the lesson of obedience and discipline and the extent to which they should follow their leader.

Should the imam stand up by mistake when he should have sat down, or should he sit down when he should have stood up, then those praying behind him have been instructed to draw his attention to such lapses by saying, 'How Perfect Allah is!' (*subḥān Allāh*). This simply means that the congregation is invoking Allah's blessings by reaffirming the tenet of faith that it is the Lord alone Who is far above all mistakes. When the imam's attention is drawn in this manner to his mistake, it is imperative for him to respond positively and without hesitation or complacency to correct his mistake. In addition to correcting the mistake, he has to perform two additional acts of prostration (*sajdatayn*) before ending the prayer, in token of his admission of error. Should the imam be absolutely certain that he has not made a mistake, he can continue the prayer according to his own judgement in spite of the call of those behind him. The congregation would then have to follow the imam even if they are sure he has made a mistake. They may take up the matter afterwards with their imam to convince him that he was wrong and then ask him to repeat the prayer.

Such conduct by the congregation towards the imam only concerns those mistakes which are minor in nature. In the case of serious lapses or wilful distortions, the congregation is duty-bound to replace the imam and to appoint another in his place. These serious lapses include major changes by the imam to the format of the prayer or its components in violation of the holy Prophet's Sunnah, reciting a distorted form of the Qur'anic verses, committing sinful acts of apostasy, polytheism, open disobedience or doing anything that might indicate his deviation from the Divine law, or his suddenly becoming insane. In the first situation, it is a sin not to follow the imam, but in the latter case it is a sin to follow him.

Exactly the same applies on a broader scale to the Muslim nation and its leadership. So long as the leader of an Islamic state functions according to the dictates of the Qur'an and the Sunnah,[8] Muslims are obliged to obey him and their disobedience is a major sin. In minor mistakes, they should at least draw their leader's attention to these and if he continues in the same manner in spite of their repeated cautions, they can continue to follow him because they have done their duty. However, should the leader transgress the bounds of the Islamic constitution and the law, then they are not bound to obey him and he can no longer remain the Muslim nation's leader.

Although the discussion so far about the objectives and impact of *ṣalāh* has not covered all of its aspects, it may help in explaining why it has been called the greatest pillar (*rukn aʿẓam*) of Islam. The Arabic word *rukn* means the pillar that supports the building. The most important support needed to raise and sustain the edifice of the Islamic social order is that those qualities and attributes are created in Muslims, both in their individual capacity and as a community, which are essential for the proper discharge of their duties as bondsmen of Allah Most Glorified and Exalted and in assuming the onerous responsibility of His deputyship in this world. Individually and collectively, Muslims should have a perfect and vibrant faith in the Unseen. They must show their total allegiance to the Lord as their One and Only God and the supreme Sovereign and remain His dutiful and obedient servants. Islam as a way of life should be so deeply engrained in their personalities so as to form the basis of their character, and that their entire social conduct may become its practical manifestation. They must have firm control over their physical and emotional capabilities in order to use them according to their faith and creed. If hypocrites emerge from amongst them or infiltrate their ranks, it should be hard for such elements to survive. Their community life has to be well-organized around the fundamentals of Islamic social values so as to allow no anti-Islamic trend to pollute the environment.

These are the aims and objectives intended to be attained through the system of *ṣalāh*. Should this greatest pillar of Islam grow weak, the individual conduct of Muslims as well as their community life would both be irreparably affected and they would indeed be incapable of upholding the great mission for which

[8] I.e. the constitution of the Islamic state. — Editor.

the Islamic community came into being. This is why the holy Prophet, may Allah bless him and give him peace, declared: 'Ṣalāh is the main pillar of Islam as a way of life' (الصَّلٰوةُ عِمَادُ الدِّين). The system of *ṣalāh* provides the support that if removed would cause the collapse of Islam's entire grand edifice.

7.11. Has Prayer Lost Its Power?

As a corollary to the above discussion, it is only natural for the following questions to arise within one's mind: Why is it that prayer, good and beneficial as it is, seems to make no difference in our lives today? Why does it neither improve our morals nor transform us into a force dedicated to Allah? Why do we continue to have disgraced and subjugated lives?

The answer to these questions will normally be that we are not offering our prayers regularly or in the manner prescribed by Allah and His Messenger, may Allah bless him and give him peace. However, such an answer may not be sufficient to satisfy completely an inquiring mind. Let us, therefore, try to explain the matter in some detail.

7.11.1. *A Parable of the Clock*

Let us look at the clock fixed upon the wall: there are lots of small parts in it connected with each other. When one winds it up, each one of these parts starts working and, as they move, the result appears externally on the clock face, which anyone can observe. Both hands of the clock move to denote the hour and the minute. The purpose of the clock is to indicate the correct time. Every part necessary for this purpose has been fitted together and the winding mechanism has been made so that each of them moves as required. Only when all these parts are correctly assembled and the clock is wound regularly does it fulfil the purpose for which it was made.

If we do not wind the clock up, it will not show the time. If we wind it up but not in the prescribed manner, it will stop or, even if it works, it will not give the correct time. If we remove some of its parts and then wind it up, the clock will not function. If some of its parts are replaced with those of a sewing machine, it will neither show the time nor will it sew cloth. If we keep every part inside the case but do not properly connect them to each other, then no part will perform its function even after winding the clock up. The clock, with all its parts intact but not interconnected, similarly fails to serve its purpose and is there in form only but not in substance. An observer from a distance cannot say that it is not a clock and he may well expect it to function the way a clock does. Similarly, when from a distance he observes us winding it up, he will take it as a genuine effort, anticipating the result that comes from such an action. However, this expectation cannot be fulfilled because what looks like a clock from a distance has in reality lost its character and potential.

7.11.2. *The Objective Before the Muslim* Ummah

Let us for a moment suppose that a Muslim is like a clock. In the same way the purpose of the clock is to indicate the correct time, a Muslim stands as the standard-bearer of truth and a witness unto mankind of his Lord, Whose deputy he is on earth. This is his assigned role and if he fails in this, he is bound to be as useless as the clock that fails to tick.

Regarding this assigned role of a Muslim, Allah Most Exalted declares as follows in the holy Qur'an:

كُنتُمْ خَيْرَ أُمَّةٍ أُخْرِجَتْ لِلنَّاسِ تَأْمُرُونَ بِٱلْمَعْرُوفِ وَتَنْهَوْنَ عَنِ ٱلْمُنكَرِ وَتُؤْمِنُونَ بِٱللَّهِ ... ﴿١١٠﴾

You are indeed the best community brought forth for mankind: you enjoin the doing of right and forbid the doing of wrong, and you believe in Allah.

(*Āl ʿImrān* 3: 110)

وَكَذَٰلِكَ جَعَلْنَٰكُمْ أُمَّةً وَسَطًا لِّتَكُونُوا۟ شُهَدَآءَ عَلَى ٱلنَّاسِ وَيَكُونَ ٱلرَّسُولُ عَلَيْكُمْ شَهِيدًا ... ﴿١٤٣﴾

And it is thus that We appointed you to be the community of the middle way[9] *so that you might be witness to all mankind and the Messenger might be a witness to you.*[10]

(*al-Baqarah* 2: 143)

---

[9] The Arabic expression that has been translated as 'the community of the middle way' is too rich in meaning to find an adequate equivalent in any other language. It stands for the distinguished group of people who follow the path of justice and equity, of balance and moderation, a group who occupy a central position among the nations of the world and its friendship with all is based on righteousness and justice and none receives its support in wrong and injustice. — Author.

[10] The verses signify that when the whole of mankind is called to account, the Prophet, as God's representative, will stand witness to the fact that he had communicated to the Muslims and had put into practice the teachings, postulating sound beliefs, righteous conduct and a balanced system of life that he had received from on high. The Muslims, acting on behalf of the Prophet after his return to the mercy of God, will be asked to bear the same witness before the rest of mankind and to say that they had spared no effort in communicating to mankind what the Prophet had transmitted to them, or in exemplifying in their own lives what the Prophet had, by his own conduct, translated into action. (*Towards Understanding the Qur'ān*, abridged version of *Tafhīm al-Qur'ān*, p. 40, nn.44 and 45).

وَعَدَ ٱللَّهُ ٱلَّذِينَ ءَامَنُوا۟ مِنكُمْ وَعَمِلُوا۟ ٱلصَّٰلِحَٰتِ لَيَسْتَخْلِفَنَّهُمْ فِى ٱلْأَرْضِ كَمَا ٱسْتَخْلَفَ ٱلَّذِينَ مِن
قَبْلِهِمْ وَلَيُمَكِّنَنَّ لَهُمْ دِينَهُمُ ٱلَّذِى ٱرْتَضَىٰ لَهُمْ وَلَيُبَدِّلَنَّهُم مِّنۢ بَعْدِ خَوْفِهِمْ أَمْنًا ۚ يَعْبُدُونَنِى لَا يُشْرِكُونَ بِى شَيْـًٔا ۚ
وَمَن كَفَرَ بَعْدَ ذَٰلِكَ فَأُو۟لَٰٓئِكَ هُمُ ٱلْفَٰسِقُونَ ﴿٥٥﴾

Allah has promised those of you who believe and do righteous deeds that He will surely bestow power on them in the land even as He bestowed power on those that preceded them, and that He will firmly establish their religion which He has been pleased to choose for them, and He will replace with security the state of fear that they are in. Let them serve Me and associate none with Me in My Divinity. Whoso thereafter engages in unbelief, such indeed are the ungodly.

(*al-Nūr* 24: 55)

7.11.3. *The Wholeness of Islamic Teachings*

To fulfil the objective of a Muslim's role as bondsman of his Lord, various parts that are required, like those of the clock, have been set together. Beliefs and principles of morality, rules for day-to-day conduct, the rights of Allah, of His servants, of one's own self, of everything in the world that one encounters, rules for earning and spending money, laws of war and peace, principles of governance and limits of obedience to the state authority – all these are the parts of Islam one would like to see in place and in perfect order in a true Muslim. As in a clock, they are linked to each other in such a way that as soon as the winding up is done, each one of these parts starts moving and, with their movement, the desired result is obtained. The supremacy of Divine law and blessings of the Islamic social order similarly become manifest once a Muslim is properly equipped to be an effective member of his community, combining within himself all the essentials of his *dīn*. This means that like the clock that functions properly and shows the correct time, he is performing the duties expected of him as a Muslim.

In just the way a clock needs all its parts, including small pieces of metal and screws, to be fastened together in the correct order to produce a result, so is a believer required not to live as an isolated being but as an integral part of the organized structure of the Islamic community (*al-jamāʿah*). To create a perfect Islamic social order Muslims have been enjoined to organize themselves into a party of Islam, endowed with the qualities of knowledge and *taqwā*.

When all parts of a clock are properly assembled, regular winding up is necessary to keep them in motion and to regulate their movement. Offered five times a day, *ṣalāh* provides that winding up, creating the necessary energy that sets an Islamic life in motion. Cleaning the clock is also necessary. Observed for thirty days a year, *ṣawm* cleanses the hearts and morals of the believers. Lubrication, too, is required. *Zakāh* is like the oil which is applied to its parts once a year. Then it is also necessary to overhaul it periodically. Hajj is that overhauling which should be performed at least once in a lifetime. And the more often it is done, the better.

7.11.4. *Abusing the Clock*

The processes of winding, cleaning, lubricating and overhauling are only of use when every part is present in the frame and joined together in the order designed by the clockmaker. They also need to be so programmed that immediately upon being wound up they start moving and showing results. Unfortunately, however, the situation has become very different today. For a start, the very *jamāʿah*, the organizational structure that was supposed to link the parts of the clock together, has ceased to exist. The result is that all the fittings have come apart, each going its own way. Everybody does whatever takes his fancy. There is no one to question anything. Everyone is self-centred. If it so pleases someone, he may follow the Islamic code; if it does not, he may go his own way. We are more concerned about our right to freedom of action but are hardly bothered about the moral side of that action.

That is how we have pulled out many parts of the clock and replaced these with anything and everything that catches our fancy. We may call ourselves Muslims, yet we render loyal service to unbelief, take interest on our money; 'insure' our lives, file false lawsuits, are hardly concerned about seeing our sons, daughters, sisters and wives giving up Islamic manners and morals and opting for a wayward lifestyle, and hardly care to equip our children with proper religious education and training. Despite this, we expect the clock to work the moment we start winding it up. We presume that cleaning, lubricating and overhauling it will produce the desired result. With a little reflection, however, we may realize that in the condition to which we have left the clock in, we may go on winding it up, lubricating, and overhauling it for the rest of our lives without any effect. Nothing positive will happen unless and until we remove the parts brought in from other appliances, replace them with the original ones, and restore them to their proper positions. Then, and only then, will the act of winding up and so forth produce the desired results.

No doubt there are many amongst us who do discharge their religious duties conscientiously. Why does that make no difference? As pointed out earlier, in our individual capacity we may be good Muslims but as a *jamāʿah,* or a collective force symbolizing the party of Islam, we stand nowhere. To use the same parable, when the parts of the clock become unhinged and numerous foreign bodies are inserted into it, it makes no difference if we wind it up or not, clean it or not, or lubricate it or not. From a distance the object may look like a clock but actually it has ceased to be one. An external observer may say that this is Islam and these people are Muslims. What he cannot see, however, is the bad shape of the entire machinery within the good-looking frame.

7.12. The Significance of the *Qiblah*

In the beginning, for prayers Muslims used to face in the direction of Jerusalem (al-Quds). Al-Quds is situated to the north of Madinat al-Munawwarah. As there were no definite instructions in this regard, the direction of al-Quds was the obvious choice for them due to its having been the focal point of worship (*qiblah*) for the followers of the apostles of God before the holy Prophet, may God bless him and give him peace. In the second year of the Hijrah, the instruction that the holy Prophet had anxiously awaited was finally revealed about the change in direction for prayers towards the holy Kaaba. Our master the Messenger of Allah, may Allah bless him and give him peace, was leading the Ẓuhr prayer when the injunctions were revealed, and it led to the exalted Imam, may Allah bless him and give him peace, and the illustrious congregation behind him turning instantaneously from the north to the south. The event has been recorded thus in the holy Qur'an:

قَدْ نَرَىٰ تَقَلُّبَ وَجْهِكَ فِي ٱلسَّمَآءِ ۖ فَلَنُوَلِّيَنَّكَ قِبْلَةً تَرْضَىٰهَا ۚ فَوَلِّ وَجْهَكَ شَطْرَ ٱلْمَسْجِدِ ٱلْحَرَامِ ۚ وَحَيْثُ مَا كُنتُمْ
فَوَلُّوا۟ وُجُوهَكُمْ شَطْرَهُۥ ۗ وَإِنَّ ٱلَّذِينَ أُوتُوا۟ ٱلْكِتَـٰبَ لَيَعْلَمُونَ أَنَّهُ ٱلْحَقُّ مِن رَّبِّهِمْ ۗ وَمَا ٱللَّهُ بِغَـٰفِلٍ
عَمَّا يَعْمَلُونَ ﴿١٤٤﴾

We see you oft turning your face to the heaven; now We are turning you to the direction that will satisfy you. Turn your face towards the holy Mosque, and wherever you are, turn your faces towards it in prayer.[11] *Those who have been granted the Book certainly know that*

[11] The change in the direction of prayer was of prime importance in the history of Islam's forward movement. The injunction contained in the verse above was revealed in the month of either Rajab or Sha'bān, 2 AH. Let us revert to the author's magnum opus *Tafhīm al-Qur'ān* for the necessary details in this context. According to a tradition in the *Ṭabaqāt* of Ibn Sa'd, the Prophet was at the house of Bishr b. Barā' b. Ma'rūr where he had been invited to a meal. When the time of Ẓuhr prayer came, the Prophet rose to lead it. He had completed two *rak'ah*s and was in the third when this verse was revealed. Soon after the revelation of this verse everybody, following the leadership of the Prophet, turned the direction of prayer away from Jerusalem to the Kaaba. A public proclamation of the new order was then made

this [injunction to change the direction of prayer] is right and is from their Lord. Allah is not heedless of what they do.

(*al-Baqarah* 2: 144)

The change of the direction of the *qiblah* was not just a routine matter: it was a revolutionary step. It marked the return to the pristine glory of the Abrahamic tradition and the elevation of the Muslim *ummah* to an exalted position of leadership of the nations of the world. This has been explained so succinctly in the following verse:

وَكَذَٰلِكَ جَعَلْنَٰكُمْ أُمَّةً وَسَطًا لِّتَكُونُوا۟ شُهَدَآءَ عَلَى ٱلنَّاسِ وَيَكُونَ ٱلرَّسُولُ عَلَيْكُمْ شَهِيدًا ۗ وَمَا جَعَلْنَا ٱلْقِبْلَةَ
ٱلَّتِى كُنتَ عَلَيْهَآ إِلَّا لِنَعْلَمَ مَن يَتَّبِعُ ٱلرَّسُولَ مِمَّن يَنقَلِبُ عَلَىٰ عَقِبَيْهِ ۚ وَإِن كَانَتْ لَكَبِيرَةً إِلَّا عَلَى ٱلَّذِينَ
هَدَى ٱللَّهُ ۗ وَمَا كَانَ ٱللَّهُ لِيُضِيعَ إِيمَٰنَكُمْ ۚ إِنَّ ٱللَّهَ بِٱلنَّاسِ لَرَءُوفٌ رَّحِيمٌ ﴿١٤٣﴾

And it is thus that We appointed you to be the community of the middle way, so that you might be witnesses before all mankind and the Messenger might be a witness before you. We appointed the direction which you formerly observed so that We might know who follows the Messenger

---

throughout Madinah and in the suburbs. Barā' b. 'Āzib says that at one place the announcement was heard by people while they were in the state of *rukū'* (bowing down). On hearing this order they immediately turned their faces towards the Kaaba.

The words, 'We see you oft turning your face to the heaven', and 'Now We are turning your face to the direction that shall satisfy you', show clearly that even before the revelation of this injunction the Prophet was expecting something of this nature. He had begun to feel, with the termination of the era of Israelite leadership, that the time had come for the central position of Jerusalem to cease and a return to the original centre of the Abrahamic mission to commence.

The 'holy Mosque' refers to the sanctuary invested with holiness and sanctity; the sanctuary in the centre of which the Kaaba is located.

To turn one's face in the direction of the Kaaba does not mean that wherever a man might be he should turn to the Kaaba with absolute accuracy. It would obviously be extremely difficult for everyone to comply with such an order. Hence the order is to turn one's face in the direction of the Kaaba rather than to the Kaaba itself. According to the Qur'an, we are required to find out the direction of the Kaaba as accurately as possible. We are not required, however, to locate it with absolute precision. We may pray in the direction which appears correct as a result of our enquiry. However, if a man is either at a place where it is difficult to determine the direction of the Kaaba or if he is in a position where it is difficult to maintain the correct direction (e.g. when traveling on a train, a boat or an aeroplane), he may pray in the direction which seems correct, or in whatever direction it is possible for him to face. If he then comes to know the correct direction while he is in the state of Prayer he should turn his face in that direction. (*Towards Understanding the Qur'ān*, English translation of *Tafhīm al-Qur'ān*, vol. 1, n.146, pp.122–3). — Editor.

> *from him who turns on his heels. For indeed it was a burdensome thing except for those whom Allah guided. And Allah will never leave your faith to waste. Allah is full of gentleness and mercy to mankind.*
> (*al-Baqarah* 2: 143)

7.12.1. *Does Facing the* Qiblah *Resemble Idol Worship?*
It may not be out of place to dispel here the misgivings created in certain minds that by facing the *qiblah* the Muslims too are guilty of worshipping the holy Kaaba.

Queries like that have often been raised by those who are either ignorant of the actual position of the *qiblah* in the Islamic system of worship or whose sole purpose is to point fingers at Islam and Muslims in whatever manner that suits them. As for those unfavourably inclined to Islam, it is better to ignore their outbursts because these are not inspired by a genuine desire to know the truth but by a deep-rooted hatred against Islam and Muslims. The first category of people, however, needs to be properly educated and their misgivings removed.

Idol worship actually has its roots in the misconception that some persons or beings other than Allah are also worthy of worship for they share divine qualities and powers with the Almighty. There are those who believe that the Supreme Being incarnates Himself in earthly manifestations and hence these too deserve worship as reincarnated deities and gods. Due to this wrong belief, pagans and polytheists erect statues, idols and altars in the names of their deities or divines. On the other hand, human history bears witness to the fact that no one past or present has ever created an idol or statue of Allah Most Glorified and Exalted, the One and Only God. There has never been any attempt by polytheists or monotheists to establish His likeness for worship. Those who do not believe in monotheism profess of their faith in a Supreme Being too, Who is free from any definite shape or form. This is why they also could never claim any image or idol exactly resembles Him. They could only conceive imaginary gods and deities, whom they sanctified as mediums or means to reach the Almighty. This is the actual position of polytheism and idol worship.

No one with the slightest knowledge of this fact could ever confuse the Islamic system of worship with that of the idol worshippers. He will have no doubt that when Muslims face the direction of the *qiblah*, circumambulate of holy Kaaba (*ṭawāf*) during hajj, or kiss the Black Stone (*al-Ḥajar al-Aswad*), it in no way resembles idol worship. Islam in its essence and spirit is absolutely a monotheistic (*tawḥīdī*) way of life. It recognizes no deity as worthy of worship except Allah. It neither believes in reincarnation nor His reappearance in any physical form.

Non-Muslims may not have physically seen the holy Kaaba but there is hardly anyone who will not have witnessed the scenes of *ṭawāf* of this simple structure. Can they claim with all sincerity that this structure represents the statue or idol of Allah Most Glorified and Exalted? Similarly, can anybody claim that the sacred Stone, fixed in one of the four corners of the holy Kaaba, in any way represents His image or His idol? The Stone simply marks the starting point of the *ṭawāf* and therefore has no relevance or resemblance with idol worship in any of its existing or extinct forms.

As for the question about why Muslims face the direction of the *qiblah* in prayers, the reason is quite simple. Allah Most Exalted has enjoined them to do so. The Muslim *ummah* has been blessed with a uniform system of worship and a single direction to turn towards to create harmony and a sense of unity among them. Instead of each individual, nation or group facing their own *qiblah*, the *ummah* as a whole has been woven in a single universal network, as with a string of prayer-beads. This is why every Muslim anywhere in the world faces towards the same point and observes the well-appointed timings for *ṣalāh*. He may live in the north or south, east or west, but he invariably turns five times a day in the direction of the holy Kaaba. Since Islam started as a monotheistic movement more than 4,000 years ago from that particular point of the valley of Makkah, the holy Kaaba naturally merited its consecration as the focal point of worship of the One and Only God. There is no other place in the world that can claim this singular honour.

7.12.2. *How to Determine the* Qiblah *on the Moon and Other Planets?*

Inspired by the possibility of human habitation on the lunar surface, one may ask how to determine the direction of the *qiblah* there. We can say that in light of the verse quoted below, the best course then would be to establish a definite point as the *qiblah* to facilitate the observance of obligatory prayers on the moon or on any other planet found habitable by man:

إِنَّ أَوَّلَ بَيْتٍ وُضِعَ لِلنَّاسِ لَلَّذِى بِبَكَّةَ مُبَارَكًا وَهُدًى لِّلْعَـٰلَمِينَ ﴿٩٦﴾

> *Behold, the first House [of Prayer] established for mankind is the one at Bakkah: it is full of blessing and is a centre of guidance for the whole world.*
>
> (*Āl ʿImrān* 3: 96)

8 Obligatory Fasting (*Ṣawm*)

Islam attaches so much importance to the objectives for which the system of *ṣalāh* has been established that in support of these another pillar *ṣawm* has been added. Like *ṣalāh, ṣawm* has also been Islam's pillar (*rukn*) since ancient times. Its ritualistic details may have differed, but the very practice of fasting has always been present as an integral part of all Divine legal codes. The holy Qur'an tells us:

يَٰٓأَيُّهَا ٱلَّذِينَ ءَامَنُوا۟ كُتِبَ عَلَيْكُمُ ٱلصِّيَامُ كَمَا كُتِبَ عَلَى ٱلَّذِينَ مِن قَبْلِكُمْ لَعَلَّكُمْ تَتَّقُونَ ﴿١٨٣﴾

> *Believers! Fasting is enjoined upon you, as it was enjoined upon those before you, that you become God-fearing.*
>
> (*al-Baqarah* 2: 183)

Thus it may be deduced that there is definitely some relevance in this form of training to the very nature of Islam. Unlike obligatory charity (*zakāh*) and obligatory pilgrimage to the holy Kaaba (hajj), *ṣawm* is not an independent pillar of a separate category. It has the same character as *ṣalāh* and has been enjoined as a support and buttress to that great pillar. Its function is to further accelerate and strengthen the impact *ṣalāh* leaves on human life. Prayer is a daily routine that occupies the life of a believer five times a day. It administers portions of spiritual light in small doses. Fasting represents an annual 'special training course' of extraordinary significance held for one month. It keeps man within the framework of its strong discipline for around 720 hours at a stretch to boost the impact left by *ṣalāh* on his character. Let us now see how this extraordinary system of special training functions and in what way it leaves its impact on us.

8.1. The Impact of *Ṣawm* as a Training System

According to the laws of *ṣawm,* eating, drinking and sexual intercourse are forbidden for a Muslim from pre-dawn early in the morning for the whole day until sunset. During this period of fasting, it is forbidden to swallow knowingly even a single morsel of food, a drop of water, or to indulge in sexual relations.

Once the sun sets in the evening, these restrictions are lifted. All that was forbidden a moment earlier becomes permissible and remains so for the whole night until the appointed moment of prohibition for the next day's fast. This is a process which begins from the first day of Ramadan and continues without a break for the whole month. Thus man is kept under strict discipline for fully thirty days. He has to take his last meal at an appointed time before early signs of daybreak (*suḥūr*), break his fast at the fixed time, offer special supererogatory prayers in congregation, and fulfil his personal desires during night-time as permitted, yet the moment this permission is withdrawn he has to stop doing these now forbidden things.

8.1.1. *A Life of Worship*

When we look at this training system, the first thing that strikes us is Islam's focus on firmly implanting in the human psyche the affirmation of Allah's sovereignty. It wants this awareness to be so strong that each individual willingly surrenders his independence and autonomy to his supreme Sovereign. This affirmation and total surrender are the essence of Islam and on them depend a person's life as a Muslim.

Islam aims at transforming the whole life of man into one of worship. He is born a bondsman and to serve his Creator is in his very nature. Not for a single moment is he to live without worship, or surrendering to his Lord in his thoughts and actions. He must remain conscious of what he ought to do to earn Allah's pleasure and what he ought to avoid to escape His punishment. He then has to walk on the path leading to the Almighty's pleasure and shun that leading to His displeasure the way he avoids the embers of a burning fire. Only when our entire lives have become modelled on this pattern can we be considered to have worshipped our Lord as is His due and fulfilled the purport of the following verse:

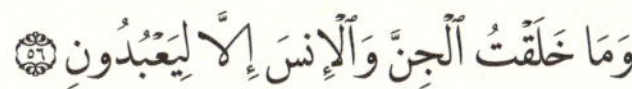

I have not created jinn and men except to worship Me.
(*al-Dhāriyāt* 51: 56)

The real purpose of all obligatory acts of worship in Islam – *ṣalāh*, *ṣawm*, *zakāh* and hajj – is to help us live a life of total worship and bondsmanship of Allah Most Glorified and Exalted. We should never feel content that we can acquit ourselves of what we owe to our Lord the Creator by simply observing the obligatory acts of worship. If we bow and prostrate in prayer five times a day, suffer hunger and thirst from dawn to dusk for the thirty days of Ramadan, and if the well-off amongst us contribute the prescribed due, and undertake the pilgrimage at least once in a lifetime, we have done just what we had to do as part of our duty. By doing all this we are not released from His bondage. We do not become free either to do whatever we may like in our day-to-day life. Rather, one of the underlying objectives of enjoining these rituals on us is to develop and groom us in such a way that we can transform our whole lives into His *ʿibādah.*

Islam as a way of life (*dīn*) does not just demand from us a firm faith in the Lord of the worlds, nor that He be accepted as the only superior Authority and Sustainer of the universe in the metaphysical sense alone. Islam also wants the individual to accept the logical and natural corollary of these fundamental truths. For instance, when man acknowledges that his Creator and the Creator of the whole universe, its Sustainer, Patron and Sovereign, is none other but Allah, and when he reaffirms that He has no partner, neither in His creation nor in its sustenance or management, it is but natural then that this firm belief is followed by practical surrender before the Almighty. A true believer, therefore, gives up all notions of his being independent and master of his own self. His attitude towards Allah Most Exalted is the same as that of a servant towards his master. It is this attitude that marks the dividing line between unbelief (*kufr*) and faith (*īmān*). Apostasy and unbelief are nothing but the assumption that one is free and not answerable to the Supreme Being. On the contrary, Islam is a reaffirmation of the fundamental truth that each one of us is Allah's bondsman: he is accountable to Him in all his words and deeds and he has to lead his life as a practical demonstration of this sense of bondsmanship and accountability. As it is essential to move from apostasy to Islam to reaffirm one's firm faith in Allah's supremacy from the core of one's heart, it is similarly imperative that to remain within the fold of Islam a Muslim must always keep his sense of bondsmanship alive and active. The moment this awareness is lost, it is bound to be taken over by the notion that one is answerable to no one and that one is free to do what one likes.

Like *ṣalāh, ṣawm* also has the same objective, with the only difference that while *ṣalāh* refreshes this position intermittently on a daily basis, *ṣawm* maintains this discipline for around 720 hours over the course of a full month each year. Its purpose is to so firmly implant within a Muslim's heart and mind his sense of bondsmanship that its impact may last for the remaining eleven months of the year. It is difficult to think that anybody can impose such hard and tough regulations on himself unless he sincerely believes that Allah is his supreme Sovereign. In so doing, the individual voluntarily forgoes his independence and free will. He abstains from eating, drinking and sexual needs from pre-dawn to sunset for around twelve to thirteen hours daily; refrains from the intake of any solid or liquid food; and hastens to break the fast the moment the *adhān* is sounded. It would appear as though it is not his animal appetites that rule over his biological needs but Someone Else: these are sealed under His command and are set free by His order. This demonstrates practically how a Muslim is governed at all times by a strong sense of Allah's supremacy and his own servitude. It also means that this overpowering thought has never for a while been away from his mind or subconscious during the whole month, otherwise who would have stopped him from breaking the regulations during the fast?

8.2. How does Fasting Develop Our Inner Selves?

Every act of worship consists of some outward physical movements, but not *ṣawm*. In *ṣalāh*, one stands, bows down, prostrates and sits. All these acts are visible to everyone. In hajj, one undertakes a long journey and travels with thousands of people. *Zakāh* too is known to at least two persons, the giver and the receiver. None of these acts can remain secret: when they are performed, others naturally come to know of them.

Although collective in spirit and observance, *ṣawm* is, however, a form of *ʿibādah* that is entirely personal and invisible. The All-Knowing God alone knows that His servant is fasting. One is required to take food before dawn (*suḥūr*) and abstain from eating and drinking until the time comes after sunset to break the fast (*ifṭār*). However, if one secretly eats and drinks in-between, nobody except God will know about it.

8.2.1. *A Sure Sign of Faith*

This invisible nature of the fast ensures that one has strong faith in Allah as the One Who knows everything. Only if one's faith is true and strong, will one not think of eating or drinking secretly. Even in the hottest of summers, when throats dry up with thirst, one will not drink a drop of water. Even when life itself seems to be ebbing away due to hunger, one will not eat anything. One does all this because of one's firm conviction that nothing can ever be concealed from the Lord and because of one's fear of His displeasure. A person only keeps fasting for a full month because of his profound belief in the reward and punishment of the Hereafter. With the slightest of doubts about the appointed day of his meeting with his Lord, the Creator and Sustainer, he would not have completed such a rigorous drill. This is how our Lord tests our faith severely over the course of a month. If we emerge triumphant from this test, the strength to refrain from other sins develops within us.

Another characteristic of *ṣawm* is that it makes us obey the injunctions of the Shariah with sustained intensity for prolonged periods of time. *Ṣalāh* lasts for a few minutes at a time. *Zakāh* is only paid once a year. Although the time spent on hajj is long, it may come only once in a lifetime, and for many not at all. With *ṣawm*, on the other hand, we are trained to obey the Shariah day and night for a whole month each year. Like a soldier in an army, we live a disciplined life continuously, following certain rules all the time. We are then sent back to continue with our normal duties for eleven months so that the training we have received in this one month may be reflected in our conduct, and if any deficiency is found it may be made up the next year. Thus the sense of bondsmanship is ingrained deeply into our psyches.

8.2.2. *A Sense of Allegiance*

The feeling that emerges automatically as a corollary to the sense of bondsmanship is that man should submit to the commands of the One Whom he regards as his Master. Both faith and allegiance are so naturally and logically interlinked that neither can be separated from the other. There can never be any inconsistency between the two, because allegiance is the result of faith in Allah.[1] We can

---

[1] It may be appropriate here to consider some frequently-used religious terms for the Supreme Being. The word *Khudā* in Persian and Urdu has the same meaning as *ilāh*, or *Rabb* in Arabic. The word 'god', with a small 'g', has almost the same connotation in English. The Hindi word *devta* is also almost synonymous. Different nations have used these terms for the Being they considered to have the power to do good or harm, whose writ they believe runs on a smaller or larger scale in the cosmic system and whose worship they regard as indispensable for human well-being. Ignorant communities have always been of the view that there is not One but many such beings and these include not only extraterrestrial bodies, like angels and jinns (demons), but also humans like kings, saints and those practising magical or extraordinary feats. These words have, therefore, their plural and feminine genders in almost all languages. For example: *ālihah* is the feminine of *ilāh* and *arbāb* a plural for *Rabb* in Arabic; *khudāigān* and *Khudāwandān* in Persian for *Khudā;* 'gods' and 'goddesses' in English; and *devtaon* and *deviān* in Hindi. These communities have also invariably believed that over and above these 'lesser gods' there is a Supreme Being Who is the Creator and the Lord of everything in this world. 'Allah' in Arabic, *Khudāi Khudāigān* in Persian, 'God' with a capital 'G' in English and *Permaishwar* in Hindi are the names of this Supreme Being. These words have no plural in these languages. Islam's message for humanity is that the powers and authority for which different nations have conceived different deities by the names of '*ilāh*', 'god'/'goddess', *khudawand*, *devta*, and *devi*, are all centralized in the One and Only Supreme Being. It is His writ that runs through the whole universe. All our gains and losses are within His Hands and anything else which we may worship as a deity because we think that it might share some of the authority and power of the One and Only God, is nothing but His subject like ourselves. These deities do not even share even the tiniest bit of real authority with the Lord.

never submit to the commands of anyone unless and until we have accepted him our lord and master, and once we have actually accepted him as such, we cannot help but obey him and show our allegiance to him. No human being is so foolish as to uphold allegiance to someone whom he does not regard as his master and ruler. Similarly, nobody has the courage to disobey his Supreme Sovereign once he has acknowledged, from the core of his heart, that He is the Ruler and He alone can do him good or ill. Thus there is an intrinsic relationship between faith in the Divine Being and the act of allegiance and bondsmanship.

The foundational principle of faith in the unity of God (*tawḥīd*) leads to the unity of life, bondsmanship and allegiance. Conversely, the natural corollary of 'polytheism' is pluralism of masters, bondsmanship and allegiance. If one believes in One God, one will obey only His command, but if one believes in ten, one's allegiance will naturally be divided between the ten of them. It is impossible for a devotee to acknowledge ten as gods but obey only One. By determining his Lord the Master, a person automatically determines the course of his bondsmanship.

The rise and fall in one's level of faith naturally leads to the rise and fall in one's level of allegiance. The stronger the belief that the Lord is our Master and we are His servants, the stronger will be the urge to obey Him. Conversely, the weaker this belief, the weaker is our sense of allegiance.

According to these premises, it is evident that the purpose of Islam's call is to reaffirm the supremacy of Allah Most Glorified and Exalted and renounce the lordship of all else; it is nothing other than to let the human being worship and obey none but Him. The Lord proclaims: *Indeed, religion is exclusively devoted to Allah* (أَلَا لِلَّهِ ٱلدِّينُ ٱلْخَالِصُ) (*al-Zumar* 39: 3). This means that allegiance is sincerely and wholeheartedly given to Him alone and it cannot be mixed up with other devotions. The Lord firmly declares: *Yet all that they had been commanded was that they serve Allah with utter sincerity, devoting themselves exclusively to Him* (وَمَآ أُمِرُوٓا إِلَّا لِيَعْبُدُوا ٱللَّهَ مُخْلِصِينَ لَهُ ٱلدِّينَ حُنَفَآءَ) (*al-Bayyinah* 98: 5). This means that the human being is duty-bound to worship Him alone and there must not

---

There are, therefore, not many *ilāh*s, *khudawand*s, gods or *devta*s, but the One and only Allah, for Whom you may be having similar words in your languages. — Author. [One should not misconstrue from the above that the proper noun 'Allah' is synonymous or interchangeable with God, *Permaishwar* or *Khudāi Khudāigān*. There is no word other than 'Allah' in any human language which connotes so well all the attributes of the One and Only God. It has neither a plural form nor a feminine gendered form, although Allah is far removed from having any gender. It is sacrosanct and sanctimonious on the authority of the holy Qur'an as well. No similar term or appellation has the same sanction on the basis of any known authentic religious text in any of the world's old or modern languages. — Editor.]

be any partnership in allegiance to the Lord. The Supreme Sovereign says: *And fight against them until the mischief ends and the way prescribed by Allah prevails* (وَقَـٰتِلُوهُمْ حَتَّىٰ لَا تَكُونَ فِتْنَةٌ وَيَكُونَ ٱلدِّينُ كُلُّهُۥ لِلَّهِ) (*al-Anfāl* 8: 39).

This clearly lays down that the Muslim's entire allegiance belongs to Allah and that he is at war with any other authority that seeks to have a share of that allegiance and demands obedience of Muslims along with that of the Lord of the worlds, or to obey it instead of the Lord of the worlds.

Allah Most Exalted proclaims that the religion of truth He sent down for humanity's guidance is there to prevail over all other ways of life human beings may adopt for themselves:

هُوَ ٱلَّذِىٓ أَرْسَلَ رَسُولَهُۥ بِٱلْهُدَىٰ وَدِينِ ٱلْحَقِّ لِيُظْهِرَهُۥ عَلَى ٱلدِّينِ كُلِّهِۦ ... ﴿٢٨﴾

> *He it is Who sent His Messenger with the true guidance and the religion of truth that he may make it prevail over every religion.*
>
> (*al-Fatḥ* 48: 28)

This definitely means that Allah's allegiance must transcend all other allegiances: the entire system of allegiance and worship, with all its branches and facets, must be subservient to His allegiance. Whosoever is obeyed must have sanction for obedience and without sanction or command from Him all worship and allegiance ceases forthwith. This is the demand of the religion of truth and the guidance that Allah has sent through the last of His Prophets, may Allalh bless him and give him peace. Whether it is one's parents, family, nation, government, head of state, whether religious scholars or divines, the organization where one is employed for one's livelihood, or one's own self and one's personal desires and vested interests, there is no allegiance that is independent of the dictates of allegiance to the Lord. Whoever believes truly that Allah is the Lord will obey no one except within the parameters of his total allegiance to Him. He will follow only the permissible limits of other allegiances. Where these limits end, the sanction to obey them will also end and he will then rebel against everyone else and be obedient only to his supreme Sovereign.

Ṣawm ensures that for many hours a day for a whole month. A person is in such a state throughout the month that he has to follow the instructions and permission of his Lord even to fulfil his elementary needs. He cannot have a morsel of food or a drop of water but only when he is permitted to. It is only the permission of his Lord that matters to him. No command other than His has any significance, nor is any ban meaningful for him unless it has His sanction. No power on earth, not even his own self, can order him to leave or break the fast. There is no obedience in this, neither of one's father, son, husband, nor of the master for his servant, of the government for its citizens or the leader for his followers. In other words, the true and extensive obedience to Allah prevails on all other forms of obedience. The act of fasting thus takes one away from all other kinds of submission and servitude to the submission and bondage of a single supreme Authority.

For this training course in allegiance, apparently just two human needs have been chosen, i.e. the need for food and sex. All disciplinary restrictions are imposed on these two alone. Yet the real spirit of fasting is that the man should be guided and governed by an all-pervasive feeling of submission and servitude. One should avoid everything Allah Most Glorified and Exalted has desired that one avoid and hasten to do everything He has ordered one to do. Fasting has been made obligatory for the same purpose, and not just to stop one from eating, drinking and having sex. The stronger the feeling of submission the more perfect is the fast, and the weaker it is the more imperfect it is. If someone abstains from these forbidden things during the fast but continues committing transgressions and indulging in other things that are haram, his fast would be like of a dead body, which may have all its limbs intact but is without a soul. Therefore, the holy Prophet, may Allah bless him and give him peace, has said:

مَن لَّم يَدَع قَولَ الزُّورِ وَالعَمَلَ به فَلَيسَ لله حَاجَةٌ فِى اَن يَدَعَ طَعَامَهُ وَ شَرَابَهُ.

> He who does not give up telling lies and acting upon lies, Allah is in no need of his leaving his food and drink.
>
> (Bukhārī)

The holy Prophet's remarking upon 'acting upon lies', along with 'telling lies' is very significant. It is in fact a comprehensive summation of all transgressions. Anybody claiming to believe in God and then disobeying Him is in fact falsifying his own claim. The real purpose of the fast is to testify to this claim through action, but when one openly repudiates it, there is nothing left there of one's fast except for hunger and thirst and, of course, God has no need for an empty stomach.

The same aspect was further elaborated by the holy Prophet, may Allah bless him and give him peace, in a different manner:

كَم مِن صَائِمٍ لَيسَ لهُ مِن صِيامِهِ اِلَّا الظَّمَاءُ وَكَم مِن قَائِم لَيسَ لَهُ مِن قِيامِهِ اِلَّا السَّهر.

> There are many who observe Fast, but get nothing out of it except thirst and hunger. And there are many who keep awake at night praying to their Lord, but they get nothing from it except sleeplessness.
>
> (Dāraquṭnī)

8.2.3. *The Spirit of* Taqwā

Rationally, this training in allegiance and self-discipline infuses and promotes the spirit of *taqwā* in man and *ṣawm* does it so well and effectively. This fact has been explained very succinctly by Allah Most Exalted in the following verse:

> يَـٰٓأَيُّهَا ٱلَّذِينَ ءَامَنُوا۟ كُتِبَ عَلَيْكُمُ ٱلصِّيَامُ كَمَا كُتِبَ عَلَى ٱلَّذِينَ مِن قَبْلِكُمْ لَعَلَّكُمْ تَتَّقُونَ ﴿١٨٣﴾
>
> *Believers! Fasting is enjoined upon you, as it was enjoined upon those before you, that you become God-fearing.*
>
> (*al-Baqarah* 2: 183)

Thus, the basic objective of prescribing fasting is to infuse the quality of *taqwā* in the believer. The word *taqwā* literally means to fear God, to be pious, and to ward off evil. As a Qur'anic term, it means to love and fear Allah Most Glorified and Exalted and to refrain from His disobedience. The best explanation of the term can be found in what Ubayy bin Ka'b, an eminent Companion of the holy Prophet, may Allah bless him and give him peace, said when the second caliph 'Umar asked him to explain *taqwā*:

> 'Leader of the Faithful (*amīr al-mu'minīn*), have you ever had a chance to walk on a track that is narrow and surrounded by thorny bushes?' 'Umar replied: 'Many times.' Ubayy asked: 'What do you do then?' 'Umar's reply was: 'I then wrap up my clothes and walk carefully lest any part of my clothing gets entangled in the bushes.' Ubayy remarked: 'This is exactly what *taqwā* means.'

The path of life being traversed by man is beset on both sides with the thorny bushes of omission and commission, desire and craving, goading and temptation, delusion and disobedience. To walk carefully to avoid entanglement with the thorny bushes of loose morals, ugliness of character, and deviation from the road of allegiance to the Lord is what the Shariah term *taqwā* stands for.

Allah Most Glorified and Exalted has made fasting the month of Ramadan obligatory to create the spirit of *taqwā*, which is an energizing catalyst that has the power to revitalize the qualities of piety and spiritual resurgence. However, it depends on one's own capacity for that potential. If man is aware of the purpose of *ṣawm*, is ready to imbibe the energy it generates and tries to develop with the help of his fasting the characteristics of piety and obedience to God, then it will create within him the quality of *taqwā* that is enough not just for the month of Ramadan but for the rest of the year. He will then be in a position to proceed on the right path in life unperturbed by the thorny bushes surrounding it. Thus, there will be no limits to the blessings and benefits he will get from his fasting in terms of reward and recompense. Yet should he remain unmindful of the real purpose of his fasting, and pay no heed to creating the quality of *taqwā* within himself, he will get nothing but hunger, thirst and sleeplessness. In a famous hadith, this same aspect has been elaborated upon as follows:

كُلُّ عَمَلِ اِبنِ آدَمَ يُضَاعِفُ الحَسَنَةَ بِعَشرِ اَمثَالِها اِلٰى سَبعِ مِائَةِ ضِعفٍ، قَالَ اللهُ تَعَالىٰ: «اِلَّا الصَّومُ فَاِنَّهُ لِى وَاَنَا اَجزِى بِهِ».

> Every deed a person does grows [before the Lord]. One good deed grows from ten to several hundred times. Allah Most Glorified and Exalted, however, says that: '*Ṣawm* is an exceptional act. It is for Me and I shall reward it in the way I please.'
>
> (Bukhārī and Muslim)

In the case of *ṣawm*, this means that there is an immense possibility of its tremendous growth in terms of spiritual benefit and reward in the Hereafter. It can grow a billion-fold from zero depending on the level of *taqwā* attained, and the exclusiveness of reward is due to the fact that *ṣawm* is an exclusively personal act of worship by the slave for his Lord, Master and Sustainer.

We may note yet another significant point here. Verse 183 of *Sūrah al-Baqarah* did not say that through *ṣawm* one will surely have the quality of self-restraint and become God-fearing. The phrase used is *la''alakum* (لَعَلَّكُمْ), which means that 'you may' or 'you are expected' to acquire the quality of *taqwā* through the fast of Ramadan. This is because it depends entirely on one's ability to get, or not to get, the advantages of the fast and on the level of *taqwā* one attains.

8.2.4. *Building Character*

Taqwā is the essence of Islamic character. The term best denotes the quality of character Islam seeks to produce in every Muslim both individually and collectively. Unfortunately, these days this Islamic term is generally understood in a very limited sense. The misconception is that *taqwā* means just to adopt a particular mannerism, a certain style of dress or physical appearance, abstention from some major sins and avoiding certain undesirable things, which may have become taboo for the general public. In fact, *taqwā* is a very comprehensive term that encompasses all aspects of human life.

In principle, the holy Qur'an classifies human attitudes and behaviours into two broad categories. According to the first category, a person may have the following attitude to life: (1) he may consider the worldly powers as his sole guides and guardians and that he is accountable to no Supreme Authority; (2) he may take earthly life to be the only life, worldly gains as the only gains, and worldly losses as the only losses and act accordingly; (3) moral and spiritual values may be of no consequence to him when compared to material advantages; and (4) he may have no permanent moral code of conduct to observe and frame his own principles according to a particular situation or occasion and so he may change them when the situation changes.

The second category of human attitudes and behaviours is as follows: (1) a person may believe firmly that he is a subject of the All-Knowing Supreme Lord and thus conducts his life with a sense of accountability for all his deeds; (2) he is aware of the earthly life being transitory and the gains and losses experienced here being temporary and deceptive and therefore decides the course of his action on the basis of the permanent gains and losses which are to accrue to him in the eternal life of the Hereafter; (3) he views moral and spiritual values and gains as more precious than material gains and moral and spiritual losses; and (4) he follows the code of moral conduct, which is eternal, and he has no freedom to amend or annul it for personal objectives and interests.

The holy Qur'an has termed the first category of human attitudes and actions as *fujūr*[2] and the second category as *taqwā*.[3] In fact, these are two distinct ways of life, which are totally opposed to each other and 'never the twain can meet'. By taking to the path of *fujūr*, man's life assumes a definite shade, which outwardly may have the sprinkling of *taqwā* but will never have its spirit. This is because all the intellectual components of *fujūr* logically form a single whole, and none of the components of *taqwā* can find a way into its well-knit system. On the other hand, the life-pattern of a man following the course of *taqwā* changes accordingly. He thinks in a different way, acts differently, and has a different approach towards the issues and problems of this world. The difference between these two distinctly separate attitudes is not restricted to man's life as

[2] *Fujūr* can be taken to be synonymous with the modern-day terminologies of materialism, utilitarianism, pragmatism and opportunism (all combined). — Author.

[3] As this category is to a great extent alien to the Western mind, it is difficult to find a term that may comprehensively cover the meanings of *taqwā*. The word 'piety' has been rendered too obnoxious by the priestly class to be its synonym. Moreover, it is not as comprehensive and rich in meaning as *taqwā*. — Author.

an individual alone, but equally concerns his community life. A community composed of *fājir* individuals, or a majority of such people, who also hold the reins of power, will give rise to a libertine, debauched and profligate culture.[4] The spirit of *fujūr* will permeate all walks of life from social norms to moral values, economy, education, and politics to international conduct. It is possible that some people in such a social set-up may well appear above the rest in their personal capacity, but the highest pedestal of goodness that they may soar to would not go beyond submerging their personal interests into the national one, as their own rise and fall depends on the rise and fall of national interests. Thus, the personal element in a *fājir* or 'permissive' social set-up makes little difference to the overall complexion of that order, the hallmark of which remains 'utilitarian', 'opportunistic' and 'materialistic'.

In the same way, *taqwā* is not just a personal attitude. When the whole community is composed of God-fearing and right-thinking (*muttaqī*) individuals or the majority of the people are *muttaqī* and they also hold the reins of power, the entire social outlook and approach of that community is bound to reflect the spirit of *taqwā*. Such a society does not determine its conduct and approach to life on a day-to-day basis. Instead, it follows a permanent and well-defined code of conduct and devotes all its energies to the achievement of its ultimate goal, regardless of the temporary worldly gains or losses that it might face in this process. Such a society does not run after material gains, but keeps as its goal the more dependable and permanent moral and spiritual gains. It does not make or break the rules according to new situations, but invariably follows the abiding principles of right and justice. It is not in the least bothered by hostile forces, but is entirely moved by the fear of God, as it knows that it will have to account for all that it does before Him – a thought that is the guiding light for it.

According to Islam, *fujūr* is the root cause of all corruption and humanity's degeneration and destruction. Islam aims at killing that deadly snake, or at least removing its fangs so that even if the snake lives it may not bite humanity. For this purpose, it seeks to carefully pick from among human beings those people who are endowed with the quality of *taqwā* and make them part of the nation of Islam (*ummah*). Those with a *fājir* mindset, though the scions of noble Muslim families, are of no use to it, even if they are deeply committed to the cause of the nation of Islam. Islam needs those who are aware of their responsibilities as

---

[4] *Fājir*, the active participle from the Arabic noun *fujūr*, ordinarily means a libertine and a depraved and profligate individual, taken together. It is opposed to *muttaqī*, the active participle of the Qur'anic term *taqwā*. — Editor.

Muslims, who are self-introspective and watchful of their words and deeds, who need no external pressure to observe the law but have an ombudsman within themselves to make them law-abiding, unseen by any police or magistrate. Islam needs individuals who believe that the Supreme Being is watching them all the time; who are fearful of the Judge Whom they will shall to face any case; those who do not run after worldly gains, temporary benefits and narrow personal or national interests. These are the people whose endeavours are targeted entirely towards Allah's pleasure, and who believe firmly that it is eventually the bondsmanship of the Lord that pays, and the servitude of falsehood that causes the ultimate loss. Islam wants people who resolutely follow the right path regardless of its hardships, failures and risks and remain undeterred by the ease, comfort, gains and attractions of the wrong path; who confidently entrust the eventual success of their endeavours to the Lord, however frustrating and disheartening the outcome might be in this worldly life. These are the believers who can be trusted for their character. The nation of Islam needs such a reliable cadre of workers for the success of the mission it has undertaken for humanity's salvation.

There can be no better or more effective means than *ṣawm* to develop and strengthen further the element of *taqwā* in man. A look at the regulations for the fast reveals how perfectly it develops and sustains the desired qualities. The fasting person knows that he has forsaken food and drink for a long spell as ordered by his Lord. He is doing that drill to please none but his Lord and Master and Sustainer. As he is fasting for Allah's pleasure, he is not in the least bothered by considerations of dieting, health gains, public approval, or any worldly punishment or reward. He believes firmly that his reward and punishment will only be there in the Hereafter. No policeman, government official or spy is there to keep a watch on a fasting person. Public pressure may force him only to the extent that he avoids eating and drinking in front of others, but no one is there to stop him from doing this in private. Furthermore, there is no one to check his motives on whether he is fasting for Allah's pleasure or for any other reason.

Let us now have an insight into a person who fulfils all conditions of *ṣawm.* (1) He firmly believes that Allah Most Glorified and Exalted is All-Knowing, All-Seeing and the Absolute Authority and as His bondsman he is accountable to Him for all that he does. (2) He also believes firmly in Life after Death, accountability on the Day of Reckoning, its reward and punishment. (3) He is mindful of his obligation and is his own ombudsman and guardian of all that brews within his mind and heart. He uses the force of his willpower to crush any urge within him to commit a sinful act, which means that he is independent of any external pressure to abide by the law. (4) He has the capacity to bear material loss for the sake of moral gain and accept worldly troubles for the sake of the blessings of the Hereafter. (5) He does not wait for an opportune moment to fast, but is ready to observe the timeframe prescribed under the law, regardless of the exigencies of weather, unfavourable personal circumstances, or demands and needs. (6) He has the capacity to control voluntarily all his temptations. In the scorching summer heat he may be parched and starving due to thirst and hunger, but neither ice-cool water nor delightful delicacies of all sorts would entice him to break his fast. A young newly-wed couple may be together alone and have a powerful urge for sex, but they do not violate the rules of fasting. Such firmness in those keeping the fast is not for worldly gains but for the dividends that may accrue to them in the Hereafter.

These are the qualities that fasting cultivates in an individual who sincerely observes it. The qualities thus generated by *ṣawm* are necessary not only for fasting or for Ramadan alone, but are also required as the basic ingredients for character development. No one can think of a better training course than *ṣawm* for this purpose, or a better time for action in building a truly Islamic personality.

8.2.5. *Self-Restraint*

Essentially, *ṣawm* involves disciplining just two basic human desires – the desires for food and sex. Cravings for indiscreet pastimes are also simultaneously covered as this is especially affected when one has to spend additional time for *tarāwīḥ* prayers (a special Ramadan exercise, performed after the obligatory 'Ishā' prayer) or to get up late in the night for *qiyām al-layl* (night prayer) before the pre-dawn meal (*suḥūr*).

The basic and real needs of an animal existence are constituted by food for sustenance, sex for self-perpetuation, and rest and relaxation to regain lost energy. Indeed, this instinct is so powerful that under its impulse the living being is forced to do whatever it must. Amongst the physical frame of all living beings, the human body is of the highest quality. Its demands are also enormous. It not only needs just any food to survive, but prefers the best food in quality and quantity. Its demand for food alone is so multifaceted that it needs a world of resources to fulfil just this one demand. Its demand for sex is not just for the perpetuation of humankind. Thousands of delicate notions and nuances are contained within this demand alone. It wants diversity, beauty, romantic settings, and a seductive atmosphere. Furthermore, the human desire for leisure is not confined, like animals, to the rejuvenation of lost energies. It not only wants to regain lost energies, but also never to lose them. Therefore it shirks from labour and tries to get things done without hard work. It attempts to use whatever ways and means are available to achieve its objectives with the minimum possible effort. It is especially averse to labour for goals beyond its animal desires.

From these three basic demands an endless network of desires comes into effect. Thus, these are in fact the three major weapons with the help of which the human body – this headstrong servant of man – tries itself to become the master and turn the master into its slave. It is always keen to reverse the correct and natural position of the relationship between itself and man, so that instead of man riding his beast of burden the beast is the rider, taking man wherever it wishes him to go. If man is slack in imposing his authority with all his might, and lets loose the reins of his discretion and willpower, the beast eventually gets hold of him and then the servant becomes the master and the master the servant. The knowledge he has been bestowed about the nature of all things and the faculties he has been granted by Allah Most Glorified and Exalted of thinking, reasoning, exploration and invention are all then pressed into service of this blind, ignorant and thoughtless animal. Instead of using them in scaling new heights, they are utilised in a downward slide towards the lowest level. They become tools for the attainment of mean animal demands instead of sublime human objectives. These faculties, then, have no use other than their exploitation for the fulfilment of animal instincts. Consequently, the animal called the human body is reduced to the level of the worst of creatures.

Who can imagine the extent of mischief to which a beast of burden can go once he has the man as his servant to carry out his desires dutifully? Let us suppose that a bull was capable of manufacturing a whole fleet of warships, which pasture could then resist the onslaught of his economic interests? Could a dog that built tanks or fighter jets not acquire vast amounts of raw meat and bone? How far could the earth can go to serve as *lebensraum* for the wolf that has the guts to form his own nation of wolves and was capable of making use of a whole host of modern gadgets — from the mass media and its propaganda machine to long-range weapons of mass destruction? Who might put a check on animal libido of the ram that could invent every type of fiction, stage play, paintings, music, dance and beauty-aid and was capable of raising colleges, clubs, theatres and casinos for training his flock of sheep in the art of satisfying his lust?

To save humanity from falling into the depths it may not be enough to explain in speech or writing what human life means and what it stands for. It is equally essential that the natural position of man's relationship with this animal is also practically established and that the rider is so thoroughly trained through various exercises and drills that he rides well, holding firmly on to the reins of his willpower and with so much control over the beast that instead of following the beast's dictates, the beast follows him. This animal has been given to us by the Almighty to help us make the best use of him and thus ride to our goal in life. This animal's brain is a vehicle for us to think, its sensory organs our means to gather knowledge and its hands and feet the tools for our actions and manoeuvres. Of everything that the Lord Almighty has harnessed for us in this world, these animal frames, our bodies, are the most useful of them all. Whatever natural instincts the body has are all related to its real needs and we are under an obligation to fulfil them. We are obliged to take care of its rest, give it nutritious food, and satisfy its demand for self-preservation. Islam neither asks us to crush our natural instincts nor to ignore the genuine demands of our bodies. Nonetheless, it is clear in Islam that our physical frame is there to serve us and our higher goals; we are not to serve it and its carnal desires. This physical frame has to be subservient to our will and we must not be led by it. It is much beyond its status to command us like a ruler for the fulfilment of its demands. Like a servant, it has to submit instead its needs to us and then it is up to our discretion and well-trained self to approve or reject its request.

One of the basic aims and objectives of *ṣawm* is to bestow this power to man over his body. It takes hold of the human body's three basic demands that are the source of all animal desires, and with the help of these three powerful weapons this animal seeks to subdue human beings. The fast takes these into its tight embrace and by reining them in passes their bridles into our hands — into the hands of our 'self' that believes in Allah and is determined to follow the path approved by Him. Thus, the animal is absolutely left at our mercy. It continues to implore us for food and drink, but it is only after sunset that we fulfil this demand. It does not have the liberty even for a sip of tea. Nor is it free to transgress its limits at the sight of its mate. When at last the time comes for it to have its food and drink after a whole day's labour, it would also like to take some rest. Yet we have our own schedule. It must now be taken to the mosque for 'Ishā' and *tarāwīḥ* prayers. Then comes the time to sleep and the animal within wishes to retire to bed and rise late the next morning. It has to be woken up, however, in the dead of night. As desired by our Lord, it is told that it must have something to satisfy its hunger until the following evening.

This is the drill that we engage in for thirty days each year so that we have absolute command over this servant of ours. That is how we become masters of our bodies and their physical powers. The impulsive force of our animal instinct is curbed and we are made capable of checking our desires to the extent we deem necessary and using our potential the way we like. Anybody unused to controlling his desires, who has been habitually surrendering to each and every demand of his body and to whom the call of his animal instinct has been like a directive from his superior that must be obeyed, is absolutely incapable of the larger, bigger and better things in life. In order to be able to perform optimally, a man's ego has to have the ability to keep his personal desires and ambitions in check and to make the best use of his faculties of mind and body given to him by Allah Most Exalted. For the same reason, it is also desirable to observe voluntary fasts during the year in addition to the mandatory fast of Ramadan. This helps to strengthen further a person's control over his physical frame.

8.2.6. *Not An Ascetic's Self-Restraint*

However, there is a big and basic difference between the power *ṣawm* gives a man's self over his person and physique and the power sought for self-rejuvenation through self-torture, self-abnegation, strenuous exercises, or any other un-Islamic means. In fact, the power sought through such artificial means is the brute force of an ignorant and self-willed ego that has allegiance to no superior authority, one that feels responsible to no laws, rules or regulations and follows no right source of knowledge. Thus, whatever power is gained by an ascetic over his physical and mental faculties can neither be used for any right purpose nor in the right way. The malaise of self-mortification, self-negation and renunciation of worldly pleasures are a product of this very phenomenon. It is because of this that the rights due to the human body and the self have often been taken away. As man has often fought against his own instincts and consumed his potential this has in a way led to the degeneration of civilization and culture, instead of using them properly for their emancipation and progress. It is because of this undesirable attitude, and the seeking of power through artificial means, that many prominent personalities have often sought to impose their 'godhood' over God's subjects and used their capabilities in a manner contrary to the cause of truth and justice.

As against this, the power that *ṣawm* gives to the human ego over the body and mind is not unbridled. It is the sublime ego that obeys Allah and His Divine guidance. It is neither an ignorant ego nor one that is self-guided, but one that follows the guidance and the Book sent down for mankind by the All-Merciful Lord. It does not take the body and the mind as its property to rule over them according to its own discretion, but instead regards them as a trust to be managed as desired by the supreme Sovereign. A man of faith and fear in God whose ego has surrendered to His will can do no wrong in this world – and not least towards his own animal frame. He feeds his body properly, clothes it properly, provides it with the best available shelter and gives it the rest it needs. He takes care to satisfy all its natural demands within permissible limits. This he does not because it is the demand of his body, but because it is the right of his body as granted by his Lord, and by giving it its due he is also entitled to Allah's pleasure.[5] The believer's ego uses its authority with full might to take the physical frame away from the path of rebellion and disobedience when the latter calls for unlawful means to afford it good food and violation of Divine law for the sake of a good outfit, vehicle, house, etc. The elaborate exercise of the holy month of Ramadan is meant for this very purpose. Thus man is energized to have full command over his mind and body at all times, because each moment is a test for him and his successful disciplining of his self can alone be a guarantor of his ultimate and everlasting success in the eternal Life to Come.

8.3. A Road Map

The discussion so far has focused on the role *ṣawm* plays in training individuals, but before we move on to its social aspect, let us reassess the programme *ṣawm* has devised to train Muslim individuals.

As stated earlier, Islam seeks to prepare a community of good and upright individuals that may raise human civilization on the foundations of goodness and virtue. For this purpose, it has not only evolved social norms and values and created a civilizational order on the basis of those values, but it has also taken special care to prepare every individual for that order, so that each and every member of the Islamic society is in total harmony and conformity with that order in his thoughts, conduct and character. In spite of the rebel within seeking to hold him back, a true Muslim obeys the system voluntarily with the total involvement of his mind and soul, with the firmness of his faith, and the full force of his personal character. *Ṣawm* has the following role to play in this comprehensive Islamic training scheme: (1) It trains every member of Islamic society to surrender willingly his personal freedom to the supremacy of the Lord and lets his whole life be governed by the Divine guidance. (2) It firmly implants in each individual's mind, through practical exercises and drills, faith

---

[5] This is why the holy Prophet, may Allah bless him and give him peace, said: 'Do charity to your own self, then to your family, and then to others.' Charity to one's own self or to one's family is apparently a strange concept. Yet Islam's approach to life is in fact totally different. The person who eats to satisfy his hunger does just as others – including animals – do. Yet if he feeds his body, his wife, and children from his lawful (halal) earnings in fulfillment of the obligations assigned to him by his Creator, then he is then doing an act of goodness and discharging his duty, for which he is entitled to Allah's blessing and reward in the Hereafter. This is the approach about which the holy Prophet, may Allah bless him and give him peace, said: 'The position of a believer is like that of Moses' mother, who fed her own infant and got paid for it.' — Author.

in Allah, the All-Knowing and All-Seeing, and accountability in the Hereafter. Man obeys the Divine law, seen and unseen, not because of any external pressure, but because he is impelled by his sense of personal responsibility. (3) In theory and practice, it infuses such a spirit into each individual that he rejects the very idea of submission and allegiance to anyone else but Allah. (4) It morally grooms each one fasting in such a way that he has absolute control over his desires and the faculties of his body and brain and he can take work from them according to his faith, knowledge and insight. Thus he develops within himself the qualities of patience, tolerance, hard work, trust in Allah Most Glorified and Exalted, resoluteness and uprightness, and gains such strength in character to be able to resist all external temptations and undesirable personal inclinations.

These are the objectives for which Islam has enjoined upon every individual member of the Islamic community to fast during Ramadan. No sane, adult person, man or woman, is exempted from this command. In the event of illness, travel and other certain exigencies sanctioned by the Shariah, if someone is unable to fast, he has to make it up later on when that condition no longer applies. In case of failing health he has to offer expiation. In short, it is obligatory for every Muslim and no one can avoid it.

It is obviously not necessary for *ṣawm* to create all the desired qualities to the same degree within every individual, because this naturally depends on each individual's capacity and capability. However, this system of training has an inbuilt mechanism that helps to generate these qualities within a person, and no device better than this could be conceived for this purpose. Seen rationally and impartially, one has to admit that no social order other than Islam has such a broad-based and comprehensive system to prepare individuals in such a way that the whole society within its ambit is trained in the desired manners and morals automatically.

It further goes to the credit of the Islamic social order that if an individual within society is so incorrigible that he cannot be a part of this order, he is identified automatically. The moment he stops fasting without any religious sanction, society at once takes note that there is a transgressor and deviant (*fāsiq*), within its fold, one who has refused to remain loyal to Allah's supreme authority and has opted to revert to the servitude of his own animal instinct. Through this distinct system of identification, society is able to obtain timely knowledge of a festering tumour within its body. It thus has the opportunity to treat the tumour and save itself from any spreading of the malaise. Islam has taken care to pinpoint such transgressors and has offered every Muslim society the opportunity to detect such elements in a timely fashion and try to reform them or else expel them from its fold. Thus it is up to a particular society how it is to react to a situation like this.[6]

8.4. The Social Aspect

Like *ṣalāh*, *ṣawm* too is a personal act. However, just as the condition of congregational prayer turns *ṣalāh* into a collective and communal affair, so too has fasting been made a collective social event, instead of leaving it as an individual act alone. Thus its advantages and benefits have been extended to an unimaginable limit. According to that seemingly minor yet brilliant measure, a particular month has exclusively been sanctified for *ṣawm*. Had the Lawgiver only desired that the individual should be reformed this much morally, He could have decreed that every Muslim should fast for thirty days at any time during the calendar year. That too would have served to fulfil almost all the objectives of *ṣawm* mentioned above. In fact, if fasting had been made an individual act, then the ease one feels in observing the fast as part of a collective social affair would have been absent, and the individual would have been required to assert his willpower rather more vigorously, which might have been more effective for self-restraint. However, for the All-Wise Lawgiver, Who blessed humanity with the benign laws and precepts of Islam, the preparation of individuals carries no meaning unless it leads to the raising of an upright and sound community. Therefore, the Supreme Lord did not want *ṣawm* to remain a purely personal affair. Instead, He specified a particular month during the year so that the entire Muslim community could have a collective schedule of fasting. In this way, the system of training that prepares individuals has been made simultaneously effective in evolving a righteous social order.

Training of such a profound nature cannot be imparted to each individual separately. Therefore, we see that an army is trained by making every soldier react at the same time to the bugle's call so that each one may develop team spirit, learn to act in unison, and assist each other in their tasks. Whatever one person lacks is made up by another; whatever deficiency remains in him is compensated for by another.

The month of Ramadan is earmarked for all Muslims to fast collectively in order to ensure similar results. This measure turns an individual act of worship into collective *ʿibādah*. Just as one when multiplied by thousands becomes a

---

[6] If a so-called Muslim society nourishes transgressors and deviants within its fold and offers them all available avenues to flourish, it in fact cuts away at its own roots and, as history testifies, it may soon find that there is no friendly soul to shed tears on its gradual degeneration, decay and eventual demise. — Editor.

formidable number, similarly the moral and spiritual benefits accruing from *ṣawm* to one person alone grows manifold times if a million people fast together. The month infuses the whole environment with a spirit of righteousness, virtue and piety. As flowers blossom in spring, so does *taqwā* in Ramadan. Everyone strenuously tries to avoid sin, and in case of a lapse the individual knows he can count on the help of his other brothers who are fasting with him. The desire automatically arises in every heart to do good work, to feed the poor, to clothe the naked, to help those in distress, to participate in whatever good is being done anywhere in society, and to prevent evil. Just as plants have their season of flowering, Ramadan too is the time of the year for the growth and flourishing of goodness and righteousness.

As mentioned earlier, the holy Prophet, may Allah bless him and give him peace, has declared for the same reason:

كُلُّ عَمَلِ اِبنِ آدَمَ يُضَاعِفُ الحَسَنَةَ بِعَشرِ اَمثَالِهَا اِلٰى سَبعِ مِائَةِ ضِعفٍ، قَالَ اللهُ تَعَالىٰ: «اِلَّاالصَّومُ فَاِنَّهُ لِي وَاَنَا اَجزِى بِهِ».

> Every deed a person does grows [in the sight of the Lord]. One good deed grows from ten to several hundred times. However, Allah Most Glorified and Exalted says: '*Ṣawm* is an exceptional act. It is for Me and I shall reward it in the way I please'.
>
> (Bukhārī and Muslim)

This shows that every good deed grows both in proportion to the intention of the doer and its outcome. However, while there is a limit to their growth, fasting has no such limit. In Ramadan, the season for the blossoming of goodness and piety, not one but millions of people water the garden of virtue together. The more a person sincerely performs good deeds during this month and the greater he avails of its blessings, the more will he radiate their benefits to his other brothers. The more he sustains the impact of *ṣawm* on his life during the subsequent eleven months, the more his garden (i.e. society) flourishes, and flourishes without limit. Should its growth become inhibited, the fault must lie with him. It may be difficult to sum up the extent of the moral and spiritual advantages of *ṣawm*, but we can pinpoint a few of these in the paragraphs that follow.

8.4.1. *The Environment of Piety and Goodness*

The first characteristic of social activity is that it creates a definite psychological environment. If a person is individually engaged in a certain activity with a certain mind-set and finds no similar atmosphere around him nor sees anybody sharing his activity, he is bound to feel the odd man out and a total stranger in his environment. Intellectually, since he receives no support from his surroundings, he would remain confined to his own self and dependent on his psychic power. In fact, different environmental effects are bound to affect him adversely. As opposed to this, if the entire atmosphere shares the same mind-set, and if all the people are engaged in the same activity with the same frame of mind and are moved by the same spirit, then it will be an entirely different matter. Then a social climate in which the whole community can share will emerge. The intrinsic goodness of the individual keeps on growing with the active support available from his external environment.

We can explain this better with the following example: if an individual is nude and those around him wear clothes, how ashamed would he feel? What amount of indecency and impudence would he need to bare himself, and even then how often would his shamelessness give in to the pressures of his environment? On the other hand, when everyone in the swimming pool is naked there will hardly be any scope for decency and shame. Thus, the shamelessness of each individual receives sustenance from others to grow further. To give another analogy, how difficult is it for a soldier to wage war individually and bear the horrors of war singlehandedly? Conversely, when the entire army is on the march, each soldier is inspired to do his best for his country and nation. Whether for vice or virtue, the collective social psyche plays an enormous role in its promotion. If the community is engaged collectively in vicious acts, then the sentiments of debauchery and profligacy know no bounds; but if the community's collective thrust is towards goodness and virtue, then the whole atmosphere is bound to become virtuous and even the bad may turn good, even for a short time.

By declaring Ramadan as the month of fasting, the supreme Lawgiver has used this month the way different seasons are used for various crops. We find that the fields bloom with each crop as the season comes. Thus, Ramadan is the harvesting season of goodness, virtue, piety and purity. Evil is subdued and righteousness prospers. The whole population is anointed with the blissful balm of the fear of God and love for goodness and charity. The harvest of *taqwā* is in full bloom. A person is ashamed of his acts of omission and commission and tries to avoid to the maximum possible extent anything that is not allowed by his faith; he also checks others from wrongdoing. In a general atmosphere of charity, every person feels inspired to do some good by way of feeding the poor, providing clothing to those in need, helping someone in trouble, sharing the work of goodness and charity with those engaged in such work, and resisting evil almost effortlessly. This is the season when hearts soften and hands refrain from wrongdoing. There is distaste for evil and craving for virtue. In short, through this brilliant arrangement, the Lawgiver has ensured that the whole Muslim community for a month each year passes through an overhauling and cleansing process in order to remove the impurities gathered during the previous eleven months.

Therefore, the holy Prophet, may Allah bless him and give him peace, has said:

اِذَا دَخَلَ رَمَضَانُ فُتِحَت اَبوَابُ الجَنّة وَغُلِّقَت اَبوَابُ جهَنَّم وَسُلسِلَتِ الشَّياطِين.

> With the advent of the month of Ramadan, the Gates of Paradise are opened and the Gates of Hell are shut and the devils are put in chains.
>
> (Bukhārī)

In another Tradition, the same truth has been elaborated in these morals:

اَذَا كَانَ اَوَّلُ لَيلَةٍ مِن شهرِ رَمَضَانَ صُفِّدتِ الشّياطِينُ وَمَرَدَةُ الجِنِّ وغُلِّقَت اَبوَابُ النَّارِ فَلَم يُفتَح مِنها بَابٌ وَفُتِحَت اَبوَابُ الجَنة فَلِمَ يُغلَق مِنها بَابٌ وَيُنَادِى مُنَادِيا بَاغِىَ الخَيرِ اَقبِل وَيا بَاغِىَ الشَّرِّ اَقصِر وَلله عُتَقَاءُ مِنَ النَّارِ، وَ ذٰلِكَ كُلَّ لَيلَةٍ.

> With the first night of the month of Ramadan, the devils and the rebellious jinns are chained up. The Gates of Hell are closed leaving no gate open and all the Gates of Heaven are opened leaving no gate shut. A herald then proclaims: 'O seeker of good, move forward! O seeker of evil, halt!' Many are set free from the Fire, and this happens every night [of Ramadan].
>
> (Tirmidhī and Ibn Mājah)

A patient in coma is tested by putting a glass close to his nose: any sign of breathing on the glass or its absence indicates if he is alive or not. In the same way, if one is to test a Muslim community, one should observe it during Ramadan. If one discovers within it the signs of *taqwā*, this would mean that it is alive. However, if the signs are otherwise and the doors of piety are found to be shut and the manifestations of *fujūr*, profligacy and anti-Islamic trends are more pronounced even during the holy month, then the spiritual demise of the community is a foregone conclusion. There is then no further chance for its survival Islamically.[7]

8.4.2. *Communal Harmony*

The second major advantage of the social activity of Ramadan is that it gives rise to a feeling of oneness and a sense of natural and real unity. Commonality of race, language, place of birth and economic interests do not create the spirit of natural nationhood. According to the popular maxim 'closer to mind, closer to heart', one is naturally closer to the person with whom one shares one's thoughts and actions. It is only the bond of spiritual harmony that firmly binds two persons together. Conversely, someone with whom we share no proximity of thought or action never gets close to our heart, even though he may be our own brother. When someone finds people around him who differ in their mind-set and activities, he definitely feels himself to be a stranger among them. However, when so many people do the same thing collectively with a similar frame of mind, this leads automatically to a strong bond of commonality, solidarity and brotherhood. They are no longer strangers to one another, and the partnership of heart and soul as well as of harmony in action bind them together into one big whole.

Whether for vice or virtue, the collective social psyche acts in a similar fashion. A partnership of burglars in thievery and a comradeship of drunkards in drinking can create a sense of brotherhood. However, there is one big difference. An individual's egotism is more pronounced when engaged in vice, which has a natural tendency to tear individuals apart. This is why no 'brotherhood' of evil is sound and selfless. At the opposite end of the spectrum, one's self will is subdued when on the path of virtue. Here, the human soul has a true sense of self-gratification and the individual moves along this path with sentiments of purity and righteousness. Therefore, there can be no social ties stronger than the bonds of brotherhood created by the collaboration of good ideas emanating from *īmān* and the righteous deed (*al-ʿamal al-ṣāliḥ*).

Like congregational prayers, the collective observance of the fast creates a similar kind of brotherhood. The collective quest for Allah's pleasure, the urge

[7] Such a community may be economically prosperous and materially advanced in different fields, but a Muslim society is certainly distinct from its non-Muslim counterparts. Unless it comes up to the standards set by the holy Qur'an and the holy Prophet's Sunnah, it remains a society spiritually devoid of its soul. Its material progress is of no help in preventing its eventual decay. This is also the lesson of history. — Editor.

to bear willingly the hardships of thirst and hunger for His blessing, to give up vice and to prevent each other from committing wrong out of fear of the Lord, and to pursue good and encourage others to do good out of love for Him – all this creates the most congenial atmosphere of communal harmony, unity and brotherhood and the kind of comradeship and fellow-feeling that is free from the adulterations and impurities of the material world.

8.4.3. *The Spirit of Cooperation*

The third major advantage of Ramadan's collective programme of worship is that it levels out the different socio-economic divisions in society. Although the rich remain rich and the poor remain poor, for a certain period of time at least the rich also taste the flavour of hunger and thirst as experienced all too often by less-privileged brethren in the community. The affluent are therefore motivated to lend their help and support to the less-privileged with the sole objective of winning Allah's pleasure. While this may apparently sound trivial, the moral and civilizational benefits of the exercise are many. In such a community, where the 'haves' are aware of the hardships faced by the 'have-nots', where they feel for them and are ready to help, and where efforts are consciously made to find out the deserving and the needy to satisfy their needs, the poor segments of society are always safe from becoming social outcasts. Furthermore, the collective will for charity and goodness remains robust, and there grows between the rich and the poor a relationship of love and not one of hatred, and a kinship of thanks and benign gratefulness and not one of rebellion and revolt. Such a society is generally free from the curse of class conflict as may be found in communities where the rich have their own domain and in times of crisis often wonder why the have-nots go hungry when they could have taken 'cake' if they did not have the 'bread' to eat.

This is the social significance of the second pillar of Islam. Through *ṣawm*, Islam prepares its followers by training them individually as moral beings and then forging them into a special community. The ultimate goal that Islam has before itself is to bring into being an upright and spiritually-motivated civil society. The constituent parts of this society are carefully prepared through the regimen of *ṣalāh*, *ṣawm* and the other pillars of Islam. It is due to this rigorous training that officials, government functionaries, ministers, teachers, intellectuals, judges, religious scholars, traders, labourers, mill-owners, farmers, public representatives, the common man, and every other member of society becomes capable of evolving collectively into that righteous and noble socio-political order, which in Islamic terminology is known as the caliphate on the model set by the holy Prophet (*al-khilāfah ʿalā minhāj al-nubuwwah*).[8]

8.5. Why does Fasting Not Produce the Desired Results?

With a bit of introspection, it is not that difficult to ascertain why our *ṣawm* is not as effective in its moral impact as it might have actually been. It is because the very meaning and purport of *ʿibādah* has become distorted in our minds. We think that mere abstention from day-long eating and drinking is what is meant by fasting. Therefore, we are very particular to observe the smallest of details concerning it. We fear God to the extent that we avoid even the slightest violation of the rules. However, we seldom care to consider whether merely being hungry and thirsty is only the form but not the purpose of fasting.

Ṣawm has been prescribed to create within us such awareness of Allah Most Exalted, love and fear of Him, and such strength of will and character that we avoid, in contradiction to our desires, seemingly profitable things that displease Allah and do those things that may entail risk and loss but definitely please the Lord. Unfortunately, however, as soon as Ramadan is over we throw away all that we may have gained from fasting. Our example then is like that of a person who ate food to his heart's content, but vomited it out later by thrusting his fingers down his throat. Just as physical strength cannot be obtained from bread until it is digested and transformed into blood flowing through every vein, similarly spiritual strength cannot be obtained from *ṣawm* until the person who fasts is conscious of its purpose and allows it to permeate his heart and mind and dominate his thoughts, motives and deeds.

After enjoining *ṣawm*, this is the reason why Allah Most Blessed and Exalted declared that fasting has been made obligatory for the believers so that they 'become God-fearing' (*laʿʿallakum tattaqūn*) (*al-Baqarah* 2: 183). Thus, we can easily understand why our *ʿibādah* has become ineffectual and devoid of meaning and purpose. The greatest mistake of all is to take the outward forms of

---

[8] There is no place in an Islamic polity for hereditary rule or the dynastic system of succession. The people's participation in the affairs of the state has been ensured through a system of governance known as *al-khilāfah ʿalā minhāj al-nubuwwah*. In this system, the caliph is the people's representative and the upholder of the holy Prophet's legacy. This legacy covers the entire spectrum of the Islamic state's activities from public welfare, socio-cultural and economic development to the religious, moral and material needs of individual citizens as well as society's well-being as a whole. For all times to come, the pattern was set for the system by the golden model of the ideal times (*khayr al-qurūn*) of our master the Messenger of Allah, may Allah bless him and give him peace, and his illustrious successors, the four rightly-guided caliphs (*al-khulafāʾ al-rāshidūn*). — Editor.

prayer and fasting as the real *ʿibādah*. If we do so, we are exactly like the person who thinks that by merely performing the four acts of taking a piece of food, putting it in his mouth, chewing it and then swallowing it that the process of digestion is complete. Such a person imagines that whoever does these four things has digested the food. He then expects the food to give him the nourishment necessary for his survival, but he should not forget also to provide the environment necessary for the digestion of the food and the required conditions of health and hygiene for the body. The act of taking food in and of itself cannot be a guarantor of sound health. Similarly, to merely fast without the essential qualities of *taqwā*, faith, allegiance and the spirit of self-restraint is no *ṣawm*. It is like going hungry and thirsty without any purpose.

8.6. The Meaning of Putting the Devils in Chains

That the devils are chained up with the advent of Ramadan signifies the fact that a true believer willingly accepts all restrictions and keeps his personal desires in check as he begins his fast. These are the desires that are otherwise genuine and there are no restrictions on them before or after the month of Ramadan. For example, drinking water is halal throughout the year but during the holy month of Ramadan it becomes haram between pre-dawn and sunset. Food satisfies one's hunger, provided it is taken with permitted means, but during Ramadan it is haram while fasting. When the believer willingly accepts these restrictions and restrains his desires and freedom of action, he actually restrains the devil within him. Conversely, if he ignores the restrictions imposed by the Shariah on food, drink and sex during the month of fasting, in a way he lets his devil rule over him and his desires.

8.7. Moon Sighting

Islam follows the lunar calendar for the observance of all acts of worship, including *ṣawm*, hajj and the yearly calculation of *zakāh*. The month of Ramadan begins with the sighting of the new moon and ends with the sighting of the moon of Shawwāl. According to a famous tradition, the holy Prophet, may Allah bless him and give him peace, said: 'Start fasting with the sighting of the moon and end the fast with the sighting of [the following month's] moon.' (صُومُوا لِرُؤيتِهِ وأفطِرُوا لِرُؤيتِهِ) (Bukhārī and Muslim). In another tradition, ʿAbdullāh ibn ʿUmar quoted the holy Prophet as saying:

لاَتَصُومُوا حَتّٰى تَرَوُا الهِلاَلَ وَلَا تُفطِرُوا حَتّٰى تَرَوهُ، فَاِن غُمَّ عَلَيكُم اقدِرُوا لَهُ.

> Do not start fasting until you have seen the new moon and do not stop fasting until you see it. If the horizon is clouded, you will have to ascertain properly the actual position of moon.
>
> (Bukhārī and Muslim)

This would mean that there are no predetermined dates for the beginning or the end of the month of fasting. While calculations can be made through different means for the sighting of the new moon, and a tentative calendar can be prepared for the whole lunar year, the exact dates for the beginning of Ramadan, the observance of Eid al-Fitr and Eid al-Adha, hajj, etc. should be determined properly only with the sighting of the moon.

8.7.1. *Why a Lunar Calendar?*

Islam's adoption of the lunar calendar does not in any way imply a disregard for the solar calendar. This preference is actually based on some practical aspects of greater importance and far-reaching significance. These include the wisdom of keeping the believer acclimatized with all climates and weather conditions, and training him to show his allegiance to the Lord and to faithfully discharge his religious obligations regardless of the rigours of time and tide. Whether it is biting cold or sweltering heat, whether the days are cloudy or the nights rainy, or the even if scorching heat makes it difficult to remain thirsty from pre-dawn to sunset, he has to fast and perform the hajj, unless physically incapable of doing so.

Moreover, how could one expect from the universal religion that is for all times and ages to fix a particular solar month for Ramadan or hajj? The dates and timings of *iftār*, *suḥūr*, Eid al-Fitr and Eid al-Adha determined for a certain time-zone, would naturally be different elsewhere. The bonds of brotherhood in the Muslim *ummah* are also strengthened further through the uniformity of the calendar. The believers perform all acts of worship in perfect harmony and unison. To start the fasting month one day earlier or two days later does not mean a break from their brethren engaged in the same exercise elsewhere around the globe.

There is yet another wisdom behind enjoining the lunar calendar for acts of worship, and that is bringing the Muslim community closer to nature. One does not need to be educated in the nuances of astronomy, or in keeping minute details of the solar calendar, for the calculation of his days for *ṣawm* or hajj. As someone lives through the days and nights and daily observes the natural sights of sunset and dawn, it is similarly easier for him to trace the moon. The predetermined dates of the solar calendar would have been too cumbersome for him. Furthermore, the practice of going by the solar calendar would have unnecessarily imparted religious sanctity even to those dates.[9] Whether one is in a desert, living in a skyscraper, flying in the air, or making a sea voyage, one does not feel handicapped by the absence of a diary to determine when a particular solar month ended and when the new one began. There is no such problem in case of a lunar month, which can simply be determined by the sighting of the moon.

8.7.2. *The Timetable for* ʿIbādāt

The criterion set by Islam for the timings of all its acts of worship is one that conforms to the needs of people of all civilizational backgrounds and intellectual levels so that each can determine his timetable in all times and climes. Instead of following the calculations of the clock, it has fixed these timings according to the visible features of nature. Those ignorant of the wisdom behind this occasionally refer to the difficulty that one may presumably face in observing *ṣalāh* and *ṣawm* timings in the polar regions, where the days and nights extend not to hours and minutes but by months.

However, confusion has been caused due to the lack of proper knowledge of the geographical phenomenon there, as actually neither the polar day nor the polar night last for six months. This matter cannot be judged on the basis of the experience of those who live around the equator. In the polar region the signs of both day and night appear regularly on the horizon, and these can easily be taken as definite indicators to mark the beginning of day or night. It is according to these signs that the people living in that region calculate the hours and minutes of their days and nights. That is how they determine their working hours and their time of their going to bed and waking up. Even before the invention of the watch, the peoples of Finland, Norway, Greenland, etc. used to calculate their time: the natural phenomena of regular signs appearing and disappearing on the horizon was their guide. Therefore, there has been no problem for the Muslims living there to prepare their timetables for *ṣalāh*, *ṣawm* and other acts of worship.

[9] For this we may note what has happened in the case of 25 December and the festivals observed on different predetermined dates by other religious communities. — Editor.

PART THREE

RESPONSES TO SOME CRITICAL QUESTIONS

9 The Role of Worship in Behavioural Change

The article that follows is in response to the query a reader of *Tarjumān al-Qur'ān* addressed to Sayyid Mawdūdī with reference to his writings on *ṣalāh*. A shortened version of the letter is given below. — Editor.

> As for the timings of *ṣalāh*, you have brilliantly dispelled the misconceptions in certain quarters. You have also succinctly explained the healthy impact of *ṣalāh* on the life of man and how it helps in his character-building and familiarization with the observance of Divine injunctions, devotion to duty and discipline in all walks of life. I have failed, however, to find a satisfactory answer to something that has been agitating my mind. Theoretically speaking, I do agree that *ṣalāh*, as well as all the obligatory acts of worship (*farā'iḍ*), have been ordained with the obvious purpose of having a healthy impact on human life. The format prescribed for each one of them is definitely such that it ought to leave the desired effect on human character and conduct. But why is it that we find this aspect missing in our practical lives as Muslims? It was rightly expected of those who regularly performed prayer, fasted, undertook the pilgrimage to the House of God and annually contributed *zakāh* that they would be models of Islamic social conduct and epitomes of virtue and righteousness. Unfortunately, however, the case is just the reverse. There is hardly any difference in the social conduct and dealings of those who observe Islamic acts of worship and those who do not. In fact, some 'pious' persons make their piety a shield or smokescreen for their misconduct. The modern educated lot is getting growingly disenchanted with *ṣalāh*, *ṣawm*, etc. due to the bad examples of such 'holy men'.

To a great extent, there is no denying the fact that the sentiments expressed above reflect the situation that prevails in Muslim societies today. However, this conundrum can be resolved without much difficulty. The letter writer himself has admitted that the Islamic system of worship is perfect in all respects. Reason also demands that the purpose for which the system was enjoined ought to be thoroughly achieved, because there is no practical step better than the Islamic system of *ʿibādah* for the human psyche to be attracted towards its Lord and familiarize itself with the performance of its religious duty. The history of humankind is also a witness to the effectiveness of this system. It was the phenomenon of the Islamic system of worship that helped to train millions of Arabs and non-Arabs spiritually and morally during the early days of Islam. The rituals of *ṣalāh, ṣawm, zakāh* and hajj were instrumental in forging the bonds of Islamic brotherhood and galvanizing divergent ethnic, linguistic and cultural groups into an internationally-oriented, dynamic, global nation of Islam.

Now, if we see the impact of this Divine system of *ʿibādāt* missing from the practical side of the life in an individual or a group, we have no reason to doubt its effectiveness. We should take it instead as an outcome of the Muslim psyche's lack of responsiveness. We know that the fire consumes wood, and, based on experience and observation, we have not an iota of doubt that the function of fire is to burn and that of the wood is to be burnt. With this conviction, if we see at times that wood placed on a burner does not burn we do not consider even for a moment that the fire has lost its ability to burn. At once, we realize instead that the wood contains moisture that renders it incapable of responding to the fire's impact. In exactly the same manner, we know through reason and logic how a particular course of training and orientation should have an impact on those for whom it has been devised, as confirmed by the tried-and-tested record of its efficacy. Conversely, when we see its ineffectiveness in certain cases, should we not explain it then by the analogy of moistened wood that burns poorly or not at all? In other words, we have no cogent reason to doubt the effectiveness of that training and orientation programme to begin with.

As for the physical features of *ṣalāh* and other acts of worship, these are no more than the performance of our few bodily limbs and repetition of some prescribed words and phrases. Abstention from eating, drinking and sexual acts from dawn to dusk in a particular month is *ṣawm.* The allocation of a certain amount of money once a year from our capital for disbursement under various prescribed categories is *zakāh.* Journeying to the holy city of Makkah the blessed in a particular month and then the performance of some specific acts of worship is hajj. There is apparently nothing in these actions in themselves that renders them capable of leaving a lasting impact upon the human psyche. Taken at face value, these acts of worship are obviously not much different in the case of *ṣalāh* from physical exercises, in the case of *ṣawm* from starvation, in the case of *zakāh* from government taxation and in the case of hajj from normal travelling. No rational being can claim that physical exercises produce spiritual sublimity, that starvation is good for moral training, or that the payment of taxes and travelling to certain places generate the noblest qualities in man.

However, the most vital aspect that distinguishes the Islamic system of *ʿibādāt* and makes them the best means for moral emancipation, spiritual rejuvenation and the chastening of the self is the quality of faith (*īmān*), duly supported by the righteous deed (*al-ʿamal al-ṣāliḥ*). It is the quality of *īmān* that elevates simple acts: bowing down, kneeling, rising up and sitting down to the stature of *ṣalāh*; mere abstention from food, drink and sex is thus turned into *ṣawm*; the act of tax payment is qualitatively changed into the noble act of *zakāh*; and what is otherwise an excursion emerges as hajj or an extraordinary journey into self-discovery. It is in fact the element of faith that is the essence and soul of the entire system of Islamic acts of worship. It is this that renders them meaningful, empowers their impact, and it is from this that the human psyche is groomed and emancipated.

Hence, it is not possible for a person who is resolute in his *īmān*, having firm faith in his Creator and the Day of Reckoning and staunchly believing in the prophethood of our master the Messenger of Allah, may Allah bless him and give him peace, and the teachings of Islam revealed to mankind through him, to repeat the lesson of *ṣalāh* five times a day without feeling its impact on his heart and without having the attendant fear of God and a sense of obedience towards the Divine injunctions. It is impossible for a person trained for a month every year in piety and the fear of God to remain unaffected and incapable of a revolutionary change in his life, as if he had undergone no training. It is similarly impossible for a person motivated entirely by his belief in the Unseen to spend out of his hard-earned wealth a certain amount in the way of Allah and still remain afflicted with self-conceit, lust for money and heartlessness – traits that are normally found in a faithless and self-centred person. It is also unthinkable for a man to embark on an arduous journey, leaving his hearth and home for the sake of God, clad in unostentatious unstitched dress, constantly calling upon his Lord proclaiming that he is there at His service and remaining for a long time in that state of ardent love and fervour until he finally witnesses with his own eyes some of the most hallowed and glorious signs of Allah Most Glorified and Exalted to remain unaffected or disassociated from his Lord. Hajj is an everlasting testimony to the success of the Lord's true believers and obedient servants and the failure and eventual doom of those who rebel against Him. It is thus impossible for one to return from such an extraordinary journey and find no trace of an impact on one's mind and heart.

Let us not lose sight of yet another fact. The qualitative and quantitative impact of acts of worship on each person is never the same. The level of their effectiveness rises or falls according to the capacity of each human psyche and the strength or weakness of its power of faith. However, it is impossible for acts of worship, observed sincerely, devotedly and with the full force of *īmān* and righteous deeds to go to waste and bear no fruit. We can say with certainty that anyone is not a true believer who combines his regular prayer with evil deeds, who fasts but remains morally wayward, whose personal character is a mix of the annual payment of *zakāh* and the deliberate devouring of interest, and whose pilgrimage to the House of God does not prevent him from irresponsible acts of transgression. This is why such a person's prayer is actually no prayer at all but only a lifeless ritual act. His fast is no fast but merely starvation. His *zakāh* is no *zakāh* but a simple act of charity or tax-payment. And his hajj is no hajj but an excursion trip as one does to London, Paris, or elsewhere.

Whatever has been said above is true only in respect of those whose lives have remained, according to the writer of the letter, unaffected by the impact of Islamic acts of worship. However, I absolutely refuse to accept that a Muslim who regularly offers prayer, fasts, pays his share of *zakāh*, and performs the hajj falls into that category. Leaving aside a very small number of such hypocrites, praise be to Allah, the majority of practising Muslims are not like that. The malaise that generally afflicts Muslims is not hypocrisy, but the infirmity of their faith, coupled with the total or partial absence of righteous deeds. This is the reason why the effectiveness of their acts of worship has been adversely affected. They pray, fast, pay their *zakāh* and also perform the hajj, but all these solemn acts only gently touch their hearts, just as steam disappears leaving behind only a little moisture on the surface of a mirror. This is not the absence of an impact, but its weakness. Buried deep within their hearts, the embers of faith are still there and due to that the acts of worship performed by them do produce results, though they are often quite feeble. That is why its signs are not clearly visible in the lives and characters of worshippers.

I also refuse to accept that the Muslims who regularly perform *ʿibādāt* are worse or even similar to those who do not worship at all. Factually speaking, if taken as a whole only that segment of our Muslim population would be found to be better in its overall conduct, manners and morals that is seriously regular in its observance of *ṣalāh* and *ṣawm*. The real problem is that our people generally tend to ignore the misdeeds of those who do not observe religious duties, while they take seriously even the minor lapses of the religiously-oriented. They do not complain much when they see a less religious person indulging in vice, but for even a little act of irreligiosity the one who is regular in his *ʿibādāt* is publicly noticed and condemned. This is because even a tiny black dot on an otherwise spotlessly white wall is immediately noticed and the onlooker is tempted to point the finger of blame at it. Conversely, one can smear a whole kitchen wall, already black with soot with charcoal and nobody would notice.

Thus, we may sum up the factual position as follows: we do have amongst us a large number of those who pray, perform the hajj and regularly observe other religious duties, but who have failed to benefit from their *ʿibādāt* and reform themselves. This is due not to any weakness in those acts of worship but mainly because of a weakening of their faith, which is the heart and soul of every act of worship and the principal factor behind its effectiveness.

Now the question that arises is what is the reason behind such a weakening of faith? An immediate answer is that the lack of a proper awareness of the teachings of the holy Qur'an and the Sunnah of the holy Prophet, may Allah bless him and give him peace. The Qur'an is the main source of the Islamic message, while the Sunnah is the interpretation of this message. Unfortunately, however, Muslims have generally been deprived of understanding Islam and its message and mission carefully. Hence, they are unable to understand correctly the teachings of the Qur'an and the Sunnah and their true spirit. Therefore, it is natural for faith not to grow and develop in their hearts in the way it ought to.

Another factor that has played a big role in rendering our acts of worship ineffective is the misconception that there is a division between the spiritual and the temporal, the religious and the material. This is the concept of the Days of Ignorance that Islam has totally demolished, but the notion has somehow found its way into the Muslim social milieu. During the dark ages of paganism and ignorance before Islam, people used to think that religion was just one of the various aspects of human life and that it had nothing to do with man's life as a whole. Religious rites and rituals were obligatory for the people only in order to please their gods and goddesses and seek their support in mundane matters. As soon as a person left the house of worship after performing certain rituals, he had no further obligations towards his religion and was free to conduct his day-to-day affairs the way he liked. Islam has totally and absolutely rejected this compartmentalization, and Allah Most Glorified and Exalted has declared our religion as *dīn* or a way of life. Islam is not just one of the so many other facets of human life: it is a comprehensive charter of action that covers every aspect of life. Islam has established a deeper relationship between the tenets of religion and social conduct, faith and personal character, acts of worship and public dealings, and mundane and spiritual affairs. It has brought integration in life. The so-called 'worldly' activities are thus not worldly as such. It tells us that the religion is not separate from worldly affairs, and that to follow *dīn* means to observe the Divine law (Shariah) in all spheres of life.

ʿIbādāt and matters in the public domain are thus no two different things in Islam. To seek Allah's pleasure and His blessings, to observe His well-defined parameters in all day-to-day matters, and to make conscious effort to gain proximity with the Lord are very much acts of worship. By prescribing *ṣalāh, ṣawm,* hajj and *zakāh* as obligatory duties, it is not intended to restrict Allah's worship to these few acts alone. Instead, these are meant to prepare man for a much bigger act of worship, one that encompasses his whole life. The entire universe is a house of worship for the Muslim, his whole life means worship, and he has to be a worshipper of his Master and Creator in each and every moment of his life.[1] His place of worship is not confined to the mosque alone. In fact, the mosque is his training centre, one that prepares him for the onerous responsibility of worshipping the Lord. If the relationship of a Muslim's prayer, fasting and other rituals is severed from his social life, and in his day-to-day conduct he feels free from the observance of Divine law, then he is no more a man of religion and true believer and worshipper of Allah Most Exalted.

It is unfortunate that Muslims are gradually losing sight of this comprehensive meaning of their religion. More unfortunate is the fact that there is a gradual revival among them of the same *jāhilī* notion of the division between the spiritual and the temporal that Islam had demolished. It is only because of this erroneous concept that the mutual relationship between acts of worship and social life has been cut off. Our economic activities have no conceptual relationship with the philosophy of *zakāh*, the impact and effect of Ramadan is confined to the month of fasting, and the transformatory role of hajj is similarly marginalized due to its becoming a ritual like the Hindu *yātrā* or Christian pilgrimage. Furthermore, the misconception has generally taken root among the people that *ṣalāh* and profligacy, *ṣawm* and disobedience to the Lord, and *zakāh* and interest can go hand in hand. (*Tarjumān al-Qur'ān*, November 1935)

---

[1] This may be a difficult proposition for those given to a secular approach to life. However, the actual position remains as explained by the author. A Muslim is a Muslim because he has willingly surrendered his free will to the will of God. He is an *ʿabd* from the age of maturity until he breathes his last and the only option for him is to sincerely worship his Creator. How can we ignore the fundamental truth so magnificently explained by the Lord!

وَمَا خَلَقْتُ ٱلْجِنَّ وَٱلْإِنسَ إِلَّا لِيَعْبُدُونِ ۝ مَآ أُرِيدُ مِنْهُم مِّن رِّزْقٍ وَمَآ أُرِيدُ أَن يُطْعِمُونِ ۝

I created the jinn and humans for nothing else but that they may serve Me; I desire from them no provision, nor do I want them to feed Me.

(*al-Dhāriyāt* 51: 56–57) — Editor.

10 The Language of *Ṣalāh* and the Friday Sermon

A gentleman from the state of Datiya asked for a formal legal opinion regarding the following:

(1) 'Is it a fact that the great jurist Imam Abū Ḥanīfah, may Allah have mercy on him, allowed those who did not have Arabic as their mother tongue to offer regular prayers in their native language? Was this his personal interpretation? If so, why do Muslim theologians and jurists not review the matter and issue a clear edict in this respect?

(2) Allah Most Exalted says:

يَـٰٓأَيُّهَا ٱلَّذِينَ ءَامَنُوا۟ لَا تَقْرَبُوا۟ ٱلصَّلَوٰةَ وَأَنتُمْ سُكَـٰرَىٰ حَتَّىٰ تَعْلَمُوا۟ مَا تَقُولُونَ ... ﴿٤٣﴾

Believers! Do not draw near to the prayer while you are intoxicated until you know what you are saying.

(*al-Nisā'* 4: 43)

The believers are thus forbidden to offer prayer in a state of intoxication or drunkenness and the reason given is that a person in such a state of mind does not understand what he says. This would obviously mean that as a precondition for prayer being valid it is essential for the one offering prayer to understand what is being recited. Therefore, if a person offers prayer in his mother tongue to understand each and every syllable of what he is reciting, is there any reason to consider such a prayer unacceptable?

(3) What do religious scholars and jurists say about permissibility or otherwise of delivering Friday sermons and those of Eid al-Fitr and Eid al-Adha in the native language of the congregation? It may be said that to deliver these obligatory sermons in a language other than Arabic was contrary to the holy Prophet's tradition, but the tradition actually demanded of the congregation that it listen carefully and understand what the holy Prophet, may Allah bless him and give him peace, said and then strictly observe the 'dos' and 'don'ts' and enrich themselves with the sage counsel and pearls of wisdom contained in those sermons.

> In a situation where ninety-nine per cent of the congregation does not understand what has been said, how can such a sermon be taken to conform to the holy Prophet's tradition? To me, the entire exercise thus loses its significance and the very act of delivering sermons on Friday and the two Eids becomes meaningless.'

The writer has actually sought a fatwa or formal legal opinion, for which he should have addressed his query to the relevant *ulema* and Muslim jurists. However, in his personal judgment, he thought it fitting to ask me to do some research in the matter and to arrive at an opinion. Therefore, I have attempted to explain briefly the injunctions of the Islamic Shariah concerning the questions raised. The following explanatory notes are by no means a substitute for a formal legal opinion (fatwa). I leave it to the *ulema* to look into these and, if they find my answers to their satisfaction, then they may accept them as well.

10.1. Some Important Preliminaries

Before taking up the subject under review, some preliminaries need to be carefully understood to help put these observations in their true perspective.

It is a well-known fact that the Islamic Shariah is based on the foundations of wisdom (*ḥikmah*) and welfare (*falāḥ*). No injunction given by the supreme Lawgiver is without meaning and purpose, nor has He overlooked the demands of wisdom and welfare in laying down procedures for the implementation of His injunctions. It follows naturally then that the correct observance of the Shariah is possible only through its correct understanding. It would be extremely difficult, or rather impossible, for a person to correctly follow the dictates of the Shariah who does not know the purpose and objective the Lawgiver has when He enjoins a thing or forbids it, or for someone who is unaware of the wisdom behind why a certain mode was prescribed for carrying out a certain injunction and how different features of that mode help to achieve the main objective. Without such knowledge, a person would know the Shariah in letter only and not in spirit; he would have access to the bone but not the marrow, and would apparently be generally following the injunctions of the Shariah but missing the very objectives behind them. His attention would be focused merely on form, but the intrinsic value and purpose of these injunctions would remain hidden from his eyes. Therefore, it would be impossible for such a person even to make any minor adjustments required in peripheral details of those injunctions and hence he would not get to the principal objectives of the Shariah.

It is an undeniable fact that the Lawgiver, in His Infinite wisdom and knowledge, has generally prescribed for His injunctions by those ways and means that fulfil His objectives at all times, places and circumstances. However, there may be a few minor details that do require adjustment because of changes in circumstance. The situation prevailing in and around Arabia during the days of the holy Prophet, may Allah bless him and give him peace, and His Companions cannot necessarily remain the same in every age and place. To exactly follow the same ways and means and avoid even the slightest adjustments or amendments under changed circumstances is, therefore, contrary to the spirit of the Shariah itself. For example, the holy Prophet, may Allah bless him and give him peace, determined the timings of regular prayers according to the solar position. This was not only the best schedule for Arabia but also the populated regions of the world in general. Yet if someone in the polar regions tries to apply the method of sunrise and sunset and the rise and fall of the shadow to determine prayer timings, he would actually be violating the very spirit and purpose of the Lawgiver's command, even while apparently trying to observe His injunctions. In fact, such an attempt would be taken as an abuse of the injunctions because that would naturally lead to a wilful abandonment of *ṣalāh*, which is an obligatory duty. Therefore, it is not correct to follow blindly, without proper insight into the legal system of Islam (*tafaqquh fī al-dīn*), even a clear statement of the Divine text, let alone its connotations and implications. Similarly, the spirit of *tafaqquh* demands that one should never lose sight of the Lawgiver's objectives and wisdom in each and every matter and one must not rush to make adjustments even in the minor details of the Divine injunctions due to any change in a situation. Such amendments and adjustments are to be based invariably on the Lawgiver's principles of legislation and must be set according to the precedents of the holy Prophet, may Allah bless and give him peace.

Furthermore, proper insight into the legal system of Islam (*tafaqquh fī al-dīn*), as with the scholarly reinterpretation of juridical issues (*ijtihād*) does not mean that the jurist (*faqīh*) or master scholar of juridical issues (*mujtahid*) should start wilfully following his own reason and judgment without minutely observing the limits set by the Shariah. This is in fact not *tafaqquh* or *ijtihād*, but the phenomenon which the holy Qur'an terms as the pursuit of personal whims and desires (*ittibāʿ al-hawā*). The essential feature of self-pursuit is a lack of balance, while the correct understanding of Islam's juridical system entails an approach of balance and moderation. A self-indulgent person is only concerned with that aspect of the matter that may interest him directly. He shuts his eyes to everything else that may not be personally beneficial to him. With such a lack of balance, he tries to assess the losses and gains in terms of his own standards.

On the contrary, *tafaqquh fi al-dīn* calls for a deeper understanding of the wisdom and rationale behind the 'dos' and 'don'ts' of Divine law. This naturally demands taking as beneficial that which Islam takes as beneficial and avoiding as injurious that which Islam takes as injurious. Therefore, it should not be mistaken that *tafaqquh* or even *ijtihād* stand for the unchecked supremacy of reason and that everyone has the right to interfere with the Shariah. The real spirit of *tafaqquh* demands that we should try to understand and give the same weight to good or bad as that given by the supreme Lawgiver. Amendments or adjustments in minor details must be made in such a way that the balance set by the Lawgiver is not disturbed.

The precedents set by the holy Prophet, may Allah bless him and give him peace, his illustrious Companions, as well as the leading lights of Islamic jurisprudence trained in the lofty Prophetic tradition, have once and for all determined some basic principles for us, which must be kept in mind while drawing conclusions and formulating decrees. One such principle is to differentiate between legal action (*ʿamal sharʿī*) and the normal or natural action (*ʿamal ʿādī* or *ṭabīʿī*). In terms of Islamic jurisprudence, legal action is the action necessitated in light of Shariah injunctions, while normal or natural action is that which the holy Prophet and his Companions took due to their natural inclinations or certain demands of time and circumstance. Legally, the former category of actions alone have juristic value, while the latter can be a source of guidance and inspiration, but because of their exclusive nature cannot become legal precedents. The difference between the two is quite distinct and can easily be noted even with a cursory glance. In certain cases, however, both these categories may be so intermixed as to make it difficult for jurists to differentiate between the two. It is here that mistakes have often been committed even by eminent law experts, who drew conclusions based on wrong deductions.

Our master the Messenger of Allah, may Allah bless him and give him peace, was His Messenger and at the same time was a human being, an Arab, and the resident of a certain place and social set-up. Whether it concerned the material or spiritual spheres of activity, whatever he did simultaneously reflected all the various facets of his extraordinary personality. Due to this happy blend of various factors, it is often quite hard to distinguish between that part of his action which was concerned exclusively with his status as Prophet and was thus a legal precedent, and the part that was more personal in nature. Similar or even more intermingled and various facets of life can be noticed in the lives of the Companions of the holy Prophet. They were the repositories of Islamic learning, direct beneficiaries of the training they received by the holy Prophet and the principal recipients of the Shariah injunctions. Therefore, they definitely stand out as role models and their actions provide us with legal guidance. Nonetheless, in more personal aspects of their lives, they cannot be considered the source of juridical guidance. The best criterion to distinguish between their various actions, especially those of religious significance, is to revert to the holy Qur'an and the Sunnah of the holy Prophet, may Allah bless him and give him peace. Only through a deeper and comprehensive study of the two can the required knowledge and insight be gained to discern the subtle difference between their legal and normal or natural actions. However, there remains the possibility of a difference of opinion in certain matters, but that does not entitle one to claim that one's deduction alone is correct according to the Shariah while that of others is incorrect.

With these preliminaries in mind, it may now be easier to look into the question of the language used in *ṣalāh* and the Friday sermon. Although they may appear the same, the two questions need to be addressed separately because they are essentially different.

10.2. The Language of Regular Prayer

Regarding the language of *ṣalāh*, the argument is generally based on this verse: *Believers! Do not draw near to the prayer while you are intoxicated until you know what you are saying.* (يَـٰٓأَيُّهَا ٱلَّذِينَ ءَامَنُوا۟ لَا تَقْرَبُوا۟ ٱلصَّلَوٰةَ وَأَنتُمْ سُكَـٰرَىٰ حَتَّىٰ تَعْلَمُوا۟ مَا تَقُولُونَ) (*al-Nisā'* 4: 43). However, this argument is actually incorrect due to a lack of proper understanding of the verse. Allah Most Glorified and Exalted has said *until you know* (حَتَّىٰ تَعْلَمُوا) and *not* 'until you understand or minutely comprehend' (حَتَّىٰ تَفْقَهُوا).

Confusion has arisen from ignoring the subtle difference between the Arabic words *'ilm* and *fiqh* or *fahm*. What is required of the one offering prayer (*muṣallī*) is that he should be in a position to know what is being recited by him or by his imam. It is obviously not possible for anyone, including those people who know Arabic, to grasp fully the meaning and significance of each and every word being recited in prayer. This is also contrary to the very spirit of the Shariah to have such a precondition for the *ṣalāh* to be correct. Is a person in prayer capable of remaining in a state of perfect presence of mind, attentive to each and every word, and fully understanding of everything being recited from beginning to end? That would perhaps be too difficult a precondition for anyone to offer his prayers correctly! A person goes through trials and tribulations of different sorts throughout his life. He is worried at times, pensive at others, emotionally disturbed, sometimes mentally preoccupied, and at some other time his brain might be wandering thoughtlessly without him actually realizing his lack of attention. It would have been almost impossible to offer prayer had the

Shariah imposed the condition that for *ṣalāh* to be correct that the *muṣallī* must be perfectly attentive and understand each and every word being recited.

The Lawgiver has imposed no such hardship on human beings, because He knows their natural handicaps. He has definitely declared that a state of understanding, complete harmony and devotion, and an overpowering sense of being in the presence of the Lord constitute the beauty and perfection of *ṣalāh* and that He would very much like each prayer to be as perfect and beautiful as possible. However, this have not been prescribed as a precondition for prayer to be legally correct.

Now, let us ponder over the wording of the verse. Had it been obligatory to fully understand the meanings of each and every word being recited for the *ṣalāh* to be correct, the injunction not to 'draw near to the prayer' would not have been exclusive to the state of intoxication and drunkenness (*sukr*). The Lord may as well have said: 'Do not draw near to prayer when you are worried, restless, emotionally disturbed or preoccupied.' Instead, He made it exclusive to the state of *sukr*, because this is a state of mind where one is oblivious to what one is saying or doing. This state of unawareness is different from the inability to understand and be attentive. A person who is drunk does not even know if he is standing in prayer or for something else. He does not know whether he is reciting the holy Qur'an or anything else or whether he is facing the *qiblah* or not. He is so dazed and out of himself that he may very likely start humming a tune while reciting the Qur'anic verses. While praising the Lord he may even begin mumbling nonsensical words, or whilst standing in front of the *qiblah* may stagger in a different direction, and even forget that he is in a state of prayer and then start talking to those next to him, or just walk away from the line. This is the state of mind Allah Most Exalted has alluded to when He said: *Believers! Do not draw near to the prayer while you are intoxicated until you know what you are saying.* In other words, we are being warned: *When out of your sheer stupidity you lapse into a state where you lose control of your senses, then don't take the liberty of approaching Our August Presence!*

It is evident from this explanation that 4: 43 has no relevance whatsoever to the language of *ṣalāh*. It would be absolutely absurd to draw from it the conclusion that the prayer should be offered in a language that the one praying must fully understand.

10.3. Arabic as the Language of *Ṣalāh*

As for the question of Arabic being the compulsory language of *ṣalāh* or not, Imam Abū Ḥanīfah was initially of the view that to offer *ṣalāh* in a language other than Arabic was not haram but undesirable (*makrūh*). However, he subsequently agreed with the views of his pupils and eminent jurists Imam Abū Yūsuf and Imam Muhammad that it is absolutely forbidden to offer prayer in any other language, because we have been enjoined to read from the holy Qur'an: *So now recite as much of the Qur'an as you can* (فَٱقْرَءُوا۟ مَا تَيَسَّرَ مِنَ ٱلْقُرْءَانِ) (*al-Muzzammil* 73: 20). As for those unable to read the Arabic text, Imam Abū Ḥanīfah and his pupils were of the view that only such people can offer prayers in any other language, in the way that a handicapped person is permitted to offer even through gesticulation.

Imam al-Shāfiʿī initially subscribed to the same view, but later on he held the position that those unable to read the Qur'an should offer prayer without recitation, because the Holy Book was the Word of God and no translation could be its substitute. He, therefore, opined that *ṣalāh* was incorrect where a translation replaced the sacred text.

Viewed in our present-day context, the question leads us to some even more crucial aspects of the matter: what is the position of *ṣalāh* in Islam? And what importance does the Shariah attach to it? Islam's real objective is not just the refinement and purification of the self. Instead, it seeks to forge individual Muslims into a righteous group or a nation of Islam capable of discharging its duties as the deputies of Allah Most Exalted on His earth. For this purpose, Allah has ordained all rituals of worship in such a way that through recourse to Him these should infuse the spirit of *taqwā* within every individual, while forging them into a group of righteous people at the same time. Among all acts of worship, *ṣalāh* occupies the most important position. It refines the self, preserves the Qur'an, propagates the Qur'anic message, and binds the Muslims together into a well-knit group. Therefore, it is obvious that prayer is not just an individual's act of communion with God but a means to infuse *taqwā* within him. It is rather the mainstay of Islam to which are attached much higher goals.

Individually, a person may rightly also be interested to understand what is being recited in the prayer, so that the very purpose of self-refinement and spiritual purification is achieved. Therefore, while this suggests that the prayer be offered in a language he understands that is bound however to damage the common interests of the community, which is much dearer to the Lawgiver. Let us look into this aspect in greater detail.

By allowing the use of any language other than Arabic in *ṣalāh* the very purpose of preserving and safeguarding the holy Qur'an would be lost. When people start taking a translation of the Qur'an as the Qur'an itself, and a general perception grows in favour of a translation as a substitute for the Divine text, this is bound to lead naturally to an eventual disregard for the Book itself. Furthermore, the taste for committing the Book of God to memory would also be lost. Secondly, disregard for the Arabic text itself and the mushrooming growth of translations and the popular preference for them would lead to an irreparable damage to Islam. History is a witness to the fact of how the emergence of heterogeneous and often contradictory translations, and their promotion and popularization by vested interests, had earlier caused havoc in the known world religions like Judaism and Christianity, etc. Thirdly, it would shatter the unity of the Muslim *ummah* and Islam would be divided and subdivided into thousands of linguistic factions. Each group speaking a particular language would have its own place of prayer and congregation. No Iranian would pray behind an Arab and no Turk would join Indians in congregation. Bengalis, Madrasis and Punjabis assembled at the same place would be tempted to offer their prayers separately according to their linguistic divisions. By shattering the very unifying force of *ṣalāh* into tiny splinters, the unity of the *ummah* is bound to fall apart.

To avoid such colossal damage, it is absolutely necessary to guard jealously the language of the holy Qur'an as the universal language of *ṣalāh* for Muslims all over the globe. As for the individual loss, this can be easily taken care of. The best part of *ṣalāh* consists of the same text. It is easy even for a man of common intelligence to remember, with very little effort, the meanings of *takbīr*, *tasbīḥ*, *tasmiyah*, *taʿawwuz*, *Sūrah al-Fātiḥah* and *tashahhud*. The surahs generally read and recited during prayer are also not more than ten to twelve in number, and these are very brief and can easily be committed to memory.[1] Their translation can also be remembered and that too without much effort. As for the longer surahs, even if some or many of those who offer prayer are unable to understand them, this would really make not much of a difference.

This is the juristic and legal standpoint. When the subject is viewed from the Shariah perspective we notice that the Qur'an itself explicitly tells us in so many

[1] One of the so many living miracles of the holy Qur'an is that true to its name it is the most well-read book in the world. It is easy to read, easy to remember, and easier to understand by Arabs and non-Arabs alike. Even a person of common intelligence can grasp its meaning, while a more serious reader, intellectually better qualified, can delve deeply to discover pearls of wisdom and so many shades of meaning that would leave him intellectually enriched and on a higher pedestal. Allah Most Glorified and Exalted says: *We have made this Qur'an easy as a reminder. Is there, then, any who will take heed?* (وَلَقَدْ يَسَّرْنَا ٱلْقُرْءَانَ لِلذِّكْرِ فَهَلْ مِن مُّدَّكِرٍ) (*al-Qamar* 54: 17). I have seen those who were illiterate, unable to read or write even a word of their own native language, but who could recite the Book of Allah with greater ease as though they understood each and every syllable of what they were reading. Therefore, there can be no excuse for a Muslim to avoid the Qur'an, because if he does so under one pretext or other, he is committing the greater blunder of avoiding Islam itself and weakening his ties with his Lord, with his own community and the *ummah* as a whole. — Editor.

verses that the Book of the Lord has been revealed in the Arabic language and that alone is the Word of God:

وَكَذَٰلِكَ أَنزَلْنَٰهُ قُرْءَانًا عَرَبِيًّا وَصَرَّفْنَا فِيهِ مِنَ ٱلْوَعِيدِ لَعَلَّهُمْ يَتَّقُونَ أَوْ يُحْدِثُ لَهُمْ ذِكْرًا ﴿١١٣﴾

(O Muhammad), thus have We revealed this as an Arabic Qur'an and have expounded in it warning in diverse ways so that they may avoid evil or become heedful.

(*Ṭā Hā* 20: 113)

إِنَّآ أَنزَلْنَٰهُ قُرْءَٰنًا عَرَبِيًّا لَّعَلَّكُمْ تَعْقِلُونَ ﴿٢﴾

We have revealed it as a recitation in Arabic that you may fully understand.

(*Yūsuf* 12: 2)

تَنزِيلٌ مِّنَ ٱلرَّحْمَٰنِ ٱلرَّحِيمِ ﴿٢﴾ كِتَٰبٌ فُصِّلَتْ ءَايَٰتُهُۥ قُرْءَانًا عَرَبِيًّا لِّقَوْمٍ يَعْلَمُونَ ﴿٣﴾

This is a revelation from the Most Merciful, the Most Compassionate, a Book whose verses have been well-expounded; an Arabic Qur'an for those who have knowledge.

(*Ḥā Mīm al-Sajdah* 41: 2–3)

فَإِنَّمَا يَسَّرْنَٰهُ بِلِسَانِكَ... ﴿٩٧﴾

Therefore, We have revealed the Qur'an in your tongue and made it easy to understand.

(*Maryam* 19: 97)

قُل لَّئِنِ ٱجْتَمَعَتِ ٱلْإِنسُ وَٱلْجِنُّ عَلَىٰٓ أَن يَأْتُوا۟ بِمِثْلِ هَٰذَا ٱلْقُرْءَانِ لَا يَأْتُونَ بِمِثْلِهِۦ وَلَوْ كَانَ بَعْضُهُمْ
لِبَعْضٍ ظَهِيرًا ﴿٨٨﴾

Say: 'Surely, if mankind and jinn were to get together to produce the like of this Qur'an, they will never be able to produce the like of it, howsoever they might help one another.'

(*al-Isrā'* 17: 88)

It has been declared further in the Book of God that the Lord has guaranteed the authenticity of no other book but the glorious Qur'an. His solemn pledge to safeguard and preserve it does not include the translations attempted by human beings. Translations can never take the place of the original. These are prone also to distortions either due to the inherent limitations of a translator, his lack of proper understanding and knowledge, or these could even be intentional and by design. Therefore, the Lord emphatically proclaims:

...وَإِنَّهُۥ لَكِتَـٰبٌ عَزِيزٌ ۝٤١ لَّا يَأْتِيهِ ٱلْبَـٰطِلُ مِنۢ بَيْنِ يَدَيْهِ وَلَا مِنْ خَلْفِهِۦ ۖ تَنزِيلٌ مِّنْ حَكِيمٍ حَمِيدٍ ۝٤٢

It is certainly a mighty Book. Falsehood may not enter it from the front or from the rear. It is a revelation that has been sent down from the Most Wise, the Immensely Praiseworthy.

(*Ḥā Mīm al-Sajdah* 41: 41–42)

In view of such solid reasons, the prayer must be offered in Arabic. Recitations must be made from the sacrosanct text of the holy Qur'an and not from its translation, as the latter can hardly be worthy of the Lord's acceptance.

10.4. The Language of the Friday Sermon

As for the next part of the question, concerning the language of the Friday sermon (*khuṭbah*, plural *khuṭab*) and those of the two Eids, this must not be mixed up with the question of the language to be used for *ṣalāh*. Therefore, it is essential to understand first of all the difference between the two.

The two Friday sermons (*khuṭbatayn al-Jumuʿah*), are not part of the Friday prayer itself. Some *ulema* have interpreted the tradition narrated by Ḥaḍrat ʿUmar and Sayyidah ʿĀ'ishah that 'The Friday prayer has been shortened because of the sermon' as meaning that the sermon is a substitute for the two prayer-cycles (*rakʿatayn*)[2] and therefore must be regarded as part of the Friday prayer. Based on that premise, they think that as the prayer cannot be offered in any language other than Arabic, the Friday sermon too must only be delivered in Arabic.

However, this is a very superficial interpretation. When you look at the injunctions concerning *ṣalāh* as well as the *khuṭbah*, you come to know that the preconditions laid down for prayer are not the same as those prescribed for the sermon. Let us note the points of difference: (1) The prescribed mode of cleanliness (*ṭahārah*) is a precondition for *ṣalāh* but not for the Friday sermon. (2) It is an obligation to face the *qiblah* in prayer, but not so during the

[2] Namely, that the two Friday sermons replace two of the four prayer-cycles (*rakʿāt*) normally observed in the Ẓuhr prayer on the other days of the week. — Editor.

sermon. In fact, the injunction for the imam delivering the Friday sermon is to face the congregation with his back towards the *qiblah.* (3) Any conversation or extraneous act of longer duration (*ʿamal kathīr*) renders the prayer null and void. However, in the Friday sermon, this is permissible as confirmed by the precedents of the holy Prophet and his Companions. (4) An essential precondition for *ṣalāh* is that it is time-bound, however, there is no restriction for the sermon to start before time. (5) According to the Ḥanafī school, it is a requirement for the Friday prayer to have a minimum of three people to form a legally-valid congregation. However, in addition to the imam, the sermon can be delivered with only one person in attendance. (6) The Friday Prayer has to be repeated if it is nullified because of something wrong; this is not so with the sermon.

As can be seen from the above, the sermon is not part of the Friday prayer. The eminent Ḥanafī theologian ʿAllāmah Sarakhsī wrote that 'Some of our scholars are of the view that the *khuṭbah* is a substitute for the two prayer-cycles and hence cannot be delivered until the prescribed time for *ṣalāh* has come, but the more correct position is that it does not form part of the *ṣalāh*.' (*al-Mabsūṭ, Kitāb al-Jumuʿah,* vol. 8)

10.4.1. *A Difference of Objectives*

There is no doubt that the Friday *khuṭbah* is also an act of worship like *ṣalāh*, but each has different and definite objectives, as explained in the paragraphs that follow.

What is intended to be gained from *ṣalāh* can be had even if it is offered without knowing the meaning of the text being read. This is because when one rises to pray, he is mindful of its prescribed time, takes care to fulfil all its prerequisites, regards the text prescribed for *ṣalāh* as sacrosanct, and performs his prayer with the utmost devotion and awareness that he is before his Lord and Master Who knows everything that he does. Thus, the person performing *ṣalāh* reaffirms that whatever he is doing by way of standing, bending, prostrating or sitting on his knees, indeed every part of his act of worship is for none but Allah Most Glorified and Exalted. All this is enough to achieve the objective for which *ṣalāh* has been made mandatory.

However, the Friday sermon has been prescribed for a different purpose, which cannot be achieved unless the congregation understands its contents. Its purpose is not just a remembrance of Allah and an invocation of His love and fear, but also for the propagation of the teachings of the Qur'an and the Sunnah, the preaching of Islam's moral values, and taking the audience into confidence on current issues and machinations of anti-Islamic forces and the ways and means necessary to counter them. This objective can only be achieved when the people understand each and every word being addressed to them.

Some religious scholars and commentators of the holy Qur'an are of the view that the purpose of the Friday *khuṭbah* is remembrance of Allah. Regarding the verse, *Believers, when the call for prayer is made on Friday, hasten to the remembrance of Allah* (*Sūrah al-Jumuʿah* 62: 9), they interpret the phrase *remembrance of Allah* as meaning the Friday *khuṭbah* and that the sermon is therefore similar to *ṣalāh*. However, the phrase can mean the Friday prayer as well and there is no reason to restrict it to the sermon. In fact, when we read the verse in its proper context, it definitely appears to mean the prayer, because the concluding part of the expression *remembrance of Allah* obviously refers to the prayer mentioned in the first part of the verse. Had it meant the sermon, the verse would have been phrased in the following manner: 'When the call is made for prayer on Friday, hasten earnestly to the remembrance of Allah (sermon) and the prayer'.

Furthermore, if *remembrance of Allah* is taken exclusively to mean the Friday sermon, it would then naturally follow that remembrance of Allah is only possible in the Arabic language. However, we know that neither the holy Qur'an nor the Sunnah of the holy Prophet, may Allah bless him and give him peace, have restricted the act of remembering Allah to the Arabic language alone. Imam Muhammad al-Shaybānī said: 'God can be remembered in any language.'

It may also be pertinent to note here that if the Lawgiver had only desired remembrance of God from the Friday sermon, then why was a more perfect and comprehensive form of remembrance – the Friday prayer – shortened to accommodate the *khuṭbah* and why was the sermon made a precondition for it?

Finally, as was established by the practice of the holy Prophet, may Allah bless him and give him peace, and his Companions, the *khuṭbah* was an essential part of the Friday prayer. As transmitted to us through the authentically recorded and well-preserved texts of some historic sermons, in addition to praise of the Lord, their contents included exhortations towards *taqwā*, sage counsels on righteous conduct, teaching relevant injunctions of the Shariah, and important community and individual matters as well. The Friday sermons were also used to reform personal mistakes, draw the congregation's attention towards a fellow Muslim in need of help, redress grievances and provide succour. To illustrate this, it may be appropriate to quote from some of the holy Prophet's famous Friday sermons.

As narrated by Imam Mālik in the *Muwaṭṭa'* and Ibn Mājah in his *Sunan*, the holy Prophet, may Allah bless him and give him peace, in a Friday *khuṭbah* counselled the congregation as follows: 'O People of Islam, Friday is the day that God has made an Eid for us. So [to observe it], take a bath today. If you have perfume, do not hesitate not to apply it. And you must use the tooth-stick (*miswāk*) to clean and polish your teeth.' According to another hadith narrated by Abū Sa'īd Khudrī, the holy Prophet, may Allah bless him and give him peace, once said in a Friday sermon:

> 'What I fear most in respect of you are earthly blessings.' When asked what he meant by 'earthly blessings', the holy Prophet replied: 'Worldly pomp and show.' At this, someone from the audience enquired: 'O Prophet of Allah, can something good bring evil?' The holy Prophet paused a while and then replied: 'Good comes only from good. The riches of this world are very sweet and attractive. When in spring everything is in bloom, an animal that grazes to its stomach's fill either dies or comes near to death due to indigestion. The animal that knows that it has eaten enough to satisfy its need and restrains itself from taking more is saved. Thereafter it wanders around in the sun, chews the cud, releases some of it through defecation and urination and, when its stomach becomes empty, forages again for food. Whoever gains worldly riches through fair means and dispenses with it fairly will find in it excellent sustenance, but he who takes it in a foul manner is like the person who carries on devouring food without feeling satiated.' (Bukhārī)

'Amr ibn Taghlib narrates that once an amount of money came to the holy Prophet, may Allah bless him and give him peace. He distributed it to some people but left out others. Later on, he came to know that those who were left out felt sad. In his next *khuṭbah*, he gave this clarification:

> I give to some of you and leave out others. He whom I do not give to is dearer to me than the one whom I gave to. I give to a group in whom I notice restlessness and anxiety in their hearts, but leave others with their qualities of goodness and self-contentment that Allah Most Glorified and Exalted has created within them.
>
> (Bukhārī)

According to a famous hadith, a person came and joined the congregation while the holy Prophet, may Allah bless him and give him peace, was delivering the *khuṭbah*. The Prophet asked him whether he had performed his supererogatory prayer. He replied in the negative. The Prophet, may Allah bless him and give him peace, asked him to rise and first offer the prayer. The man was in tatters and the holy Prophet really desired that the congregation should take note of his plight and help him after the prayer. When he finished the prayer, the Prophet formally exhorted those present to provide the man with relief. This hadith has been narrated by Bukhārī, Muslim, Aḥmad and others.

Abū Dāwūd and Nasā'ī relate that once when the holy Prophet was in midst of his Friday sermon, he noticed a person trying to move forward by clambering over the shoulders of other members of the congregation. He admonished him not to cause discomfort to others.

The eminent Companion Anas narrated that the holy Prophet was once delivering the *khuṭbah* during a time of drought and famine when a person beseeched him: 'O Prophet of Allah, the cattle herds have perished and the children are without food. Please pray to the Lord for rain!' The Prophet prayed during the sermon itself. By the grace of Allah, it started raining immediately, and continued for a whole week. On the following Friday, the same person rose from amongst the congregation as the Prophet was about to deliver the *khuṭbah* and said: 'O Prophet of Allah, the houses are crumbling and belongings are going to waste. Please pray to Allah.' In response, the holy Prophet's brief but comprehensive and most poignant words of supplication resounded from the pulpit: 'O our Lord, let it be around us but not over us!' At this, the people saw the clouds moving from overhead to adjoining areas.

Once when the second caliph Ḥaḍrat 'Umar was delivering the *khuṭbah*, he saw Ḥaḍrat 'Uthmān entering the mosque. He objected: 'Why is it that people take their time to come to the mosque after the *adhān*?' Then he moved towards 'Uthmān and asked him: 'Why so late?' He replied that he had been busy in some engagements and the moment he heard the *adhān*, instead of going home he performed ablution and rushed to the mosque. About this the second caliph observed: 'Well, you are not only late but you say that you were content to perform *wuḍū'* only. Don't you know that the holy Prophet, may Allah bless him and give him peace, instructed us to have a *ghusl* on Friday?' (Bukhārī, Muslim and Mālik)

These are just few examples that reaffirm how the Friday sermons were used by the holy Prophet and his illustrious Companions not only for Allah's remembrance, but also for some sublime objectives such as promoting the individual and collective well-being, instruction in Islamic values, social awareness and matters of national importance. The Friday *khuṭbah* was never intended to be part of a formal practice that people listened to ritualistically once a week, as is the case with Christian Sunday sermons. On the contrary, it was made an effective and dynamic tool in Muslim community life. The believers who come together once a week in a larger assembly are able to know the Divine injunctions, refresh their memories of Islamic teachings, redress the wrongs that may have cropped up within individuals or groups, invite the people's attention to the work of national reconstruction and public welfare, and to let the imam (either as a political leader or a prayer-leader) apprise the people of the Islamic state's policies and plans and thus make himself accessible to them for cross-questioning.

There is yet another basic difference between the Friday sermon and the Jumu'ah prayer. Everything recited in *ṣalāh* is literally predetermined. A person not knowing Arabic can easily learn its meaning and commit it to memory with little effort. Thus, those not conversant with the Arabic language are in no way deprived of its benefit. Conversely, there is no prescribed text for the *khuṭbah.* A fresh *khuṭbah* is needed every Friday and, hence, it is impossible to learn its meaning or commit it to memory beforehand. To make the Arabic language compulsory for the Friday sermon would render it incomprehensible to a non-Arab and it would thus be reduced to a lifeless ritual, thereby losing the very purpose for which the Lawgiver ordained it as an essential part of Friday's grand assembly. Anyone, even of low intelligence, would understand that to address the Turks in Sanskrit and the Persians in German would be a meaningless exercise. So how can we think that the All-Wise Lawgiver would expect that the elucidation of religious injunctions and instructions in noble conduct and deeds be done in a language unintelligible to the audience?

To sum up, let us keep in view the following three points that emerge from this discussion: (1) The Friday *khuṭbah* is not part of *ṣalāh* and, therefore, it does not follow that as Arabic is compulsory for *ṣalāh,* it must also be mandatory for the *khuṭbah.* (2) The objectives intended to be achieved through the *khuṭbah* would be lost entirely if the sermon is delivered in a language unintelligible to the congregation. However, this is not the case with *ṣalāh,* because the objectives for which it has been made obligatory are largely achieved even without a perfect understanding of the text prescribed for it. In other words, inability to understand the words recited in *ṣalāh* causes only a partial loss, but the loss is total insofar as *khuṭbah* is concerned. (3) The partial loss of understanding caused in *ṣalāh* can be redressed by subsequently consulting and if possible memorizing the text's translation. However, there is no way to repair the loss caused by the inability of the audience to understand the contents of the *khuṭbah.*

10.4.2. *Reservations Against the Non-Arabic* Khuṭbah

There were many reasons why eminent jurists and religious scholars of the past expressed strong resentment and dislike for using any language other than

Arabic in Friday sermons. During the early days of the Islamic movement, it was only natural for the torchbearers of the new civilization to jealously guard the integrity and pristine beauty of the language that was the repository of Islamic knowledge and wisdom. They saw it as among their tasks to save Arabic and Islam from the adverse impact of foreign languages, which were then obviously the vehicles of alien cultures and civilizations. Furthermore, in the early days of Islam, the Muslims were mainly Arabs and the non-Arabs (*ʿajam*) were synonymous with non-Islam. Therefore, it was logical to restrict the delivery of Friday sermons to the language that was the *lingua franca* of the Muslim community. The ever-increasing number of those embracing Islam was yet another factor and wisdom demanded that those entering the grand portals of the religion of truth should learn the official language of their new religion and state.

However, with the passage of time, the situation changed drastically. While Arabic remained the main source that sustained and symbolized the Muslim *ummah*'s solidarity as a global community, simultaneously the different native languages spoken in the Muslim world became enriched with Islamic thought, values and traditions because of their close interaction with Arabic. These languages are no longer representatives of paganism and un-Islamic culture: the language of the Qur'an runs through their veins like lifeblood. One of the countless living miracles of the holy Qur'an is that it not only saved one of the oldest human languages from dying out and becoming defunct, but that it has also turned Arabic into the most dynamic and vibrant of all modern languages. The 'Bangla' that a Muslim Bengali speaks is very different from the same language spoken by his Hindu counterpart. The Sikh or Hindu from the East Punjab often finds himself at a loss to read or understand a Muslim Punjabi's language. Urdu, Persian and Turkish are no longer the non-Islamic languages of the past. Thanks to the language of the holy Qur'an, today they are almost as rich in Islamic learning, values and culture as Arabic itself. Hence, Arabism today is no more synonymous with Islam. Even the dress worn by a non-Arab Muslim from east to west is as much Islamic as the traditional Arab robe, provided that it does not violate the Islamic dress-code. Therefore, it would be wrong to put too much stress on Arabism today, which was once so essential in the early days of Islam.

According to yet another argument, it is often contended that the Book of God and all Islamic injunctions are in Arabic and, therefore, the Friday sermon must also be delivered in that language. We agree that it is essential for a Muslim to know the Arabic language because he cannot have a better understanding of his religion without it. We also acknowledge that the major cause of the Muslims' going astray is their lack of direct access to the fountainhead of their guidance – the Qur'an and the Sunnah. Therefore, we have stressed time and again this need and so, according to our considered opinion, the Arabic language ought to be included in our curricula as a compulsory subject for Muslim students. However, in the given situation, one must not shut his eyes to realities on the ground. Our predicament today is that not even the basic religious education is compulsory for Muslims, let alone Arabic. Under such circumstances, an insistence that the *khuṭbah* must be 'recited' in Arabic is like putting the cart before the horse. Therefore, efforts should be directed towards assisting people to first know and understand the language of the Qur'an, before taking such a big leap.

There is yet another and perhaps more weighty argument in favour of the *khuṭbah* being delivered in Arabic. It is feared that if the Friday sermon were allowed in local languages other than Arabic, then this will open the floodgates of linguistic division. Irrespective of their ethnic, linguistic, social or national differences, the Friday congregation is the platform for all Muslims to assemble. However, the non-Arabic *khuṭbah* would thwart this goal of Islamic unity and pull people apart on the basis of the languages they speak.

Although this argument carries some weight, the problem is not insurmountable. The best course to take in this respect is to retain the second part of *khuṭbah* in Arabic, consisting exclusively of praise of the Lord (*ḥamd wa thanā'*), prayers and salutations (*ṣalawāt wa salām*) for our master the Messenger of Allah, may Allah bless him and give him peace, his illustrious family and Companions, may Allah be pleased with all of them, and the relevant verses from the holy Qur'an. However, the first part ought to be delivered in a language commonly understood by the people of that country or region. This part should also contain religious instruction, guidance, and Islamic teachings relevant to a particular situation facing the Muslim community. The language used for the first part of *khuṭbah* must essentially be that which is not restricted to a particular ethnic or linguistic group, but should be the *lingua franca* for the Muslims of an entire region or country. For example, Urdu is one such language that transcends ethnic and linguistic barriers and is spoken and easily understood from Bengal in the east to the North-West Frontier in the west. However, on the occasion of an international gathering, it would be advisable to only use Arabic for the Friday sermon.

10.4.3. *Some practical problems*

As discussed so far, there is no restriction from the Shariah standpoint on a non-Arabic *khuṭbah*. However, there is yet another part of the issue, which does not so much concern its juridical aspect but is nonetheless significant because of some practical problems and handicaps involved.

The delivery of the *khuṭbah* in a commonly intelligible language is desirable because the congregation benefits from that. This further means that its real objective is not just to be intelligible but also to be beneficial. Unfortunately, however, the prevailing situation in our mosques and the academic and professional level of those imams leading the prayer and the *khuṭabā'* giving the *khuṭbah* is quite dismal. We find that the responsibility of leading prayers has sadly fallen on the shoulders of those who, to say the least, are hardly qualified for this onerous task. Our mosques are generally being managed by a class of semi-literate people who are inadequately qualified even in their own vocation. The great Islamic institution of the mosque, which had once been a vibrant symbol of Muslim unity and faith and which helped to build the lofty citadel of the *ummah*, is now unfortunately at the mercy of those who are short-sighted, ill-qualified, lacking in knowledge and Islamic character. Can one expect such imams and *khuṭabā'* to deliver a sermon in Urdu that is a source of inspiration and guidance in both our spiritual and material worlds?

With the exception of a very small minority, even the mainstream of our *ulema* comprises of those whom, if they were allowed to use Urdu for Friday sermons, would soon turn their respective mosques into an arena of sectarian infighting, because each one of them belongs to a certain school of thought and considers it a sin to show large-heartedness and tolerance towards those of another school. They have been trained and live in an environment where petty issues of a controversial nature take precedence over everything else: momentous issues of religious significance and those of greater national interest matter little to them. To facilitate such 'religious scholars' to speak to a congregation in its own language would mean dividing it along sectarian lines. The impact that this eventuality might have on the younger generation of Muslims and those with a modern education would simply be disastrous. Whatever interest they might have retained in religion and an important religious institution like the mosque is likely to suffer irreparable damage.

Apart from sectarianism, the Muslim community of the subcontinent is also facing today the growing trend of political factionalism. Wherever a group of semi-literate and ill-trained political leaders have found the opportunity to address people, they have caused more schisms and factional trouble instead of helping to resolve issues of collective importance, or unifying the people as a whole. If this phenomenon is allowed to persist, its adverse fallout is even bound to affect the mosques so much so that each political faction may one day feel the need to have its own mosques.

Before allowing the use of non-Arabic sermons, we would first of all have to take some remedial measures for the ills facing the Muslim community. In my opinion, a group of well-qualified, well-balanced and moderate scholars of the Islamic sciences should take it into their hands to prepare a series of Friday sermons in Urdu. They should pen sermons that are free from controversial issues and capable of infusing the correct religious spirit within the congregation. Those managing the affairs of the mosques should then try to allow only such properly written sermons to be delivered on Fridays. If this is not possible, then it is better to continue with the old practice of reading out the Arabic *khuṭbah* instead of inviting unnecessary sectarian and political troubles through Urdu sermons by the ill-qualified imams. Should the community happily find preachers (*khuṭubā'*), who can effectively perform the job, then there is no harm in taking advantage of their scholarship for the community's collective good. (*Tarjumān al-Qur'ān*, March–April 1937)

10.5. Two More Queries Regarding the Language of Friday Sermons

[Abridged versions of two lengthy letters addressed to Sayyid Mawdūdī on the subject and his detailed response are given in the paragraphs below. — Editor.]

10.5.1. *Is It Obligatory for the* Khuṭbah *to be in Arabic?*

A reader of *Tarjumān al-Qur'ān* from Nizamabad in the state of Hyderabad wrote:

> On the question of the language of the Friday *khuṭbah*, you have very convincingly advanced your arguments, both from the juristic as well as rational standpoints. Under the prevailing circumstances, the plight of Muslims is such that to place such stress on Arabic as the language of these sermons is really very difficult to justify. Yet in terms of principles, I would venture to differ from you. The sole objective of the revelation of the holy Qur'an is to establish a Divine government. The state language of that government is to be Arabic and the language of its subjects too would have to be naturally the same. There are a number of verses in the holy Qur'an in favour of the Arabic language, which explain why the Book of God was revealed in it. If its revelation in Arabic was only because the holy Prophet was an Arab and its first audience were the people of Arabia, this was something so obvious that did not need to be described as an act of wisdom from the All-Wise Lord. However, the Qur'an

> is also universal guidance for mankind and the Prophet of Islam is a *mercy for the Worlds*, both known and unknown. Therefore, the Arabic language spread rapidly throughout the length and breadth of the Islamic world beyond Arabia as long as the Muslims were in the ascendant. With their decline and the rise of British colonial rule, however, English has now taken its place. Is it unsurprising that a nation that has the same code of conduct, the same instructions for this life and the Hereafter, and the same values, traditions, and objectives should have the same language to further cement the bonds of brotherhood and strengthen the cause of its uniformity and unity? Before the advent of Islam, Arabic was the language of the Arabs alone. After Islam, however, it no longer remained exclusive to a particular geographic or ethnic group, but became the international language of the Muslims from east to west.

It appears that the learned writer did not look into the case dispassionately enough and so different issues have become mixed up in his letter. There is a juristic aspect to this issue, according to which the main question is whether it is obligatory or not to deliver the *khuṭbah* in Arabic. To arrive at a definite conclusion in this regard, the following questions need to be looked into: Do we have a source-text indicating that the Arabic *khuṭbah* was obligatory for Fridays? Can the holy Prophet's practice of delivering the Friday sermon in Arabic be taken as part of his Sunnah, i.e. is there a binding Shariah precedent in this respect? Can the term Sunnah be applied to each and every act of the holy Prophet, may Allah bless him and give him peace? If not, then what is the difference between the customary act of practice and the Shariah precedent of the Sunnah of the holy Prophet? In the case of a difference, should the *khuṭbah* in Arabic be taken as either a customary or a binding precedent?

Another part of the issue is its social aspect, for which the following questions merit consideration. What is the purpose of the Friday *khuṭbah*? Can this purpose be achieved by following the method adopted by the holy Prophet and his Companions? In the Shariah, are the objectives more important than the means? If objectives are more important, can we follow a different method to avoid their loss in continuing to follow traditional means? How far is it permissible to make readjustments and changes in order to meet the demands of a certain situation?

The answers to these questions may resolve the *khuṭbah* issue. The line of argument followed by the writer regarding the Arabic language is nearly the same as that previously advanced by those who opposed the translation of the holy Qur'an into other languages. To accept his viewpoint would naturally lead to the conclusion that the holy text can neither be translated nor can its meanings be explained in any other language. According to a section of people, the position of Arabic as the 'official language' of the world of Islam is sacrosanct and it is binding on Muslims to learn it and failing to do so would be a sinful act. This simply means that the holy Qur'an cannot be translated into any foreign language; that all the injunctions and teachings of Islam should similarly remain intact in the 'official language' of Islam; and that it is incumbent on all non-Arab Muslims to become well-versed in Arabic so that they can read and understand everything that their religion expects them to know.

Yet don't we all know that such a standpoint is Islamically incorrect? Obviously, the reason is that to restrict legitimate access to the sacrosanct texts of the Qur'an and the Prophetic Tradition to the medium of Arabic alone while declaring the use of translations to be illegitimate would be tantamount to excluding nearly eighty per cent of the followers of a global religion from its universal message and mission. This is the reason why every seeker of truth considers the translation of and commentaries upon the holy Qur'an to be necessary and not just permissible, and it is due to this that he not only tolerates but very much endorses the propagation of the Islamic tenets, teachings and writings in non-Arabic languages as well. If this is the case, then why is there this fuss about the Friday sermon being delivered in a different language? Nobody has ever objected to someone addressing the mosque's congregation or delivering a sermon before the prayer in a language other than Arabic. So why should we object to a significant act of explaining important religious issues in a major language of the world of Islam such as Urdu?

It often happens that people fall in love with their customary habits and raise objections even to a sincere effort at reinterpretation or readjustment that a legist or expert in juridical issues may venture to make as needed by the dictates of changing times. However, such an initially adverse reaction by a section of people gradually gives way to a better understanding of Islamic teachings and once those previously unused to any change become accustomed to it, they not only approve of it but start to like it. Shāh Waliyyullāh was vehemently opposed by a group of religious scholars of his time for that very reason when he did his Persian translation of the holy Qur'an. The people even objected once to the delivery of lectures and the preaching of Islamic teachings in a language other than Arabic. During Ottoman rule, when the Ottomans tried to introduce new weapons and techniques, a group of people tried to oppose these on the grounds that they were a blameworthy innovation (*bidʿah*) or even a heresy. But can anybody take such an obscurantist stand today? If one tries to examine the reason behind such a mind-set, one would come to the conclusion that the real factors are not juristic (*fiqhī*), but psychological and based on the fascination of a person or group for customary habits and practices.

As for the pre-eminence of the Arabic language in Islam, no one can deny that it has always had a dominant position in our religion. The holy Qur'an is in Arabic. The most reliable material regarding the Sīrah of the holy Prophet, may Allah bless him and give him peace, his Tradition, and biographies of the four caliphs and the eminent Companions is well-preserved in this language. To know Arabic is essential for a correct understanding of Islam and, therefore, the *ulema* have always stressed the need to learn this language. Even today, every right-thinking Muslim believes that it must be included in the curricula of Muslim students and taught as a compulsory second language. All this is absolutely correct and there can be no room for contention in this. Yet, as explained earlier, there is a great difference between what actually is and what ought to be. While efforts must be made for something that is needed, it would be nothing but short-sightedness not to take measures to meet the demands of realities on the ground. Both reason and religion call for putting the objective before the means. If a certain means, although preferrable, is ineffective in a given situation, there is no harm in taking a different means to get better results. If insisting on certain conditions means that one loses the real objective, then that would neither be an act of wisdom nor of religiosity.

Now, let us take a look at the real objective of the religion. Is it to spread the Arabic language as the 'official' or 'national' language of Islam or is it to teach Muslims Islam's message and mission? Naturally, it is the latter. If that is so, and everyone can see with their own eyes that not even two per cent of non-Arab Muslims understand Arabic, and that Muslims today are not in the position to spread the Arabic language as was previously the case, then are we not duty-bound to think of appropriate measures to meet the challenge? It is now up to us to either achieve our objective through alternate means or to let it go by resisting the change.

As a universal religion, Islam has no exclusive kinship with any particular language. The real objective of Allah Most Glorified and Exalted is to convey His message to His servants and for this He chooses a language as a medium, just as he selects a person as His Messenger. Before the holy Prophet, He had chosen persons and languages from among other nations to transmit the same message. If, at the close of this hallowed mission, He selected the last of His Prophets from a noble family of Arabia and the language he spoke for spreading eternal guidance, it should not lead to the conclusion that Islam and Arabic are one and the same and that the use of any other language in service of the religion is taboo or tantamount to breaking the relationship that Arabic has with Islam. Had it been so, the holy Prophet would have been the first to give clear instructions in this respect and disallowed the preaching of religion in any other language. On the contrary, it is established on the authority of the Prophetic traditions that he advised some of his Companions to learn other languages. We know that Salmān Fārisī used to preach Islamic teachings to non-Arabs in their native languages.

As for the use of the Arabic language in correspondence, which the holy Prophet, may Allah bless him and give him peace, addressed to the Caesar of Rome and the Khosrau of Persia, the obvious reason for this is that it would have been contrary to the established norms of protocol and beneath the dignity of a head of state to use the language of his addressee and not his own official state language for such communication. Furthermore, it was not then practicable to train those from amongst the Companions who could at short notice acquire the necessary expertise in foreign languages for such an important task. The holy Prophet was also aware of the fact that the Arabic language was not alien to the Persian and Roman Empires, as they had under their control a number of neighbouring Arab chiefdoms and many Arab tribal elders had access to the imperial courts of Byzantium and Persia. There was also flourishing trade between the Quraysh of Makkah and the peoples of Egypt and Abyssinia across the Red Sea. Therefore, it was not difficult for the addressees to easily arrange the translation of the holy Prophet's letters, as they actually did.

Now that Islamic civilization has produced tremendous literature in languages like Urdu, Persian, Turkish, Indonesian, etc. there is no reason to insist upon excluding them from the common Islamic heritage to preach the Divine message. (*Tarjumān al-Qur'ān*, Aug-Sep. 1937)

10.5.2. *Is the Non-Arabic* Khuṭbah *also Obligatory?*

The following is the highlights of a query from a reader from Muradabad:

> It appears from your observations regarding the Friday *khuṭbah* that it can be delivered in any language other than Arabic. You have also referred to the practical problems involved in allowing the *khuṭbah* in the native language of the congregation and therefore would prefer the current practice of giving Arabic sermons to continue. From this discussion one can easily deduce that you regard the non-Arabic *khuṭbah* as permissible (*jā'iz*), but the Arabic one as essential (*wājib*). If the *khuṭbah* is *wājib* and the objectives for which it has been made essential cannot be achieved unless rendered in a

language commonly understood by the congregation, then would it not naturally be essential to deliver it in the local language?

The solution you propose to meet the practical problems involved in a non-Arabic *khuṭbah* is also apparently untenable. Even if you succeed in having a board of learned scholars to prepare sermons in Urdu on topics of religious and social significance, and even if these scholars are clearheaded and unbiased in terms of a particular school of thought, how can you guarantee a clearheaded and balanced approach from those using these prescribed sermons on the pulpit? Who can check the *khaṭīb* from delivering a sermon without any digression from the written text that would at best serve as a guideline? In any case he would be free to be as vitriolic as might please him against another sect or school of thought.

It is also difficult to understand why you would like these sermons to be absolutely free of any discussion of controversial issues. There is obviously no need to focus on such matters unnecessarily, but it is equally important to guide the congregation on things religious and irreligious, and what comes under the category of a religiously healthy practice and that which has to be avoided as blameworthy innovation (*bidʿah*), or something unsanctioned by the religion. Therefore, I am of the view that only that part of the *khuṭbah* which relates to preaching Islamic injunctions must essentially be in the local language, while the *khaṭīb* can be briefed verbally or in writing to avoid going into unnecessary details that might vitiate the atmosphere [of learning and concord]. It may also be impressed upon him to be selective in use of words and be as soft and appealing as desired by the religion itself. Special care also needs to be taken in selection of imams and *khuṭabā'* for the Grand Mosque, while the *ulema* may also consider publishing a tract based on rigorously-authentiated (*ṣaḥīḥ*) hadiths to guide them on historically correct and authentic material for use as a backgrounder for their sermons.

It is interesting to note arguments made both for and against the non-Arabic *khuṭbah.* To begin with, let it be clearly understood that the Lawgiver has neither declared that delivering the Friday sermon in a particular language is essential nor has He forbidden us from using a different language for this purpose. Whatever we find in books of jurisprudence (*fiqh*) in this context is based on the scholarly reinterpretation (*ijtihād*) of eminent jurists. We cannot pronounce one as correct and the other as wrong, just as we cannot give the findings of the jurists the same status as that of the Qur'an and the Sunnah. To differ from their views is not like differing from Shariah injunctions. Religiously the more learned among the Muslims are free to act upon the view that appears to them to be weightier and better suited to their given situation. This is the wisdom behind the Lawgiver leaving options open.

The position of a *khaṭīb* in the Islamic religious system is not merely that of a preacher but of a responsible guide, upon whose shoulders lie the burdens of guidance and leadership of the group of Muslims within his sphere of influence. Every *khaṭīb* is thus responsible for safeguarding his people's social life from the impact of various ills and helping them to discharge their duties and obligations towards individuals and society correctly. Such sustained guidance and leadership are obviously not possible from an imam or *khaṭīb* who acts in an individual capacity, who is neither under the discipline of a collective religious order nor is answerable to anyone, and who is inadequately qualified in his vocation to discharge the onerous responsibility of a well-qualified preacher.

Therefore, under the circumstances, I am firmly of the view that the Friday *khuṭbah* is too serious and important a duty to be left entirely to the whims of individuals underqualified for the job. The weekly sermons that are meant to be delivered in Urdu should be prepared by a group of well-qualified men of Islamic learning, with a special emphasis on the projection of the fundamental principles of Islam, stressing the need of the Muslim *ummah*'s unity, creating awareness about social ills and unethical practices, and forewarning the audience against all such activities which are contrary to the Shariah. Efforts must also be made to avoid controversial issues that give rise to sectarian differences, and to reunite once again the followers of different sects to help them perform the Jumuʿah prayer together in a single mosque. (*Tarjumān al-Qur'ān*, August–September 1937)

11 The Friday Congregation in a Village

A respected personality from the Punjab countryside has asked the following in his letter:

> The *ulema* of the Ḥanafī school still stress the condition of a township to hold a valid Friday prayer. In fact, the lifestyle in our towns and cities has changed so much that, if we could, it would be better to prevent our religiously-inclined simple village folks from visiting cities even to offer the Friday prayer. I own a whole village in which I have constructed a mosque and a library of religious books. People from adjoining hamlets arrive here every Friday to pray. They also get an opportunity to benefit from Qur'anic lessons and religious instruction, in addition to listening to the Friday sermon. We have a much bigger gathering and congregation during Ramadan. However, the *ulema* oppose the holding of Friday prayer here on the grounds of this being a small hamlet, yet if that is stopped now, the village folk would hardly go to the city just to offer Friday prayer. They would not agree if they were told to offer the regular Ẓuhr prayer here in lieu of the Friday prayer. They make special preparations for this weekly event and flock to this village with their children to offer the prayer. There is a town at a distance of a few miles from here, where Jumuʿah prayer is offered in a number of mosques, but none have a religious scholar of standing to conduct the prayer and, therefore, even if I somehow try to impress upon the village folk to go there they are likely to lose more than what they might actually gain. They are poor people of meagre resources and such a weekly journey to a town miles away would be tantamount to taxing them too much for nothing. I shall be grateful for your learned views in the matter.

The question of Jumuʿah prayer held in villages has remained in dispute for a long time. Therefore, it may not be possible to offer a solution acceptable to every school of thought and end the controversy once for all. However, I shall try to focus on the standpoint that appears to me to be correct in light of Shariah injunctions.

To begin with, what needs to be properly understood first of all is the status of Jumuʿah in the Islamic Shariah and the purpose behind the Lawgiver's command regarding the Friday congregation, and then to see what are the relevant instructions given in this respect, as also the objectives underlying these instructions. It should also be noted what the jurists of different schools of thought took into consideration when deciding in favour or against the holding of the Friday prayer in a village. This is how we can understand the issue in its correct perspective and decide on the lawfulness or otherwise of the Jumuʿah Prayer in a village.

11.1. The Social Side of Islam

When we look deeper into the philosophy of the commands and prohibitions of the Shariah, we realize at once that the ultimate goal of Islamic law is not just to reform and purify the individual, but to forge all reformed and upright persons together into a well-knit group of righteous people. Furthermore, this group should be equipped to perform their duties as the supreme Lord's deputies on earth and bring into existence a civilization and social order capable of nurturing and promoting the goodness of human nature and suppressing its evil side. This is among the basic goals of the Shariah and this is the reason why all its injunctions are socially-oriented and not merely individualistic in nature. Although the Shariah devotes all the power at its command to purify and reform the individual, its ultimate objective remains to prepare them to be useful members of a model Islamic society.

As explained previously, *ṣawm* is a means in itself for self-purification of the individual, but it is obligatory for every Muslim to observe thirty days of fasting during a particular month so that the community as a whole may benefit simultaneously from its blessings and emerge as a party of pure individuals. The same is true of *zakāh*. In its very essence, it is a collective act of worship and public welfare. It purifies the individual in such a way that he becomes instrumental in the relief and assistance of poorer sections of society. Similarly, the hajj assembly is a collective exercise and an important social event. Finally, *ṣalāh* or regular prayer stands out as the most effective act of collective worship. It does the same thing five times a day that *ṣawm* does for thirty days in a year, *zakāh* once a year and hajj once in a lifetime.

With the underlying objective of laying the foundation of a righteous social order, establishing a party of the pure and trained individuals as servants of God, the Lawgiver commands us to assemble five times a day at a proper place to discharge the mandatory duty of *ṣalāh*. Then once a week we are required to have a greater assembly of Muslims at a larger mosque for Divine remembrance and worship. Beyond this weekly Jumu'ah gathering, there are then the two events of grand public assembly, one marking the end of the month of fasting and the other in hallowed memory of the Prophet Abraham's great act of sacrifice in the way of God. The foundation of the great edifice laid by the daily prayers is thus expanded by the Friday Prayer and brought to its grand finale by the congregations of the two Eids.

11.2. The Real Significance of the Friday Assembly

As explained above, the prime objective of every act of obligatory worship made is to promote social living and a collectivist spirit among Muslims. In so doing, this also curbs individualistic and anarchic trends. The collective offering of the daily prayers calls for extra efforts by Muslims to assemble in a mosque five times a day at the appointed times. Therefore, it is under exceptional circumstances that an individual is allowed to offer his regular Prayer singly, but no such exception is permitted in case of the weekly Friday prayer. If one misses the congregation, he misses the Jumu'ah prayer and all its blessings.[1]

Thus, it is easier to understand why so much stress has been laid upon the observance of the Friday prayer in its true spirit as well as the significance of the *khuṭbah* delivered on the occasion. It is also easier to understand why the congregation has been enjoined to get to the mosque before the start of the *khuṭbah* that precedes the prayer and *not* before the prayer itself. Allah Most Glorified and Exalted says:

يَـٰٓأَيُّهَا ٱلَّذِينَ ءَامَنُوٓا۟ إِذَا نُودِىَ لِلصَّلَوٰةِ مِن يَوْمِ ٱلْجُمُعَةِ فَٱسْعَوْا۟ إِلَىٰ ذِكْرِ ٱللَّهِ وَذَرُوا۟ ٱلْبَيْعَ ۚ ذَٰلِكُمْ خَيْرٌ لَّكُمْ إِن كُنتُمْ تَعْلَمُونَ ۝

Believers, when the call for prayer is made on Friday, hasten to the remembrance of Allah and give up all trading.[2] *That is better for you, if you only knew.*

(*al-Jumu'ah* 62: 9)

---

[1] Lexically, Jumu'ah means 'coming together', the gathering or assembly. A central mosque is earmarked for public offering of this weekly prayer. The larger the congregation, the greater is the Lord's blessing. Every Muslim has therefore been enjoined to make special preparations to observe the event with religious fervor, as he does in respect of the two Eid prayers and with the same objective in view as elucidated by the author. — Editor.

[2] Explaining the significance of Friday prayer, Abdullah Yusuf Ali, says: 'The idea behind the Muslim weekly "Day of Assembly" is different from that behind the Jewish Sabbath (Saturday), or the Christian Sunday. The Jewish Sabbath is primarily a commemoration of God's

The importance of the Friday congregation can be better understood through the following Prophetic traditions:

> I feel like asking someone to stand in my place to lead the congregation and then go and set on fire the houses of those who sit back in their homes and do not come to the mosque for the Jumu'ah prayer.
>
> (Muslim and Aḥmad)

> He who believes in God and the Last Day, must observe [the sanctity of] the Jumu'ah prayer, but the person who is careless and remains involved in his pastime or business, God does not care for him too and God is above all need and is worthy of all praise.
>
> (Dāraquṭnī)

> People should refrain from missing their Jumu'ah Prayer, or else God will definitely set a seal upon their hearts. [Because of their deliberate sin, their senses will become impervious to good.] They would then turn neglectful.
>
> (Muslim)

Let us ponder for a moment! Why has it been said so emphatically that we must leave all business and hasten to Jumu'ah prayer? How is it that an all-loving and all-compassionate personality like the holy Prophet, may Allah bless him and give him peace, felt like setting the houses of Friday absentees on fire? What is there after all in the Jumu'ah prayer to declare its non-observance as being akin to hypocrisy? The reason is that the proper upkeep and religious and moral sustenance of the Muslim *ummah* depend on the proper observance of Friday prayer. The Friday assembly is one of the most important means for the attainment of Islam's ultimate objective: laying the foundations of a unique

---

ending His work and resting on the seventh day (Genesis II: 2; Exodus XX: 2). We are taught that the Almighty needs no rest nor does he feel fatigue (*al-Baqarah* 2: 255). The Jewish command forbids work on that day but says nothing about worship or prayer (Exodus. XX: 10). Our ordinance lays chief stress on the remembrance of God. Jewish formalism went so far as to kill the spirit of the Sabbath and called forth the protest of Jesus: "The Sabbath was made for man and not man for the Sabbath" (Mark II: 27). The Christian Church, although it has changed the day from Saturday to Sunday, has inherited the Jewish spirit. Our teaching says: "When the time for Jumu'ah Prayer comes, close your business and answer the summons loyally and earnestly, pray, consult and learn by social contact: when the meeting is over, scatter and go about your business".' (*The Holy Qur'ān: Translation and Commentary*, Abdullah Yusuf Ali, n. 5,462, p. 1,548). — Editor.

civilization and the establishment of a righteous social order. Its loss means the loss of that great goal and any wilful disruption in that respect is like jolting the very edifice of Islam.

This leads us to the following conclusions: (1) The first thing established from the discourse above is that the Shariah lays greater stress on the collective observance of the Friday prayer, because it is of vital importance for the fulfilment of Islam's grand objectives. Therefore, it is preferable to avoid unnecessary meddling with those aspects of a peripheral nature that may lead to the loss of Jumuʿah prayer and instead follow the course that may help establish this vital system. (2) The Shariah wants to forge unity among the believers and bring them together on one platform. Therefore, special care needs to be taken to keep the strength and unity of the congregation intact and not to weaken it.

11.3. Points of Consensus Regarding the Friday Congregation

As we proceed further in this respect, we notice that the Book of God forcefully enjoins Muslims to observe the day of the assembly and hasten to the call of the muezzin, leaving aside business and all other activities. From the precedents of the holy Prophet, may Allah bless him and give him peace, and his illustrious Companions, the following points of consensus emerge regarding the observance of Jumuʿah prayer, its timings, venue, etc.: (1) The time of the Jumuʿah prayer is the same as that of Ẓuhr prayer. (2) Neither the holy Prophet, may Allah bless him and give him peace, nor his Companions ever offered the Friday prayer without the *khuṭbah.* (3) The Friday Prayer is mandatory for every sane, adult, free male member of Muslim society who is physically fit to offer the prayer. Women, children and slaves are among those exempted from this obligation. (4) Jumuʿah prayer was never offered in the wilderness or the forest, in temporary accommodation or in camps, whether during the days of the holy Prophet, may Allah bless him and give him peace, or his Companions. This means that a permanent settlement is needed to establish the Friday prayer. (5) It was neither offered in a private place nor a house, but always at a venue that was freely accessible and available to every Muslim in the community. Therefore, public access is essential for the observance of Jumuʿah prayer.

11.4. Differences of Opinion

These are the points on which there is a universal consensus of the entire Muslim *ummah*, as these are firmly established by the Sunnah of the holy Prophet, may Allah bless him and give him peace, and the practice of his Companions, may Allah be pleased with them all. However, leading jurists and theologians have differed in their opinions about the following aspects of Jumuʿah prayer: (1)

the exact size of the congregation; (2) whether the Jumuʿah *khuṭbah* consists one or two parts; and (3) the observance of Jumuʿah prayer in a village.

According to Imam al-Shāfiʿī, the Jumuʿah congregation is permitted in every village with a population of at least forty sane male members of the Muslim community, but is unlawful in a village in which residents migrate to other places during summer or winter. In support of his position, he cites an eminent Companion of the holy Prophet, ʿAbdullāh ibn ʿAbbās, his cousin and a leading narrator of Prophetic traditions, that the first Friday Prayer held outside of Madinah was in a Bahraini village called Jawāthī. The second caliph ʿUmar is also reported to have told the people of Bahrain in response to their query that they should offer the Friday prayer wherever possible. However, the condition of a minimum number of forty men to hold the Jumuʿah prayer in a village is uncorroborated by either of these reports. In fact, the first report only mentions the word *qaryah* which means 'village' in Arabic. Imam Aḥmad follows Imam al-Shāfiʿī's line. For Imam Mālik, Jumuʿah prayer is permitted in a village that is neither a temporary nor a seasonal settlement, regardless of its male population being forty or less.

Imam Abū Ḥanīfah and his disciples do not approve of the Friday prayer being organized in a village. Their position is based on a saying of the fourth caliph ʿAlī: 'There is neither Jumuʿah nor Eid but in a *miṣr jāmiʿ*.' They also argue that the Companions of the holy Prophet raised no pulpits for the Friday sermon in the village mosques of the conquered territories, which means that no Jumuʿah was observed there. However, the Ḥanifīs themselves differ on the interpretation of the word *miṣr*. To some, the term *miṣr jāmiʿ* stands for a township run by a governor or administrator (*amīr*) and a judge (*qāḍī*). According to some followers of the Ḥanifī school, *miṣr* is a place with a population large enough for a grand mosque. It has also been defined as a town of ten thousand inhabitants. According to some others, it is a town of at least three thousand people. According to yet another interpretation, *miṣr* is the place that the Islamic government of the day may have notified with instructions to hold Friday prayer there. There are also scores of other definitions of the term *miṣr jāmiʿ*. Therefore, it must be kept in mind, therefore, that even the Ḥanifī jurists could neither agree on the precondition of *miṣr* for the Friday prayer nor on a definite interpretation of this term. The question then naturally arises: Would it be justified to exempt a large segment of the rural Muslim population from performing a very important and mandatory religious duty just because of an uncertain and vague precondition?

As stated above, the following two aspects are of primary importance regarding the observance of Jumuʿah prayer: (1) the obligatory nature of the

Jumuʿah prayer which means every sane, physically-fit Muslim male has to observe it; and (2) the social aspect of this important weekly assembly, which is intended to bring a larger number of people on one platform to create a feeling of togetherness and cohesion among them. Unless both these aspects are kept in view, we are likely to be unbalanced in our judgment. Therefore, senior jurists have tried to strike a balance between these two aspects.

Thus, Imam al-Shāfiʿī and Imam Aḥmad considered the minimum number of forty Muslim men as the desired requirement for organizing the Friday prayer in a village. They also viewed it as obligatory for the people in adjoining settlements to whom the sound of the Friday *adhān* reached to join the congregation at that particular village. According to Imam Mālik, the required number for the Friday assembly could be as few as twelve persons. A village with such a small number of Muslim men was declared eligible for the Friday prayer and the neighbouring hamlets within a radius of six miles were considered duty-bound to attend the prayer there.

On the other hand, Imam Abū Ḥanīfah was of the view that the permission to organize Jumuʿah prayer in every small village went against its very objective of encouraging a sense of collectivism and social harmony. He took it to be contrary also to the established practice of the Companions of the holy Prophet and the reported statement of Ḥaḍrat ʿAlī making the observance of the Jumuʿah prayer conditional to *miṣr jāmiʿ*. Therefore, Imam Abū Ḥanīfah held that the Jumuʿah prayer should be organized at a town's central mosque and those eligible should flock to that mosque from a distance of around three miles.

From an historical perspective, we know that during the days of Imam Abū Ḥanīfah Iraq, Persia and the Arabian Peninsula (al-Jazīrah) were well populated, with villages and rural areas overflowing with people. Due to the boom in commerce, trade and industry, smaller townships had grown within the large cities. The divide between the rural and the urban had become blurred. This is why we do not find a definite demographic description of the term *miṣr* and the number of adult males required to make the Jumuʿah prayer eligible varied from twelve to forty. Each jurist tried to give his own version of the features he considered necessary for a *miṣr* or a populated area fit for a Jumuʿah congregation. However, these definitions are neither binding nor final, but are essentially recommendations that may vary from time to time and place to place as it did during the days of the imams of the four schools of Islamic jurisprudence.

According to a leading jurist of the Ḥanafī school, ʿAllāmah Ibn Humām, the offering of Jumuʿah prayer in a town is obligatory for a person who lives in its suburbs and who can easily return to his village after the prayer well before the night sets in. This view is based on the authority of the Prophetic tradition related by Imam Tirmidhī from Abū Hurayrah: 'The holy Prophet, may Allah bless him and give him peace, said: "The Jumu'ah prayer is obligatory for the person [from the countryside], who can return and join his family by sunset."' With the advances in transportation and communication, it is now possible for those residing at a much longer distance from a township to visit its central mosque to offer the Friday prayer. Therefore, it is more appropriate not to fix the distance in terms of miles, but to observe the precondition prescribed by the holy Prophet, may Allah bless him and give him peace. A villager who can reach the town and after offering the Jumu'ah prayer can then return to his family before it gets dark must join the Friday congregation in his nearby town. According to the above tradition, for those who cannot do so are permitted to offer the Ẓuhr prayer instead in their village.

Some prominent jurists have tried to lay down certain special features for a *miṣr jāmiʿ* to facilitate the identification of a suburb fit to organize a Jumu'ah congregation there. These may be summed up as follows: (1) The place should have a large Muslim population; (2) it should have a mosque big enough for a larger congregation; (3) it should have a religious scholar capable and duly qualified to deliver the *khuṭbah*; (4) the place should have government functionaries for law enforcement; and (5) it may also have a market place providing the essential commodities required by adjoining villages. In sum, there are no preconditions to establish the Friday prayer, but rather there are the most appropriate features to help the local people and their religious and administrative functionaries to arrive at a consensus. (*Tarjumān al-Qur'ān*, March 1937)

11.5. In Response to a Rejoinder

In a rejoinder to my interpretation of the Ḥanafī viewpoint on Friday congregation in village, two senior members of the *ulema* wrote to me the following, firstly:

> I have only this much to say on the question of Jumu'ah in villages that while there is enough room for it in other schools of thought, we fail to understand your interpretation of the Ḥanafī viewpoint. The Ḥanafīs categorically declare Jumu'ah as not being mandatory for village folk. If there is a different perception according to your research please enlighten us.

And secondly:

> Your legal opinion on the subject of Jumuʿah and *khuṭbah* in villages is beyond our comprehension. It does not conform to the stand taken by any of the four schools of jurisprudence, because each of them has some precondition or another attached to them. However, those who follow none of the four schools (*ghayr muqallidīn*) hold the same view as held by the editor of *Tarjumān al-Qur'ān.*

At the outset, let me make it quite clear that my position is neither that of an antagonist holding his own fort in religious matters regardless of the Shariah injunctions, nor has my attitude ever been that of disdain or disregard for the arguments advanced by men of learning. I have always been and remain a seeker of knowledge and have tried faithfully to express an opinion formulated as the result of my dispassionate study and research in matters of religious significance. In case of a viewpoint established through sufficient proof and proper reasoning, I have also never hesitated to retract my earlier stand. My earlier submissions on the subject were based essentially on the Prophetic traditions, the historic record of the days of the holy Prophet's Companions and legal precedents. That was perhaps the reason for some to suspect that I am trying to advance my personal views as a 'jurist' in opposition to the Ḥanafī viewpoint and was, therefore, also dubbed as a non-conformist (*ghayr muqallid*).

Instead of opening the doors of any fresh controversy over the issue of Friday congregation in a village, let me now put forward my arguments exclusively according to the Ḥanafī school. We have before us the following four aspects that need to be reviewed to settle this matter once and for all: (1) the exact nature of Jumuʿah as a mandatory duty; (2) the preconditions for its observance; (3) were these ever amended and is there room for further amendment?; and (4) can a system be evolved for the observance of Jumuʿah, which, though at variance from the known Ḥanafī stand, may not be opposed to it? Let us look into each of these aspects separately.

11.5.1. *Jumuʿah as a Duty*

There is a consensus among religious scholars of every school of thought, including the Ḥanafīs, that Jumuʿah is an individual duty binding on every sane, adult member of the Muslim community (*farḍ al-ʿayn*). ʿAllāmah Sarakhsī in his *al-Mabsūṭ,* wrote: 'From the point of view of the Qur'an and the Sunnah, Jumuʿah is obligatory. There is a consensus of the Muslim men of learning on this.' ʿAllāmah Ibn Humām in his *Fatḥ al-Qadīr* said: 'Jumuʿah is a duty made obligatory by the Book of God and the Sunnah of the holy Prophet, may Allah bless him and give him peace. There is also a consensus of the Muslim *ummah* that anyone who renounces it is *kāfir*.' 'Allāmah Bābarqī in his commentary on *al-'Ināyah 'alā al-Hidāyah* observed: 'We have been ordered to leave the Ẓuhr prayer to establish the Friday prayer. Ẓuhr prayer is undoubtedly mandatory and something mandatory can only be left in favour of something which may be more important and much more obligatory in nature.'

It is evident from the observations of these leading scholars of the Ḥanafī school that the Friday prayer is not a duty because of the interpretations of some senior jurists, but is made obligatory by the Qur'an and the Sunnah and the injunctions in this regard are so clear that anybody refusing to accept them is liable to become a *kāfir*. If such is the nature of the Friday prayer, it calls for extreme care and precaution before excluding a whole segment of the Muslim population from its observance.

11.5.2. *The Preconditions for Observing Jumu'ah*

Now, let us see what these preconditions are that, if unfulfilled, invalidate such an important duty? According to the Ḥanafī school, there are two types of preconditions: those concerning the *muṣallī* and those related to external factors.

The preconditions of the first category are as follows: (1) the *muṣallī* should be a local resident and not a traveller; (2) he should be an adult male member of the Muslim community and not a child or a woman; (3) he should be a free citizen and not a prisoner or a slave; and (4) he should be healthy and physically fit to attend the congregation and not sick or disabled. There is a hadith to this effect, which forms the basis for this Ḥanafī position: 'The holy Prophet (peace be upon him) said: "For he who believes in God and the Last Day, the Jumu'ah is obligatory for him, except the one who is a traveller, a slave [or captive], a child, a woman or a patient."' The exemption given to these categories does not mean in any way that they are forbidden to attend the Jumu'ah prayer. It simply means that the magnanimous Shariah (*al-sharī'ah al-samḥā'*) has given special relaxation to certain categories of people due to their particular circumstances. However, if any one of them performs the Friday prayer, it will go to his or her credit and he or she will be entitled for more reward (*ajr*) from the Lord.

The following are the six preconditions with regard to the second category of requirements considered necessary by the Ḥanafīs for the correct observance of Jumu'ah prayer in a village: (1) *miṣr* (township); (2) time; (3) *khuṭbah*; (4) congregation; (5) *sulṭān* (governmental authority); and (6) free public access (*idhn 'ām*).

We are primarily concerned here with the first precondition of township, but before examining that let us first look at the other five. The preconditions of the midday time, *khuṭbah* and congregation are established by the Book of God and the Sunnah of the holy Prophet, may Allah bless him and give him peace. As for the fourth precondition, no exact number has been fixed for the composition of the Jumu'ah congregation and therefore there has been some difference of opinion among the jurists in this respect. The sixth precondition of free public access is also an established precedent. So far as the first and fifth preconditions of *miṣr* and *sulṭān* are concerned these are based not on any clear textual evidence of the holy Qur'an or Hadith, but on the deduction and induction of the jurists of the Ḥanafī school.

The Prophetic traditions about the Jumu'ah prayer as an obligatory duty do not contain a word that indicates that the presence of a *sulṭān* was a precondition for its observance. There is a hadith warning those who do not care to observe the Jumu'ah prayer, although 'ruled by a leader, tyrannical or just'. Imam Ḥasan al-Baṣrī is also said to have described Jumu'ah and Eid prayers as a public duty that the government of the day (*sulṭān*) must establish. However, these do not imply in any way that the existence of a *sulṭān* is a precondition for holding the Friday congregation. Can we deduct from the above that in the absence of a government authority from a certain place that even the obligatory duties of the Muslim community would come to a standstill? If somebody says that it is upon the girl's father to arrange her marriage, would that mean that in the event of the girl having lost her father she is to remain a spinster for the rest of her life?

As for the oft-quoted statements about the condition of *miṣr* or township, we have come across no consensual definition of the word so far, either in the holy Qur'an or in the Sunnah, or even among the senior jurists of the Ḥanafī school. The legal experts who have variously tried to define the term have never claimed their definitions to be final and binding, because that is possible only if their conclusion is supported by the textual connotation or implication of the Book of God or the Prophetic Tradition. This is the background of these two preconditions. The *ulema* of the Ḥanafī school have themselves introduced amendments to these conditions from time to time, which only confirms that they recognize there is scope for further amendments to these preconditions in accordance with the demands of the time while keeping the Shariah parameters in view.

So far as my careful studies and research go in this respect, I am firmly of the view that according to the intention and implication of the Islamic Shariah, the Jumu'ah prayer is not meant to be offered in each and every hamlet separately, because that is contrary to the very objective of cohesion and greater weekly social interaction. This is why the provision of *miṣr jāmiʿ* was laid down. The term itself is an indicator of its meaning and stands for a human habitation where people can assemble from nearby smaller villages and hamlets to offer the Jumuʿah prayer. The centrality of such a habitation is inherent in its very meaning and connotation, but not the size of its population or the number of shops or markets existing there. An imam or responsible official of the Islamic government of the day can declare any village that is centrally located among a cluster of smaller villages and hamlets as *miṣr jāmiʿ* and order the people in the surrounding locale to assemble there to offer the Jumuʿah prayer.

The Shariah intention by laying down the condition of *miṣr jāmiʿ* was obviously to let village folk assemble at a central place instead of observing this solemn weekly religious event of great social significance in a scattered manner. However, for reasons unknown, the very meaning and purpose of this precondition were reversed by exempting village folk from discharging this mandatory duty, instead of advising them to collect at a central place of their choice and convenience for this purpose. It was perhaps due to the misunderstanding of a section of the *ulema* that instead of correctly interpreting the import of the word *miṣr* they took it to mean 'the city' in its conventional sense. And as our cities are located at longer distances from villages and travellers are exempted from Jumuʿah prayer, they therefore construed that the villagers, being required to travel to such long distances to attend the Jumuʿah prayer, should be exempted from this duty. For me, the dictate of *taqwā* demands that instead of opening the door for exemptions for such a solemn act of duty, efforts should instead be made to pave the way for its proper observance.

In the way I have tried to define *miṣr jāmiʿ*, it becomes easier for a large number of our village dwellers, even including Muslim nomads, to perform Jumuʿah prayer correctly as enjoined by the Shariah. The best course for this is to regroup the rural areas within the radius of four to five or eight to nine miles, as per local conditions, into small circles or units and then with the general consent of the local population to adopt a central place as *miṣr jāmiʿ*. Adjoining villages may become part of its catchment area. It may then be officially announced that such and such a place has been chosen by the residents of the respective units or circles as the central place for the observance of the Jumuʿah prayer. If such a system were followed, it would not only be in conformity with the holy Prophet's authentic traditions, but also with the Ḥanafī juristic viewpoint.

11.5.3. *Resumé*

In order to help our right-thinking readers decide whether the system proposed by me to establish the Jumuʿah prayer in centrally-located villages is opposed to or in line with the Ḥanafī school of thought, I would sum up the discussion as follows: (1) According to the Ḥanafīs, it is unlawful to observe Jumuʿah prayer in each and every village. I too share the same view. (2) Jurists of the Ḥanafī school say that the Friday prayer should be observed in every *miṣr jāmiʿ*. I am also of the same opinion. (3) The Ḥanafīs only consider the following two types of places as *miṣr jāmiʿ*: one that may have emerged over the years as a town similar to our cities and major townships; or a place designated by the imam (in this case, the leading local figure of the Islamic government of the day) for the purpose of establishing the Jumuʿah system. I have proposed only the following amendment: Where there is no imam, the consensus of the local Muslim populace should be viewed as a substitute for the imam. There is no reason to dispute this minor change, which is in consonance with the spirit and essence of the Shariah injunctions. (4) The Ḥanafī *ulema* ruled in favour of exempting Muslim villagers from observing this duty because Muslim rulers and their deputies had failed to establish the Jumuʿah system in the countryside. As a result, the performance of Friday prayer became restricted to cities and major townships, and, due to the factor of distance, the *ulema* exempted village folk from observing Jumuʿah prayer. Therefore, the legal opinion issued as a result of this handicap needs to be immediately reviewed and justice done to the majority of the Muslim population that has so far been denied the blessings of this great religious event through no fault of their own.

Following the demise of Muslim rule in India, our social existence as a community now entirely depends on the relationship fostered and strengthened by the bonds of Shariah laws concerning our beliefs, acts of worship and socio-cultural interactions. We as a community are strong with the strength of these bonds and weak with their weakness. These ties are relatively stronger in urban areas in spite of so many adverse factors. However, the situation is different in the villages, where the population is sparsely spread over an area of thousands of square miles. The religious bonds that tie them together as a community have grown so weak that a little mishap may cause disruption. Our village people are like the scattered sheep of a flock and so have become easy prey to each and every wolf of disruption. In places where they are in a minority nothing of their lives, honour or property is safe. If no urgent attempt is made to meet this challenge, one is likely to see the Muslim population of our countryside gradually becoming alienated and eventually becoming a thing of the past. We must not forget that out of a total population of eighty million Muslims, nearly 60.5 million live in rural areas.

The best course to preserve our unity and strength as a nation is to strengthen our religious ties and social bonds. If we succeed in reuniting the community in urban as well as rural areas by further cementing these bonds through important events like the Friday and the two Eid congregations, and creating within them a sense of the religion's centrality as a binding and unifying force, then we will be doing a great service to Islam and the Muslim *ummah.* (*Tarjumān al-Qur'ān*, April–May 1938)

12 The Use of Loudspeakers for *Ṣalāh*

Some educated youth from the Punjab sent the following letter about the permissibility or otherwise of the using loudspeakers for *ṣalāh*:

> The management of our Eidgah (the prayer ground for Eid congregations) installed loudspeakers for the Eid prayer. However, the local *ulema* expressed strong disapproval and told the people that prayer conducted using loudspeakers is invalid. They gave the following reasons for their disapproval: (1) The use of loudspeakers is part of amusement and fun (*al-lahw wa al-la'ib*). (2) According to the Ḥanafī school, those standing behind the imam have to follow him in prayer. To respond to the voice from a loudspeaker would mean that they are not following the imam but an instrument. However, we are unconvinced by these arguments. The first point is in fact a claim and not an argument. The second point is also hardly tenable. It appears, these people are unaware of the basic mechanism of the tool. The voice amplified by a loudspeaker is not different from the voice of the speaker himself. It is the voice of the imam or *khaṭīb* using the loudspeaker. The stand taken by such persons tend to enrage knowledgeable Muslims and expose the ignorance of our so-called *ulema*. It is due to such elements that an educated Muslim youth is often even forced to revolt against religion itself. This was the attitude that encouraged political leaders like Ataturk and Reza Shah [Pahlavi] to take anti-Islamic steps. We look forward to a person of your insight and vision guiding us on the matter. In case you too subscribe to the views of these *ulema*, kindly provide us with cogent reasons to satisfy us that the use of loudspeakers is un-Islamic.

The above letter has been reproduced verbatim to let our religious scholars and men of learning understand the contemporary mind-set and to keep in view the realities on the ground and how our younger generation, equipped with better academic training and a broader vision, views otherwise commonplace issues of religious significance. About three years ago, a similar situation arose in Hyderabad (Deccan), where the people happily performed their Eid prayer in the local Eidgah with the help of loudspeakers installed all over the ground. However, a section of *ulema* subsequently condemned the act and an official committee was formed to take up the matter, which issued a legal opinon pronouncing the use of this technology as unlawful for *ṣalāh*. I was then in Hyderabad and know what an adverse impact it had on educated youth and how badly they felt about the local *ulema*.

I am not among those who are always keen in the name of enlightenment to fiddle with Islamic teachings in order to make them plausible to the educated class. Even the most conservative and violently orthodox from among our *ulema* understand and acknowledge my instance of relentless jihad through my pen against the un-Islamic trends of a particular class in our society. At the same time, however, it has always been my considered opinion that our religious scholars must not forget that they are not living in the age of *Hidāyah* and *Badā'iʿ al-Ṣanā'iʿ*, but in a world of scientific invention and fast-changing socio-economic and cultural scenarios. The contemporary world has a new set of issues and problems, which call for a fresh approach to tackle them. It is impossible for millions of our Muslim youth, spread across the globe, to remain unconcerned and unaffected by the issues and developments that naturally go on emerging with the passage of time. The sixth-century Hijrah discipline of logic is of no more use now. With the spirit of *ijtihād* and broader vision our *ulema* must pre-empt anti-Islamic trends and guide and lead Muslim youth today through forceful argument and an enlightened approach on the road to Islamic glory. If the way of our younger generation is blocked at each step by the misuse of the seventeenth-century *Fatāwā ʿĀlamgīrī* and *al-Fatāwā al-Tātārkhāniyyah*, the natural corollary of such a situation will be their deviation from the path of the holy Qur'an and the Sunnah and getting lost in the alleyways of their choice, as has already happened to the younger generations in many Muslim countries.

The issue under discussion can be answered in a few words, but I would first like to elucidate the general principles according to which other issues of a similar nature may also be tackled in the light of Shariah injunctions. Firstly, we must always keep in mind the first basic principle of Islamic jurisprudence, that no clear-cut ruling of the Shariah can be available to us on issues of a peripheral nature unless these had taken place during the holy Prophet's time. As for subsequent events, these are to be reviewed and examined in light of the precepts and formulas laid down by the Shariah itself. That is how emergent issues and problems were resolved by the Companions of the holy Prophet, the Followers (Tābiʿūn) and then by the leaders of the various schools of Islamic thought. These are the precedents that serve to help and guide us in finding solutions to emergent problems. It would obviously be wrong for us to follow the interpretations of a particular period blindly to resolve a certain matter today. What we need to do in such cases is to keep for our guidance the broad principles and outlines laid down by the Shariah and the way the Companions of the holy Prophet, the Followers and subsequent jurists resolved similar issues in their times.

Secondly, it is an insufficient reason for a new invention to be declared undesirable (*makrūh*) or impermissible (*ghayr jā'iz*) simply because it was not in use during the days of the holy Prophet, may Allah bless him and give him peace, and his Companions, or during the times of the founders of the various schools of jurisprudence. Allah Most Glorified and Exalted never intended His revealed laws to put an end to man's urge to invent things for his convenience. The quest for fresh resources and the discovery of new means to put them to better use are as lawful today as they were before. Those who interpret the Sunnah and innovation (*bid'ah*) in these terms do great injustice to Islam and Muslims. They actually confirm the calumny of anti-Islamic forces that Islamic teachings were only for a particular age and to follow them now would mean to shut out any prospects of future civilizational growth and advancement in human knowledge.

Thirdly, the real objective behind the Divine law of the Islamic Shariah is to teach human beings the principles of putting the resources created for them to better use instead of misusing them. This is how they can reap the real benefits and gains of these bounties instead of accruing losses and failures. The Qur'an and Hadith not only contain verbal instructions in this regard, but also the holy Prophet's practical example of how he made the best use of the available resources of his time in furtherance of Islamic objectives. The precedents thus set by him were followed by his Companions and then by the leading jurists of Islam, who understood the spirit of the principles of Islamic law so well and showed us how to apply them according to the needs of changing times. Once we understand those principles, we will have no problem in making the best use of resources that the forces of nature have laid to us and that may be under our command in future. It would be easier therefore for us to determine what is lawful and unlawful by examining these principles and how our Lord would like us to put latter-day inventions to better use. The problem faced by our *ulema* today is mainly due to their preoccupation with peripheral matters and their inhibition in tackling emergent issues in the light of the fundamentals and general precepts of the Islamic Shariah.

Fourthly, certain cardinal principles have been laid down in this context by the holy Qur'an and the Sunnah and the basic rule framed by our jurists in light of these principles comes to the following: Everything is permitted (*mubāḥ*) unless proved otherwise. Let us now briefly refer to the relevant dictates in the matter:

هُوَ ٱلَّذِى خَلَقَ لَكُم مَّا فِى ٱلْأَرْضِ جَمِيعًا ... ﴿٢٩﴾

It is He Who created for you all that is on earth.

(*al-Baqarah* 2: 29)

وَسَخَّرَ لَكُم مَّا فِى ٱلسَّمَـٰوَٰتِ وَمَا فِى ٱلْأَرْضِ جَمِيعًا مِّنْهُ ... ﴿١٣﴾

He has subjected to you all that is in the heavens and the earth, all being from Him.

(*al-Jāthiyah* 45: 13)

It is evident from these verses that Allah Most Exalted has harnessed everything that is in the heavens and on the earth for the benefit of mankind. Therefore, the human being has the right to make the best use of these things. He does not need to have a separate license for each and every thing and is justified in using and taking them as lawful so long as there is no definite injunction to the contrary.

Regarding halal and haram, the Qur'an and the Sunnah stipulate the following basic principle:

... وَيُحِلُّ لَهُمُ ٱلطَّيِّبَـٰتِ وَيُحَرِّمُ عَلَيْهِمُ ٱلْخَبَـٰٓئِثَ ... ﴿١٥٧﴾

He (the holy Prophet) makes the clean things lawful to them and prohibits all corrupt things.

(*al-Aʿrāf* 7: 157)

الْحَلَالُ مَا اَحَلَّ اللهُ فِى كِتَابه وَ الحَرَامُ مَا حَرَّمَ اللهُ فِى كِتَابِه، وَمَا سَكَتَ عَنهُ فهُو مِمَّا عَفَا عَنهُ

The lawful (halal) is that which God has sanctioned in His Book and the unlawful (haram) is that which God has proclaimed so in His Book. As for things of which He made no mention, these are permitted.

(Abū Dāwūd)

Fifthly, the matter was further explained succinctly in a hadith as follows: 'There is nothing harmful and disadvantageous in Islam' (لاضَرَرَ وَلاضِرَارَ فِى الإِسلَام). Anything for which no clear-cut injunction is available would thus be adjudged on the touchstone of these universal principles. In other words, it would be assessed as to whether a certain thing is advantageous and beneficial to the people or harmful and injurious. If it is good, it would be halal and if bad it would be haram. On the same analogy, if a thing that is otherwise good is misused or used in a wrong way to the people's disadvantage, then the manner of its use would become unlawful. On the contrary, if the same thing is used in the public interest and for the general good of the people, it would be lawful.

Sixthly, the Lawgiver has provided us with a yardstick and standards to determine right and wrong, good and bad, and loss and gain. We have not been left to grope in the dark about what is advantageous or disadvantageous for us. We have been given certain principles to determine wherein lie our gains and our losses. These also include the general principle that whatever stands as a hurdle in the way of religious duty is harmful and disadvantageous and must, therefore, be avoided, and, conversely, that everything helpful in discharge of religious obligations is useful and its use is not only permitted but is desirable.

For example, if the sighting of the new moon is impossible with the naked eye, due to the sky being overcast or the atmosphere being hazy, the use of binoculars would not only be permissible but very much desirable. To make use of a clock or a timepiece to set the timings for *ifṭār* or *suḥūr* cannot therefore be objected to on the same grounds. Who would prefer to ride by camel instead of driving in a car to Makkah the blessed for pilgrimage? Who can declare as haram the use of missiles, bombs, fighter planes, etc. in defence of Islam and the Muslim homeland on the plea that these were never used before?

Seventhly and finally, anything meant to serve the exclusive purpose that the Qur'an and the Sunnah have declared haram and that has no other use is definitely unlawful and absolutely forbidden. However, an instrument or tool that can either be used for good or bad purposes cannot be decreed unlawful simply because of its wayward and profligate use for wrong or unethical purposes. For example, the radio or tape recorder cannot be rejected outright as unlawful because they are at times misused to spread vulgarity.

In light of these few broad principles we may now look at the question of the use of loudspeakers and amplifiers for *adhān* and *ṣalāh.* The only conclusion that we can draw in light of these principles is that their use is not only lawful but rather most desirable. The basic function of this instrument is to amplify the voice and hence there is nothing undesirable in it. Being a tool of new invention, we obviously can find no injunction about it in the Qur'an or the

Sunnah. The fundamental principles provided to us by the Shariah help us to arrive decisively at the conclusion that there is nothing unlawful in this effective means of public good. That the same instrument is also used to relay cheap songs and vulgarity has nothing to do with its basic nature and utility as a most useful tool of public address, through which the message of human salvation and welfare can conveniently be transmitted to a much larger audience. It would be rather strange to let this medium be misused by the anti-Islamic elements to serve their interests, while we remain hesitant to use it for a much nobler cause.

As for the element of doubt about *ṣalāh* being spoiled if the congregation follows a voice other than that of the imam, the voice reaching the congregation through the loudspeaker is certainly that of the imam's. It is exactly like the voice amplified and transmitted and re-echoed through a vaulted structure. Moreover, according to the agreed formula of the principles of Islamic jurisprudence, the imam and the congregation make a unified whole. Human amplifiers (*mukabbirūn*) who imitate the signals of the imam (i.e. the formulae that signify change of one bodily position to another in the prayer) to transmit them to those standing in rows further behind have always had a useful role in facilitating the orderly performance of the prayer. Before the invention of this mechanical device, it was the human amplifier that made it possible for a million-strong congregation to perform *ṣalāh* in an orderly manner. The loudspeaker is even better than the *mukabbir*, because the latter was slow in transmission, while the former acts instantaneously. An irresponsible or less attentive *mukabbir* can even disrupt the whole prayer by delaying, fumbling or making mistakes in his transmission, but there is no room for such mishaps in case of a loudspeaker.

The prayer is a process in which a person's limbs, physical frame, spiritual self, and entire body and soul are all involved in unified communion with his Lord. Beyond the individual, both visible and invisible cosmic forces also partake in the exalted act of worship. Even inanimate objects of nature are one with the *muṣallī* as he stands for *ṣalāh*. The holy Qur'an says:

...وَإِن مِّن شَيْءٍ إِلَّا يُسَبِّحُ بِحَمْدِهِ وَلَٰكِن لَّا تَفْقَهُونَ تَسْبِيحَهُمْ... ﴿٤٤﴾

> *There is nothing but gives glory to Him with His praise, though you do not understand their hymns of praise.*
>
> (*al-Isrā'* 17: 44)

On what grounds can one raise an objection to the use of an inanimate object to celebrate the praises of the Lord? How can one declare unlawful in service of the Lord the use of an object created by the human mind in light of the wisdom and knowledge bestowed on him and out of the material and substance provided by none but the Almighty Himself?

According to a well-known principle in Islamic jurisprudence, if a person offering prayer acts in a manner that gives an outsider the impression that he is not praying, then it spoils his *ṣalāh*. If such an impression is not created, then no little action by the *muṣallī* can spoil *ṣalāh*. The use of a loudspeaker during *ṣalāh* is obviously not something that can ever create the impression that the one offering or leading the prayer is not praying. Hence, on that account too, its use for prayer cannot be declared unlawful.

These are the reasons and arguments on the basis of which I am firmly of the view that the loudspeaker can be used for the Friday and Eid sermons and for *ṣalāh* and there is absolutely nothing wrong in it that makes its use unlawful. (*Tarjumān al-Qur'ān*, August 1938).

13 The Islamic Festivals of Eid al-Adha and Eid al-Fitr

Festivals are the *sine qua non* of human society. Man has perhaps been engaged in festivities since the time he began his communal life on earth. In the past and today, every nation has earmarked a few days – from two to four or five to ten – each year for this purpose. These festivals in fact reflect the true spirit of a society. As the people assemble in one place, give vent to common sentiments and feelings, celebrate an event collectively, and uniformly perform some rites and rituals, they are automatically welded together to form one community. A common social psyche thus emerges and is gradually groomed and revitalized.

If we review and examine the festivals organized by different countries and communities around the world, we notice that these are generally held to celebrate either some historic event, to extol some great personality, or to observe some religious occasion. A prerequisite for any festival is that there should be an event of common interest emotionally binding the people in a common bond. This is why a people very rarely take an interest in the festivities of other peoples. Even if they wish to observe such events out of expediency, they are unable to inject the same spirit of exuberance within these as they do in case of their own festivals.

The way festive occasions are observed differs from one people to another. Some confine it to sports, musical and recreational events. Some communities cross the bounds of recreation and their celebrations degenerate into profligacy, indecency and uncivilized behaviour. In case of others these occasions may be a mix of recreational as well as serious festivities and rituals. Then there are communities for whom such social events are the means to infuse in the people a sublime spirit of healthy manners and morals and a sense of belonging to higher values in life. In short, the way a nation celebrates an event is the barometer by which one can openly judge its character and collective psyche. The more a nation stands on a higher moral pedestal, the more civilized and pleasant will be the tone and tenor of its festivals and the mode of celebration. Conversely, the more it is morally perverse, the more will its festive events reflect the same degree of perversion.

Being a global reformist movement that is not confined to any particular country or community, Islam seeks to enrol all humanity into a society of righteous culture. It has reformed every walk of life and imparted to it its own distinct colour. It has similarly given festivals a new complexion that is totally different to those observed by other communities. Islam does not disregard to a community's collective festive spirit or the significance festivals naturally have for a nation. In fact, it seeks to make the best use of this phenomenon and induces a qualitative change in the celebration of festive occasions. Therefore, it has infused these events with the spirit of moral rejuvenation and social well-being. In this respect, the following three important aspects need to be kept in mind.

Firstly, no global reformist movement can view events of boisterous and unbridled fanfare with approval. Festivals based on sentiments exclusive to a particular community that are not shared by others may serve as a divisive force, splitting humanity apart. Thus, while helping a community to organize and galvanize itself, such festivals are simultaneously instrumental in splitting and distancing one community from another. This is why a trans-communal movement that addresses humanity at large and seeks to interweave the human race into a single civilizational network cannot approve of events which are exclusively communal, race or region-based. The grand objective this global movement has before itself naturally demands that nations and communities coming under its umbrella should be lured into giving up their pre-Islamic modes of festivities and replacing these with festive events that are equally significant for every member of Islam's global community. In other words, Islam even seeks to use its festive occasions for the higher moral purpose of galvanizing the nation of Islam into a single whole.

Secondly, a worldwide movement that believes in the supremacy of the One and Only God cannot tolerate festivities that may contain the slightest shade of pantheism, hero-worship or superstitious beliefs. Due to the very nature of its mission, among all nations and countries falling under its benign civilizational umbrella, it has to check and stop their old festivities in the name of religion and unhealthy cultural trends, as these may keep reminding them of their pagan past, and worthless traditions and customs. On the other hand, Islam seeks to introduce festivals that not only cater to the instinctual human desire for jubilation and festivity but also leave a deep imprint of monotheism and righteousness on everyone taking part in them.

Thirdly, the quality of righteousness also gives rise to superior moral conduct. This demands that a monotheistic movement, which is the torchbearer of virtue and purity, should also provide its followers with festive occasions that are free from depravity, lowliness and indecency, while at the same time offering them avenues of healthy entertainment and pastimes. Such occasions should not begin and end with recreation. Instead, these should make the best use of exuberance produced by such social events for the furtherance and promotion of higher moral values.

These are the three basic characteristics, which are reflected in the festivals Islam has prescribed for the Muslim *ummah.* The communities that embraced Islam in Arabia, Persia, Egypt, Syria and elsewhere were inspired to leave behind their pre-Islamic pagan religious and national festivals and replace them with the two global festivals of Eid al-Fitr and Eid al-Adha. The first of these is organized to celebrate the successful completion of the thirty days of fasting enjoined upon the nation of Islam by Allah Most Glorified and Exalted. It is a day of thanksgiving to the Lord for His great blessings. The second festival is dedicated to the memory of the matchless sacrifice made by a great and most sincere servant of God about four thousand years ago. Both these events have evidently no concern or relationship with any particular nationality or community. These are instead based on universal values common to all God-fearing friends of humanity, whether they live in the east or the west, north or south, whether they are black or white, red or yellow, rich or poor. Both these festivals are marked by the spirit of worship and allegiance to the Lord and Master of our destinies. There is no aspect of hero-worship in these festivals either.

The way these global festivals of Islam are celebrated is so highly refined, civilized and full of socio-cultural advantages that none could ever think of any other mode of festivity better than these. However, having said that, the Muslim community did subsequently taint the Islamic festivals to some extent with the practices of the Age of Ignorance. Nonetheless, their spirit and essence remain the same even today and no major change in their tone and temperament has taken place.

13.1. How did the Islamic Community of the Golden Era Celebrate the Festivals?

Let us see how the Muslim community celebrated Eid al-Fitr and Eid al-Adha in the golden days of our master the Messenger of Allah, may Allah bless him and give him peace, so that we can know the real spirit of sanctity and jubilation expected on these solemn festive occasions.

Early in the morning of Eid day, every Muslim man, woman and child used to take a bath (*ghusl*) and put on their best clothes. On the occasion of Eid al-Fitr, before going for the Eid prayer, they gave in charity a certain measure of foodstuff or its equivalent amount to the needy and deserving so that nobody was left hungry on such a happy occasion. On Eid al-Adha, they first went to offer prayers and then rushed back home to slaughter sacrificial animals and then distribute the meat. The special prayers of the two Eids were the main and indispensable part of these festivals for which everyone, clad in their best attire, set out from home as the early morning sun had just risen on the eastern horizon. All able-bodied men, women, children, young and old, were to set out in an open display of their strength, communal harmony and social grandeur and participate in the special prayers of thanksgiving.

Thus, the two Eids also offered each member of the community the opportunity to participate in an event of collective jubilation. The prayers of the two Eids were not offered in the mosque, but in a spacious ground away from residential areas to accommodate the maximum number of people. As the congregation set out for the prayer ground, they glorified the name of their Lord on the way and chanted the following soul-stirring words, which resounded in every street, lane and by-lane, road and alleyway of a Muslim locality:

اَللهُ اَكبَرُ، اَللهُ اَكبَرُ، لاَاِلٰهَ اِلَّا اللهُ وَاللهُ اَكبَرُ، اَللهُ اَكبَرُ، وَلِلّٰهِ الحَمدُ!

> Allah is the Greatest, Allah is the Greatest! There is no God but Allah! Allah is the Greatest, Allah is the Greatest! He Alone is Worthy of all Praise!

On arrival at the prayer ground, the congregation arranged themselves in rows and at the commencement of the prayer time stood in straight lines. The holy Prophet, may Allah bless and give him peace, then led the two-*rakʿah* prayer, followed by the *khuṭbah,* which he delivered standing up. As against the Friday sermon, the sermons of the two Eids were delivered after the prayer so that the maximum number of people could benefit from this very important speech by their leader, which was given only twice a year. The Prophet then moved to that part of the ground where the women had assembled and addressed them separately so that they were not deprived of his thoughts and ideas on such an important social-religious event. In addition to different instructions, guidance and sage counsels, the *khuṭbah* contained a review of important current issues and problems facing the Islamic community. In case of any impending military or political action, the holy Prophet, may Allah bless him and give him peace, announced the broad outlines of his decision before that grand assembly. The assembly's attention was also drawn to the financial needs of the community and the state to which each one responded to instantly, to the best of his or her ability. The women often took out their jewels and ornaments to donate them generously for the cause of Islam and the Muslim community.

That unearthly crowd of angelic men, women and children then left the prayer ground and, as instructed by their Benign Guide and Lord, took a different route on their way back home. The real significance of this instruction was that no part of the township should be left out of the solemnity and jubilation of the happy occasion and also that a sense of greater assimilation could prevail within the community.

On the day of Eid al-Adha, those who were financially capable sacrificed an animal on their return from the prayer ground. The purpose of this activity was not just to refresh the memory of a great historical moment, but also to revive the sentiments of sacrifice and surrender to the will of the Lord, according to which an octogenarian native of Iraq willingly readied himself at the alien site of Makkah to sacrifice his only son for the love of God and then at that very moment the Almighty miraculously saved his son and a ram was slaughtered in his child's stead.

That is how the global Islamic Festivals of Eid al-Fitr and Eid al-Adha were celebrated by our master the Messenger of Allah, may Allah bless him and give him peace. The same tradition was followed by his rightly-guided caliphs and the same will eternally remain the guiding light for the observance of the two most sublime festivals in the world of Islam. While Eid al-Fitr reminds Muslims of the great blessing the Lord bestowed on them in the form of Ramadan, the month of fasting and the month of the Qur'an, the 10 Dhū al-Ḥijjah is celebrated as Eid al-Adha to commemorate the great sacrifice of Prophet Abraham, may Allah's peace be upon him and on the last of His Prophets. This blessed occasion is also a reaffirmation of the firm faith Muslims have that their life and death and everything they have is for their Lord. These sentiments are so tellingly couched in the following words, which the Muslims utter while slaughtering the sacrificial animal:[1]

إِنِّي وَجَّهْتُ وَجْهِيَ لِلَّذِي فَطَرَ السَّمَاوَاتِ وَالأَرْضَ حَنِيفًا وَمَاأَنَاْ مِنَ الْمُشْرِكِينَ. إِنَّ صَلاَتِي وَنُسُكِي وَمَحْيَايَ وَمَمَاتِي لِلّٰهِ رَبِّ الْعَالَمِينَ. لاَ شَرِيكَ لَهُ وَبِذَلِكَ أُمِرْتُ وَأَنَاْ أَوَّلُ الْمُسْلِمِينَ. اَللّٰهُمَّ مِنكَ وَ لَكَ. بِسمِ الله، اَللهُ أكبَر.

I have turned my face in exclusive devotion to the One Who originated the heavens and the earth, and I am certainly not one of those who associate others with Allah in His Divinity. No doubt, my prayer, my rituals of worship, my life and my death are all for Allah, the Lord of the worlds. He has no partners like unto Him. So have I

> been ordered and I am the foremost of those who submit themselves to Allah. O my Lord, whatever I have is from You and it is for You! In the name of Allah, Allah is the Greatest!'

In addition to these formal activities, which were officially observed by the Islamic state and its great leader, may Allah bless him and give him peace, during these festivals, the youth informally played their favourite games and sports and the girls got together within the boundary walls of their homes to sing chivalrous songs. These were all kept within certain limits. No one went beyond the society's well-established norms and values or ventured to cross the bounds of decency by exceeding the permissible limits.

On such occasions, the attitude of the elders in that blessed environment can be imagined from the following example, documented by history. One Eid, when the holy Prophet, may Allah bless him and give him peace, entered his house he saw some young girls sitting with Sayyidah 'Ā'ishah and singing some songs. These were not songs of romance or revelry, but the folkloric songs about the ancient Battle of Bu'āth. The singers were not professional artistes or performers, but innocent girls all from the family. The holy Prophet, may Allah bless him and give him peace, did not interfere in their recreation and went silently to a corner, wrapping himself up in a shawl and took some rest. After some time, Sayyidah 'Ā'ishah's father and the holy Prophet's closest friend, Ḥaḍrat Abū Bakr visited the house. He scolded his daughter for this activity. On hearing his voice, the holy Prophet, may Allah bless him and give him peace, removed the shawl from his face and asked him to leave the girls alone as: 'For every nation there is a festive occasion and today is our Eid.' Abū Bakr then spoke no further, but the girls stopped singing and then slowly made their way back to their homes. This is an example of the spirit of purity, piety, enjoyment and decent manners that a Muslim society is expected to inculcate and promote. On the one hand, this incident reminds us of our duty as elders to keep the festive spirit of our youth within the limits of decency, and also of the need for tolerance so long as those limits are not crossed. On the other hand, it also instructs young ones on how to be obedient and respectful to their elders. (All India Radio, 29 December 1941)

14 Blood Sacrifice: The Islamic and un-Islamic Approaches

Blood sacrifice has remained an essential part of the worship ritual that human beings have observed since time immemorial. The practice had included manslaughter as an offering to deities, generally depicted with gruesome faces. The very sight of such bloodthirsty gods and goddesses provoked revulsion in the average onlooker. A section of those with a secular mind-set among Muslims often related the concept of blood sacrifice in Islam with the pagan practice of the past. The following three articles by Sayyid Mawdūdī help us to understand the subject in its correct perspective and the Islamic approach to the matter. — Editor.

14.1. Blood Sacrifice in Islam

Around four thousand years ago, a great man arose from the soil of Iraq to forever leave his indelible mark on human history. At the time of his birth, the whole world was given to polytheism and idolatry. The community into which he was born worshipped the sun, moon and stars. The royal dynasty that ruled his land was revered and worshipped as the lord and master of his countrymen because of its self-proclaimed status as the descendants of deities. The priestly family into which he was born were chiefly responsible for keeping his people entrapped in the myth of star-worship. The father of this man was no ordinary mortal, but the chief priest of his country's main temple.

He was born at a time and into a community and family that would naturally have led him to follow the hallowed tradition of his family, a path replete with incentives and privileges. Like his father, he would have risen in eminence to a position second only to that of the king's. There was apparently no light or source of guidance anywhere in the world to show him the way to a different path. His family background and personal interest also demanded that he should never ever contemplate a different way of life. Yet he was a man of different mettle. He refused to be swept away by the tide and unquestioningly accept the prevailing unhealthy norms and customs because of family pressure or his own status in that society. As he grew older, he felt obliged to ask himself if the precepts and principles upon which his ancestors and his entire nation had erected the whole structure of their social life were right. During his own search for the truth, he looked up at the sun, the moon, the stars and all those deities about whose divinity he had heard so much about since his childhood. He examined each of them one by one to ascertain if it would be right to accept or reject their divine status. He finally arrived at the firm conclusion that all the so-called deities were servants of the One and Only God, Who created the heavens and the earth and whatever inhabits them.

When the light of the truth thus dawned on him, he did not hesitate for a moment to renounce the false gods and beliefs and practices he had inherited from his ancestors. The firmness of his faith led him to reaffirm and proclaim:

إِنِّي وَجَّهْتُ وَجْهِيَ لِلَّذِي فَطَرَ ٱلسَّمَٰوَٰتِ وَٱلْأَرْضَ حَنِيفًا ۖ وَمَآ أَنَا۠ مِنَ ٱلْمُشْرِكِينَ ۝٧٩

Behold, I have turned my face in exclusive devotion to the One Who originated the heavens and the earth, and I am certainly not one of those who associate others with Allah in His Divinity.

(*al-An'ām* 6: 79)

Following this declaration, he announced to the notables of his clan and the community in general that he had parted ways with them and could no longer follow their idolatrous way of life. This was the first sacrifice he made in the way of the Lord. In one stroke, he cut at the roots of the blind following of ancestral tradition, and family and community ways and delusions.

Great man that he was, he did not rest content with this declaration. The truth had dawned upon him that the Oneness and Uniqueness of God (*tawḥīd*) alone was the right course, and ascribing partners to God in his Divinity (*shirk*) was a false notion without firm foundation. He had also become aware of the fact that his countrymen had built up their religion, morality and culture on polytheism, a precarious basis far removed from monotheism. This made him restless and he now had an overpowering sense of duty to warn his community against *shirk* and to invite them to *tawḥīd*. He knew that by openly propagating his ideas, he would lose his position as the heir apparent of the chief priest and all the powers and privileges that accompanied that position. He was also aware that through his preaching he would expose himself to the wrath of his entire community. He further knew that he stood in direct opposition not only to his father but to the royal family as he would challenge their claim to be the infallible offspring of the deities, from which emanated all their authority and power. Fearlessly, however, he rose to this call of duty. He invited his father, his family, his community and even his king to desist from *shirk* and follow the golden path of *tawḥīd*. The more he was opposed, the more resolute he became in his mission. Finally, the decisive moment came when he was standing alone. Against him stood everyone else, from his family and community to the ruling hierarchy. In the entire country, he had no friendly soul in his favour, not even the feeblest of voices. Even so, he did not lose heart and continued to propagate his monotheistic creed. Finally, those in authority decided to punish him for his 'atrocious act of profanity' by burning him alive. Fear of this horrific punishment failed to deter him from his Divine mission. He willingly accepted being thrown into the inferno, but did not retreat from the course of his faith in the Ultimate Truth he had chosen for himself with full conviction. This was his second grand sacrifice.

At the appointed date he was thrown into the raging fire, but was miraculously saved from burning. How this happened God alone knows, but the whole populace and the high gentry who had gathered to witness the spectacle were aghast, first by seeing him thrown into the fire and then by the extraordinary sight of it refusing to consume him. Following his miraculous emergence from the inferno unharmed, it was difficult for him to then remain in his native land any longer. He thus opted for exile. Yet the problem he again faced was that the neighbouring lands were all idolatrous and there was not even a tiny community of people anywhere who believed in the One God who could give him refuge and follow his mission. The only option left to him for safe refuge was to desist from preaching his monotheistic creed and to remain forever silent. Yet he refused to be cowed and even in exile did not falter in his mission. Wherever he went he called the people to leave the worship of false deities and return to the One and Only God as His true servants. He told them that it is He alone Who could satisfy all their needs in this world and grant them everlasting bliss in the Hereafter. As a migrant, he did not remain peacefully anywhere, sometimes in Syria, Palestine, Egypt and then in Hijaz on the coastal belt of Arabia. In short, he spent this entire period of his life moving from one country to another. He was neither in search of shelter nor was he looking for the comforts of hearth and home, a farm or livestock or a flourishing business. He did not pine for the luxuries of life. His sole desire and objective in life was to see the faith in which he believed emerge as supreme and see a humanity lost to ignorance and falsehood return to the right path. That was the mission that kept him restless and moving from place to place. It was for this that he had given up all his personal comforts. That was the third sacrifice offered by this great man in the way of Allah Most Glorified and Exalted.

Wandering like a nomad with no worldly assets or succour, he was rewarded by the Almighty towards the end of his life with a son. The son was born to him at an age when it is normally not expected. This child grew up in an atmosphere of piety and purity until he was in the prime of his youth, when his parents could rightly look to him as their future hope and support in old age. It was in his only son whom his aged father could see the flowering of his own personality and mission. Anyone could surmise the high degree of love and affection the octogenarian father must have had for him, yet nothing is dearer in life to a true Muslim than the supreme Lord and His pleasure. All the sacrifices the father had made in times past would have been too great and beyond the capacity of any ordinary mortal, yet God had still another and the greatest of all sacrifices in store for this great man. He was put to a test not many could endure, one for which he will be extolled until eternity as the supreme model of love for his Creator. In this respect, he was asked to sacrifice his precious son in the way of Allah, to prove that his fatherly love of his only son did not supersede his love for the Lord. He did not waver for a moment but passed this test too and was prepared to sacrifice his son by his own hand. Yet, just as before, he was once again saved from an incalculable loss. As he was about to place his sharpened knife on his beloved son's throat, the All-Merciful Lord so arranged that his young and vivacious son Ismāʿīl was miraculously saved and replaced by a well-fed and robust ram. The sacrifice was accepted as the most memorable and momentous ever made by any human being in the way of the Lord. Allah Most Glorified and Exalted did not need the blood of the great man's son. It was meant instead to test his fidelity and love for his Lord, and to the mission to keep aloft the banner of His Name, and he did succeed in this most difficult of tests. But for the will of the Lord, the sharpened knife might have done its job. That was the greatest sacrifice the great bondsman of Allah made to prove his loyalty and allegiance to Islam and his faith in the Lord, and God rewarded him with the leadership of humanity and elevated him to the loftiest pedestal as 'God's intimate friend' (*khalīl Allāh*).

This is an account of the glorious life and mission of the man whom we all know as our master Ibrāhīm, may Allah's peace be upon him. It is this great sacrifice that we Muslims commemorate the world over by slaughtering animals on this particular day called the Festival of Sacrifice or Eid al-Adha. The purpose of this celebration is to revive within us Muslims the same spirit of sacrifice, the same sentiments of unquestioning surrender to the will of the Lord (Islam), unwavering faith in Him (*īmān*), and sincere devotion (*ikhlāṣ*), which our master Ibrāhīm demonstrated in the way of Allah throughout his life. If a person slaughters an animal but his heart is devoid of this spirit, he is unnecessarily shedding an animal's blood. God needs neither the blood nor the flesh. What is desired instead is that a man who has proclaimed himself a Muslim by reaffirming his faith in Allah and His Last Messenger, may Allah bless him and give him peace, must live as His true servant and bondsman. No bias, self-interest, pressure, fear, material loss, no internal weakness or external force should ever remove him from the path of truth. He should never accept any other bondsmanship after having declared his allegiance to Allah. It should not be difficult for him to sacrifice all his affiliations and loyalties for the sake of his bond and loyalty to his Lord.

Islam believes in such sacrifice and more than ever before we are today in need of injecting this noble spirit within our personal characters. Whenever the Muslims have suffered in this world it has mainly been due to the absence of this Islamic spirit of sacrifice for the noble cause. (Radio Pakistan, October 1947)

14.2. Is Animal Sacrifice a 'Pagan and Wasteful Exercise'?

Some pamphlets were distributed on the eve of Eid al-Adha last year urging Muslims not to misuse the national wealth of livestock in a 'senseless, thoughtless, harmful and wasteful ritual' of animal sacrifice on 10 Dhū al-Ḥijjah. A bunch of few misguided zealots exhorted Muslims instead to use the amount of money thus saved on various social welfare schemes and activities. They believe that animal sacrifice was a pagan ritual that has no sanction in the holy Qur'an. As for the hadiths [on this subject], they refused to accept their veracity. This group of pseudo-intellectuals has been busy misleading the people through their anti-Hadith and anti-Islamic campaigns, especially on the advent of Eid al-Adha each year. A person with no proper knowledge of Islam is liable to fall prey to such mischievous propaganda. It was therefore considered necessary to dispel any doubts and misunderstandings raised by what this group was energetically spreading against the relevance of blood sacrifice and its significance in Islam.

From whatever has been reported to us of their writings, their views may be summed up as follows: (1) The first objection raised against blood sacrifice is that the ritual is a remnant of the pagan custom, and religious figures (*mawlawīs*) have sanctioned it because of their sheer ignorance of the Islamic teachings. One of the luminaries of this group claimed that: 'The ritual of offering blood sacrifice was prevalent among all uncivilized and uncultured communities of the world. Today, none other than Muslims are involved in this.' (2) Secondly, they regard blood sacrifice as an economically harmful practice. In their view, the amount of money spent on sacrificial animals is a waste and no rational or material gain is achieved in return. (3) They claim to have found no injunction regarding sacrifice in the holy Qur'an, while they subscribe to nothing narrated in the Hadith. By totally rejecting the holy Prophet's tradition, it is easier for them to pronounce as 'un-Islamic' anything that may not be plausible to the non-Muslim world, or that which they are unable to grasp the meaning and purpose of.

As these objections have been raised by people who claim to be Muslims and declare the Qur'an as their ultimate criterion and the only authority to settle religious issues by, we will explain the question of blood sacrifice only in light of the Qur'anic injunctions. We will also try to elucidate through the Book of God the significance of including animal sacrifice among the prescribed Islamic acts of worship.

The injunctions given by the holy Qur'an regarding blood sacrifice can be classified under three categories. The first category of sacrifice is related to the hajj rituals. Allah Most Exalted says:

وَأَذِّن فِي ٱلنَّاسِ بِٱلۡحَجِّ يَأۡتُوكَ رِجَالٗا وَعَلَىٰ كُلِّ ضَامِرٖ يَأۡتِينَ مِن كُلِّ فَجٍّ عَمِيقٖ ٢٧ لِّيَشۡهَدُواْ مَنَٰفِعَ لَهُمۡ
وَيَذۡكُرُواْ ٱسۡمَ ٱللَّهِ فِيٓ أَيَّامٖ مَّعۡلُومَٰتٍ عَلَىٰ مَا رَزَقَهُم مِّنۢ بَهِيمَةِ ٱلۡأَنۡعَٰمِۖ فَكُلُواْ مِنۡهَا وَأَطۡعِمُواْ ٱلۡبَآئِسَ ٱلۡفَقِيرَ ٢٨

And publicly proclaim pilgrimage for all mankind so that they come to you on foot and mounted on lean camels from every distant point, to witness the benefits in store for them, and pronounce the name of Allah during the appointed days over the cattle that He has provided them. So eat of it and feed the distressed and the needy.

(*al-Ḥajj* 22: 27–28)

The order to establish the system of *Ḥajj* was given to Prophet Abraham, may Allah's peace be upon him, immediately after he completed the construction of the Kaaba. The purpose of this pilgrimage was described so as to enable the people to benefit from the blessings of both the temporal and spiritual worlds and to offer a blood sacrifice in the name of Allah. The Muslim *ummah* being heir to the Abrahamic tradition, the ritual was then ordained for them as part of the obligatory hajj rituals (*manāsik al-ḥajj*). Addressing the nation of Islam in *Sūrah al-Ḥajj,* the Lord declares:

وَٱلۡبُدۡنَ جَعَلۡنَٰهَا لَكُم مِّن شَعَٰٓئِرِ ٱللَّهِ لَكُمۡ فِيهَا خَيۡرٞۖ فَٱذۡكُرُواْ ٱسۡمَ ٱللَّهِ عَلَيۡهَا صَوَآفَّۖ فَإِذَا وَجَبَتۡ
جُنُوبُهَا فَكُلُواْ مِنۡهَا وَأَطۡعِمُواْ ٱلۡقَانِعَ وَٱلۡمُعۡتَرَّۚ كَذَٰلِكَ سَخَّرۡنَٰهَا لَكُمۡ لَعَلَّكُمۡ تَشۡكُرُونَ ٣٦

We have appointed sacrificial camels among the symbols of [devotion to] Allah. There is much good in them for you. So make them stand [at the time of sacrifice] and pronounce the name of Allah over them, and when they fall down on their sides [after they are slaughtered], eat and also feed them who do not ask and those who ask. Thus have We subjected these animals that you may give thanks.

(*al-Ḥajj* 22: 36)

The second category of sacrifice is that which is offered as part of the mandatory rites in the *tamattu*ʿ or *qirān* categories of hajj, or in the case of the pilgrim being prevented from completing hajj rituals due to some mishap, or imposed as a penalty for any transgression or violation of the prescribed rites. This has been explained in the following verses:

وَأَتِمُّوا۟ ٱلْحَجَّ وَٱلْعُمْرَةَ لِلَّهِ ۚ فَإِنْ أُحْصِرْتُمْ فَمَا ٱسْتَيْسَرَ مِنَ ٱلْهَدْىِ ۖ وَلَا تَحْلِقُوا۟ رُءُوسَكُمْ حَتَّىٰ يَبْلُغَ ٱلْهَدْىُ مَحِلَّهُۥ ۚ ... ﴿١٩٦﴾

Complete hajj and ʿumrah *for Allah. And if you are prevented from doing so, then make the offering which is available to you, and do not shave your heads until the offering reaches its appointed place.*

(*al-Baqarah* 2: 196)

... فَمَن كَانَ مِنكُم مَّرِيضًا أَوْ بِهِۦٓ أَذًى مِّن رَّأْسِهِۦ فَفِدْيَةٌ مِّن صِيَامٍ أَوْ صَدَقَةٍ أَوْ نُسُكٍ ۚ ... ﴿١٩٦﴾

If any of you should have to shave your head before that because of illness, or injury to the head, then you should make redemption by fasting, or almsgiving, or ritual sacrifice.

(*al-Baqarah* 2: 196)

... فَإِذَآ أَمِنتُمْ فَمَن تَمَتَّعَ بِٱلْعُمْرَةِ إِلَى ٱلْحَجِّ فَمَا ٱسْتَيْسَرَ مِنَ ٱلْهَدْىِ ۚ فَمَن لَّمْ يَجِدْ فَصِيَامُ ثَلَـٰثَةِ أَيَّامٍ فِى ٱلْحَجِّ وَسَبْعَةٍ
إِذَا رَجَعْتُمْ ۗ تِلْكَ عَشَرَةٌ كَامِلَةٌ ۗ ... ﴿١٩٦﴾

And when you are secure, then he who avails of ʿumrah *before the time of hajj shall give the offering he can afford; and if he cannot afford the offering, he shall fast for three days during hajj and for seven days after he returns home; that is, ten days in all.*

(*al-Baqarah* 2: 196)

يَـٰٓأَيُّهَا ٱلَّذِينَ ءَامَنُوا۟ لَا تَقْتُلُوا۟ ٱلصَّيْدَ وَأَنتُمْ حُرُمٌ ۚ وَمَن قَتَلَهُۥ مِنكُم مُّتَعَمِّدًا فَجَزَآءٌ مِّثْلُ مَا قَتَلَ مِنَ ٱلنَّعَمِ يَحْكُمُ
بِهِۦ ذَوَا عَدْلٍ مِّنكُمْ هَدْيًۢا بَـٰلِغَ ٱلْكَعْبَةِ ... ﴿٩٥﴾

Believers! Do not kill game while you are in the state of pilgrim sanctity. Whoever of you kills it wilfully there shall be a recompense, the like of what he has killed in cattle – as shall be judged by two persons of equity among you – to be brought to the Kaaba as an offering.

(*al-Mā'idah* 5: 95)

In the above verses, sacrificial animals have been called *hady*, which means an offering or a domestic animal that is sacrificed in the name of the Lord as part of the obligatory hajj rituals (*manāsik*).

The third category of blood sacrifice is the one enjoined upon the holy Prophet, may Allah bless him and give him peace, and through him to all Muslims:

قُلْ إِنَّ صَلَاتِي وَنُسُكِي وَمَحْيَايَ وَمَمَاتِي لِلَّهِ رَبِّ ٱلْعَٰلَمِينَ ﴿١٦٢﴾ لَا شَرِيكَ لَهُۥ ۖ وَبِذَٰلِكَ أُمِرْتُ
وَأَنَا۠ أَوَّلُ ٱلْمُسْلِمِينَ ﴿١٦٣﴾

Say: 'Surely my prayer, my service of sacrifice and all worship rituals, and my living and my dying are only for Allah, the Lord of the whole Universe. He has no associate. Thus have I been bidden, and I am the foremost of those who submit themselves [to Allah].'

(*al-An'ām* 6: 162-163)

In the first of the two verses quoted above, the word *ṣalāh* is followed by *nusuk*, which means worship ritual and also blood sacrifice. The words *nusuk* and *mansak* (plural, *manāsik)* have generally been used by the holy Qur'an to mean sacrifice, as in the following verse of *Sūrah al-Ḥajj*:

وَلِكُلِّ أُمَّةٍ جَعَلْنَا مَنسَكًا لِّيَذْكُرُوا۟ ٱسْمَ ٱللَّهِ عَلَىٰ مَا رَزَقَهُم مِّنۢ بَهِيمَةِ ٱلْأَنْعَٰمِ ۗ ... ﴿٣٤﴾

For every people We have laid down a ritual of sacrifice that they pronounce the name of Allah over the cattle He has provided them.

(*al-Ḥajj* 22: 34)

... فَمَن كَانَ مِنكُم مَّرِيضًا أَوْ بِهِۦٓ أَذًى مِّن رَّأْسِهِۦ فَفِدْيَةٌ مِّن صِيَامٍ أَوْ صَدَقَةٍ أَوْ نُسُكٍ ۚ ... ﴿١٩٦﴾

If any of you should have to shave your head before that because of illness, or injury to the head, then you should make redemption by fasting, or almsgiving, or ritual sacrifice.

(*al-Baqarah* 2: 196)

Thus, these Qur'anic verses determine the meaning of the term *nusuk*. It should be noted also that the phrase *my prayer* (*ṣalātī*) in 6: 162 are followed by *my service of sacrifice and all worship rituals* (*nusukī*), and for both it has been said in the next verse (6: 163): *Thus have I been bidden*, while it concludes with these words: *and I am the foremost of those who submit themselves [to Allah]*. This means that the injunction is not specific to the holy Prophet, but is for every Muslim man and woman who bows his or her head in submission to the will of the Lord.

This is the reason why the holy Prophet, may Allah bless him and give him peace, stressed that every financially capable Muslim should sacrifice an animal on Eid al-Adha. This is what we know from various hadiths as well. Our master the Messenger of Allah, may Allah bless him and give him peace, said:

مَن كَانَ لهُ يَسَارٌ فَلَم يُضَحِّ فَلَا يَقرَبَنَّ مُصَلاَّنَا.

> Whoever could have but did not sacrifice, then he should not even come near to the place of our prayer.
> (Narrated by Abū Hurayrah, *Aḥkām al- Qur'ān*, al-Jaṣṣāṣ, vol. 3, p. 248)

اِنَّ اَوَّلَ نُسُكِنَا فِى يومِنَا هٰذا اَن نَبدأ بِالصَّلوٰة ثُمَّ نَرجِعَ فَنَنحَر. فَمَن فَعَلَ ذٰلِك فَقَد وَافَقَ سُنَّتَنا.

> Our first ritual worship on this day of ours [Eid al-Adha] is that we begin with *ṣalāh*, then return [home] and offer sacrifice. Whoever does that has followed our Tradition.
> (Bukhārī, Muslim and Aḥmad)

مَن ذَبَحَ قَبلَ الصَّلوٰةِ فَاِنَّمَا يَذبَحُ لِنَفسه وَمَن ذَبَحَ بَعدَ الصَّلوٰة فَقَدتَمَّ نُسُكهُ وَاَصَابَ سُنَّة المُسلِمِين.

> He who slaughtered [the sacrificial animal] before prayer, then his act is for his own self, but one who slaughtered after prayer, his sacrificial rite was complete and he observed the tradition of Muslims correctly.
> (Bukhārī and Muslim)

The Divine injunctions about blood sacrifice thus are confirmed in a crystal clear manner by the Book of God. These are further reaffirmed in the Prophetic traditions, thereby leaving no room for any doubt or misgiving, nor any excuse for further elaboration or re-interpretation. Unfortunately, however, the group that claims to be in the vanguard of those who firmly believe in the holy Qur'an has the audacity to think differently and misinterpret the injunctions to suit their purpose. However, their posture can only be called a blatant distortion of the holy Qur'an. The Qur'ān enjoins something, but, while claiming to be believers, they opt to misinterpret it on avowedly rational and practical grounds. The Supreme Lord declares: *There is a blessing for you in this* (*lakum fīhā khayr*), yet they call animal sacrifice a wasteful exercise. The Qur'an pronounces something as being *among the symbols from God* and prescribed by the Lord Himself, but they prefer to borrow from the Western orientalist lexicon to call it a pagan custom. This is nothing but a sign of ignorance of the worst kind.

Among the innumerable living miracles of the holy Qur'an is that it responds with convincing answers to the misgivings that might have arisen in the past or may arise in the future regarding its injunctions. Let us now see what the Book of God does say about various reservations expressed against the act of sacrifice.

During the pre-Islamic days of Jāhiliyyah, altars were erected to offer blood sacrifice to deities of all sorts and the pagans of Makkah invoked their support and assistance in every mundane matter. That was not the hallowed practice of these pagans alone, but also the polytheists of India, Iran, Egypt, Rome and elsewhere, who raised altars and temples to slaughter animals and even human beings in the name of their gods and goddesses. Even the otherwise monotheistic Jews were prone to indulge in such pagan practices and repeatedly went with their offerings and sacrifices to the altars of various idols, for which they were also frequently censored by the apostles of the Old Testament. There is a reference in the holy Qur'an as well to these pagan rites and rituals of the *jāhilī* period:

وَجَعَلُواْ لِلَّهِ مِمَّا ذَرَأَ مِنَ ٱلْحَرْثِ وَٱلْأَنْعَٰمِ نَصِيبًا فَقَالُواْ هَٰذَا لِلَّهِ بِزَعْمِهِمْ وَهَٰذَا لِشُرَكَآئِنَا ... ﴿١٣٦﴾

They assign to Allah a portion out of the produce and cattle that He has created, saying out of their fancy: 'This is for Allah' – so they deem – 'and this is for the associates [of Allah] whom we have contrived.'

(*al-An'ām* 6: 136)

وَقَالُواْ هَٰذِهِۦٓ أَنْعَٰمٌ وَحَرْثٌ حِجْرٌ لَّا يَطْعَمُهَآ إِلَّا مَن نَّشَآءُ بِزَعْمِهِمْ وَأَنْعَٰمٌ حُرِّمَتْ ظُهُورُهَا وَأَنْعَٰمٌ
لَّا يَذْكُرُونَ ٱسْمَ ٱللَّهِ عَلَيْهَا ٱفْتِرَآءً عَلَيْهِ ... ﴿١٣٨﴾

They say: 'These animals and these crops are sacrosanct: none may eat of them save those whom we will' – imposing interdictions of their own contriving. And they declare that it is forbidden to burden the backs of certain cattle, and these are the cattle over which they do not pronounce the name of Allah. All these are fabrications against Allah.

(*al-An'ām* 6: 138)

As the book of eternal and universal guidance for mankind, the holy Qur'an changed the course of all forms of worship and rituals of worship and offerings from other than God to God alone. It commanded the believers that unlike the infidels they are to bow and prostrate in humility and offer sacrifices only to the One and Only God and that they should always proclaim the following the verses from *Sūrah al-An'ām* 6: 162–163 cited above: *Say: 'Surely my Prayer, my service of sacrifice....*

The infidels pronounced the names of their deities on their sacrificial animals. The believers were ordered never to pronounce any name other than Allah's, Most Glorified and Exalted is He, while slaughtering their cattle. The unbelievers left their animals free in the name of their idols and took no work or benefit from them, as though their freed bulls and cows had become idols themselves. The Muslims were told to take normal benefits from their animals until these were sacrificed in the name of the Lord:

لَكُمْ فِيهَا مَنَـٰفِعُ إِلَىٰٓ أَجَلٍ مُّسَمًّى ... ﴿٣٣﴾

You may derive benefit [from sacrificial animals] until an appointed time.

(*al-Ḥajj* 22: 33)

... فَإِذَا وَجَبَتْ جُنُوبُهَا فَكُلُوا۟ مِنْهَا وَأَطْعِمُوا۟ ٱلْقَانِعَ وَٱلْمُعْتَرَّ ... ﴿٣٦﴾

And when they fall down on their sides [after they are slaughtered], eat and also feed them who do not ask and those who ask.

(*al-Ḥajj* 22: 36).

It was then proclaimed in unequivocal terms:

لَن يَنَالَ ٱللَّهَ لُحُومُهَا وَلَا دِمَآؤُهَا وَلَـٰكِن يَنَالُهُ ٱلتَّقْوَىٰ مِنكُمْ ... ﴿٣٧﴾

Neither their flesh reaches Allah nor their blood; it is your piety that reaches Him.

(*al-Ḥajj* 22: 37)

Anyone with even a minimum level of insight into the legislative wisdom of the Islamic Shariah will have no difficulty in understanding how effective and powerful the method applied by the Divine Law is in eliminating once and forever the idolatrous rites and rituals of the pagan days. There could have been no other way more naturally effective in this than dedicating all civilized forms and types of worship, prevalent among the world's polytheist communities, exclusively to the One and Only God, and banning them forever from [the worship of] any other deity. But for this measure, the world could never have witnessed the blossoming of *tawḥīd* in acts of worship and the unity of faith.

The act of sacrifice has yet another significant aspect that is elucidated in the holy Qur'an. There has always been yet another category of people, whose number may now be on the rise, to whom it is simply obsolete to believe in God and if they do so due to rational imperatives it is like accepting a mathematical formula. Unfortunately, these people do not realize that every material gain that accrues to them, the produce they get from the soil to sustain them, the riches they reap from the available resources, the livestock and cattle herds placed at their disposal to their immense benefit, none of these is of their own creation or due to any personal privilege of theirs, nor are they their real owners. Everything human beings possess is a gift from God, a reward from the Lord. It can easily be noticed that the state of indifference from which such people suffer causes them much damage spiritually, morally and materially. As a cure and a preventive measure, Allah Most Exalted has prescribed certain acts of worship, which include *zakāh* on wealth and agricultural produce and sacrifice of animals from the livestock in one's possession or acquired from the market. We have also been ordered to do such acts in His name to remind us that we are not masters of what we have but are merely its custodians and so are not free to dispose it at will.

Islamic *ʿibādāt* keep impressing upon us the fact that we have been blessed with things – none due to our personal privilege but entirely because of the munificence of our Lord. Therefore, we will always have to take His pleasure into consideration while making use of His bounties. The following Qur'anic verses make a fine reference to this fact:

وَهُوَ ٱلَّذِىٓ أَنشَأَ جَنَّـٰتٍ مَّعْرُوشَـٰتٍ وَغَيْرَ مَعْرُوشَـٰتٍ وَٱلنَّخْلَ وَٱلزَّرْعَ مُخْتَلِفًا أُكُلُهُۥ وَٱلزَّيْتُونَ وَٱلرُّمَّانَ
مُتَشَـٰبِهًا وَغَيْرَ مُتَشَـٰبِهٍ ۚ كُلُوا۟ مِن ثَمَرِهِۦٓ إِذَآ أَثْمَرَ وَءَاتُوا۟ حَقَّهُۥ يَوْمَ حَصَادِهِۦ ۖ وَلَا تُسْرِفُوٓا۟ ۚ إِنَّهُۥ لَا يُحِبُّ ٱلْمُسْرِفِينَ ١٤١
وَمِنَ ٱلْأَنْعَـٰمِ حَمُولَةً وَفَرْشًا ۚ كُلُوا۟ مِمَّا رَزَقَكُمُ ٱللَّهُ وَلَا تَتَّبِعُوا۟ خُطُوَٰتِ ٱلشَّيْطَـٰنِ ۚ إِنَّهُۥ لَكُمْ عَدُوٌّ مُّبِينٌ ١٤٢

It is He who has brought into being gardens – the trellised and untrellised – and the palm trees, and crops, all varying in taste, and the olive and pomegranates, all resembling one another and yet so different. Eat of their fruits when they come to fruition and pay His due on the day of harvesting, and do not exceed the proper limits, for He does not love those who exceed the proper limits. And of the cattle [He has made] some for burden, and some whose flesh you eat and whose skins and hair you use to spread on the ground. Eat of the sustenance that Allah has provided you and do not follow in the footsteps of Satan, for surely he is your open enemy.

(*al-An'ām* 6: 141–142)

وَلِكُلِّ أُمَّةٍ جَعَلْنَا مَنسَكًا لِّيَذْكُرُوا۟ ٱسْمَ ٱللَّهِ عَلَىٰ مَا رَزَقَهُم مِّنۢ بَهِيمَةِ ٱلْأَنْعَٰمِ ۗ فَإِلَٰهُكُمْ إِلَٰهٌ وَٰحِدٌ فَلَهُۥٓ
أَسْلِمُوا۟ ۗ وَبَشِّرِ ٱلْمُخْبِتِينَ ﴿٣٤﴾

For every people We have laid down a ritual of sacrifice that they pronounce the name of Allah over the cattle He has provided them. Your Lord is One God; so submit yourselves to Him alone. And give, (O Prophet), glad tidings to those that humble themselves before Allah.

(*al-Ḥajj* 22: 34)

This is yet another aspect of the ritual of sacrifice's significance. Even a person of common intelligence can find out the difference between the immense benefits accruing to him through this and the relative disadvantages if he is prevented from discharging this Islamic duty in favour of saving his money for donation to a charitable institution, as pleaded for by some heretics.

14.3. The Economic Aspect of Animal Sacrifice

Now, let us examine the economic aspect of sacrificial ritual. The heretics opposed to Prophetic Tradition dismiss sacrifice as an extravaganza. On the other hand, the holy Qur'an tells us that the ritual of sacrifice carries benefits for us and that the meat of the sacrificial animal is not entirely for us to consume but also to *feed them who do not ask and those who ask* (*al-Ḥajj* 22: 36). In our own country, one will find millions of the poor and the needy, who have no proper source of sustenance and go without a meal for days, and who eagerly wait for Eid al-Adha for at least a few days of free and profusely available beef and mutton. Even a person of common intelligence cannot take this to be contrary to the principles of economics.[1]

Then, there are thousands of poor herdsmen and those who live by rearing livestock. Eid al-Adha offers them the best opportunity to get maximal financial benefit by selling their animals at profitable prices. Would it be a good service to the nation and its economy if the sacrifice is banned and these people were rendered jobless? Millions of low-income people also find Eid al-Adha an occasion of additional means to raise their income. They include men who slaughter animals and get paid handsomely, as are those who get their share of money from the sale of hides and skins. Would it be a wise step to deprive all of them from their guaranteed source of earnings simply because someone thinks it a wasteful exercise?

It is also surprising that a bunch of heretics champion the cause of national economy only when the money is required for a religious cause. Perhaps they think that welfare schemes and projects of charity can only be launched in the country when people stop spending once a year on sacrificial animals, and the moment this expenditure is banned there will be a downpour of resources for every charitable and public welfare scheme.

If one is really serious and sincere about his love for the poor, then he should at once come forward and close down thousands of cinema halls, brothels, night clubs and dens of moral corruption in the country to save the huge amount thus squandered by our profligacy, not annually, but daily on their ungainly, unhealthy, and extremely wasteful extravaganza. Such a well-meaning person must also make it binding on the affluent to divert their income to public welfare needs. Instead of trying to destroy the institution of sacrifice, why can't we patronize and promote the institution of *zakāh,* as that alone can generate the revenue required to meet the essential needs of public welfare.

To conclude, I would like to add that once Muslims are made to think in term of material gains alone and are brainwashed to stop investing in religious events of public welfare, the matter would then not stop with the banning of Eid al-Adha alone. Somebody might next propose that instead of spending millions of rupees annually on the hajj, the utility of which he is unable to comprehend,

---

[1] The economic system of Islam is welfare-oriented. It seeks to create a just social order where the poor and indigent get their due without even asking for it. The ritual of sacrifice is just one of its aspects. Among the five pillars of Islam, the mandatory system of *zakāh* lays the foundations of a polity where it is incumbent upon the rich to share their affluence with the needy. It is the magnanimity inherent in Islamic social justice that the poor and the rich enjoy equal status and neither the affluent is allowed by society to grow filthy rich nor are the indigent allowed to live perpetually on alms. — Editor.

the amount should be saved to open a commercial bank. (*Tarjumān al-Qur'ān*, July 1937)

14.3.1. *A Tract on Blood Sacrifice Reviewed*

As my article on the question of sacrifice in Islam was in press, I received a copy of the monthly *Iblāgh* of Amritsar in which Mr. Arshi Amritsari had contributed his 'research work' on the subject. Although many of his arguments against the institution of sacrifice have already been dealt with in my earlier article, I would like to review this piece of 'research' in more detail.

The writer starts his paper with a quotation from the *Encyclopedia Britannica* to tell us how *homo sapiens* viewed the act of sacrifice in the earliest of times; on what set of dogmas sacrificial rituals were based on in ancient Rome and Greece; among the Semitic religions, under what pretext the Jews retained pagan practice; what the Jewish Rabbis and Greek philosophers believed about God and spirits; what were the sacrificial rites among the ancient Aryans, the peoples of Rome and Arabia; and how Christianity dispelled popular notions among all those pagan nations and introduced to humanity the 'wise concept' that a little charity to the poor is as good as offering a big sacrifice, and the bread and wine offered and taken at the Eucharist ceremony in the Christian Church is better than any sacrifice offered to the Lord.

The statements taken from the Gospel and mentioned in detail by the writer while introducing the subject do help to add to our knowledge. However, we fail to understand their relevance and significance in the context of the topic under discussion. To begin with, the entire Gospel quotation is misplaced, simply because the issue in question is whether the act of sacrifice has been enjoined upon us as Muslims by Allah Most Exalated and His holy Prophet or not? If it is established that no such injunction exists from the Lord and His Prophet, then the testimony of the *Encyclopedia Britannica* is simply uncalled for. However, if it is confirmed that sacrifice is an Islamic tradition on the orders of Allah and His Messenger, then it is then binding on all Muslims, regardless of what any book or author may say. Our allegiance to Islam has never been nor can it ever be subject to any approval and reaffirmation by world 'encyclopedias' or from any other quarter.

Moreover, it is extremely surprising that those who claim to be missionaries of the Qur'an with their slogan being 'We follow nothing but the Book of God' should revert to a European source to understand an Islamic subject. If that was intended to throw light on the history of sacrifice and the pagan practices of *jāhilī* days, enough material was available on the subject in the Qur'an itself. This would have also helped the author to understand and elucidate the difference between the blood sacrifice of the days of ignorance and that of Islam.

It is no less surprising too that the few self-styled champions of the Book of God summarily reject as 'unreliable' the testimony of the much-celebrated and universally-acknowledged books of Prophetic Tradition such as the *Ṣāḥīḥ* of Bukhārī, the *Ṣāḥīḥ* of Muslim, the *Muwaṭṭa'* of Imam Mālik and so on, in spite of the universal consensus of Muslim scholars, theologians, jurists and researchers about their authenticity. On the other hand, it is difficult to understand on what basis the statements coming from Western sources about ancient peoples and civilizations of Rome, Greece, Egypt, the Aryan and Semitic races, etc. conform to the parameters of veracity of those 'scholars'. The factual position is that the ancient peoples and civilizations existed in the 'dark ages' thousands of years ago, much before the glorious era of the holy Prophet, may Allah bless him and give him peace. Whatever research material is available on them today comes nowhere near in veracity to the authentic data about the holy Prophet's life history, which were scientifically recorded and documented in hadiths and the books of Sīrah by generations after generations of Companions, Followers, scholars of Hadith (*nuḥaddithūn*), and renowned biographers. The sources upon which Mr Arshi relies in his 'scholarly discourse' on ancient civilizations and peoples, even the most authentic of these are nowhere nearer in reliability to the *ḍa'īf* category of traditions, narrated by Ibn Majah, Ḥākim and Bayhaqī.[2] Relying upon the scientifically substandard and unreliable sources and taking the liberty of transmitting to us the dogmas and beliefs of people lost in the hoary past, the writer is hardly justified in denying us the right to narrate what the Prophet of Islam, may Allah bless him and give him peace, did or said in a certain situation, or regarding a particular issue and that too on the authority of the scientifically-recorded traditions.

According to the conclusion, which the author of the 'research paper' has based on the material he gathered from the *Encyclopaedia Britannica*, 'the progress of civilization has exposed the undesirability of sacrifice'. The sentence seeks to convey perhaps nothing more than total aversion to a sacred Islamic ritual. Therefore, let us see how the supreme Lord has conveyed to us the significance of blood sacrifice and how much good it has for us the Muslims:

---

[2] The Prophetic tradition that the *muḥaddithūn* categorize as 'weak' (*ḍa'īf*) is not because of its 'questionable authenticity', but only due to a missing link in the chain of narrators (an essential criterion of *isnād* or ascription through a chain of narrators). Nevertheless, the authenticity of such traditions is not in the least questionable, although not as strong as that of the *ṣāḥīḥ* or *ḥasan* hadiths (or those with uninterrupted chains of narrators). — Editor.

وَٱلْبُدْنَ جَعَلْنَٰهَا لَكُم مِّن شَعَٰٓئِرِ ٱللَّهِ لَكُمْ فِيهَا خَيْرٌ فَٱذْكُرُوا۟ ٱسْمَ ٱللَّهِ عَلَيْهَا صَوَآفَّ فَإِذَا وَجَبَتْ
جُنُوبُهَا فَكُلُوا۟ مِنْهَا وَأَطْعِمُوا۟ ٱلْقَانِعَ وَٱلْمُعْتَرَّ كَذَٰلِكَ سَخَّرْنَٰهَا لَكُمْ لَعَلَّكُمْ تَشْكُرُونَ ﴿٣٦﴾

We have appointed sacrificial camels among the symbols of [devotion to] Allah. There is much good in them for you. So make them stand [at the time of sacrifice] and pronounce the name of Allah over them, and when they fall down on their sides [after they are slaughtered], eat and also feed them who do not ask and those who ask. Thus have We subjected these animals that you may give thanks.

(*al-Ḥajj* 22: 36)

Even a man of common intelligence can note how Mr. Arshi's statement is in open conflict with the verse quoted above. The ritual that has been described by the Lord as being *among the symbols* of Allah and an act of charity has been dismissed by the author as an 'undesirable' legacy of the pagan past. Basic questions that automatically arise from what he has sought to covey are as follows: Does the act of sacrifice have the sanction of the holy Qur'an, as evident from the above verse? If the Qur'an attributes to it even the minimum level of virtue and goodness, can the Book of God be absolved of the charge of belonging to the time when human civilization had not progressed much? Would it then be fit for this glorious book of *guidance unto mankind* to be declared as the Book of God? Is the writer of the tract not wittingly or unwittingly guilty of trying to reduce it to the level of a product of some semi-civilized brain of the sixth century AD? May Allah Most Glorified and Exalted forgive us for such unabashed blasphemy!

Questions like these are bound to crop up when someone gives precedence to an *Encyclopaedia* or any book of reference over the hallowed Qur'anic text. The very starting point of Mr Arshi's crusade against blood sacrifice led him to an entirely different course. The logical outcome of this great slip would have been his refusal to accept the holy Qur'an as the Book of God. Yet, contrary to his misguided reason, his intuition prevented him from falling headlong into the ditch of apostasy and he could remain content with misinterpreting the Qur'anic text.

A man's position is painfully paradoxical when he seeks to remain within the ambit of a particular system while practically deviating from it on intellectual and ideological levels. In such an eventuality everything of that system appears to him unsuited to his temperament and he tries to untie each and every thread of its fabric to reweave it on lines set by his whims. However, his dilemma is that he is keen to keep his designs secret and let nobody discover them. Therefore, at each and every step, he has to use the tools of misinterpretation, distortion, deception, verbosity and wordplay. It is sad to say that the author of the article in question faces a similar dilemma. His views on sacrifice are opposed to the Islamic standpoint. According to the holy Qur'an, the Sunnah of the holy Prophet, the exegeses and commentaries of the Book of God, the books of Islamic jurisprudence and the consensus of the Muslim scholars and jurists, the sacrifice ritual of Eid al-Adha is part of the Islamic credo. It is an act of virtue and goodness, the performance of which has been enjoined upon Muslims and a set of rules and regulations have been framed for it. Thus, he is left with no option but either to accept what has clearly been stated by the holy Qur'an, corroborated further by the Sunnah and reconfirmed by the consensus of Muslim jurists and scholars, or to reject it point blank saying that he believes neither in the holy Qur'an, nor in the Sunnah of the holy Prophet and may therefore be taken as an unbeliever.

Quoted below are just two specimens of Mr Arshi's attempted intellectual distortion of the holy Qur'an with the hope that it may help him and his ilk to correct their misperceptions and return to the right path. The Qur'an mentions in clear terms the memorable incident of Prophet Abraham's vision, according to which he saw in his dream as slaughtering his only son Ismāʿīl and, in total submission to the Lord's command, he proceeded to sacrifice his son. When he was ready to do so, the Most-Merciful Lord called out to him:

وَنَـٰدَيْنَـٰهُ أَن يَـٰٓإِبْرَٰهِيمُ ۝ قَدْ صَدَّقْتَ ٱلرُّءْيَآ ۚ إِنَّا كَذَٰلِكَ نَجْزِى ٱلْمُحْسِنِينَ ۝

We called out to him: 'O Abraham, you have indeed fulfilled your dream. Thus do We reward the doers of good.'

(*al-Ṣāffāt* 37: 104–105)

The verses that follow extol the remarkable incident further:

إِنَّ هَـٰذَا لَهُوَ ٱلْبَلَـٰٓؤُا۟ ٱلْمُبِينُ ۝ وَفَدَيْنَـٰهُ بِذِبْحٍ عَظِيمٍ ۝ وَتَرَكْنَا عَلَيْهِ فِى ٱلْـَٔاخِرِينَ ۝ سَلَـٰمٌ عَلَىٰٓ إِبْرَٰهِيمَ ۝

This was indeed a plain trial. And We ransomed him with a mighty sacrifice, and We preserved for him a good name among posterity. Peace be upon Abraham.

(*al-Ṣāffāt* 37: 106–109)

It is evident from the above verses that Allah Most Exalted desired to test His intimate friend (*khalīl*). Instead of directly commanding him to sacrifice his son in His name, He alluded to it through a vision. The love the Prophet Abraham, may Allah's peace be upon him, had for Allah superseded the love of all earthly things, including for his own son, and so he did not wait for a direct command through revelation but got ready to act upon what he saw in his dream. He did so because he knew that a Prophet's dream was unlike that of an ordinary mortal and the vision he had while sleeping could not be dismissed as mere hallucination. That was the real sacrifice, and when it was actually fulfilled the Lord prevented His intimate friend from shedding his son's blood and ransomed him with 'a mighty sacrifice'. As one thinks of it, one comes to the conclusion that this was an extraordinary incident – a practical demonstration of this spirit of the following verse:

لَن تَنَالُوا۟ ٱلْبِرَّ حَتَّىٰ تُنفِقُوا۟ مِمَّا تُحِبُّونَ ...

> *You shall not attain righteousness until you spend [for the sake of Allah] out of what you love.*
>
> (*Āl ʿImrān* 3: 92)

Now let us demonstrate how this glorious Qur'anic narrative of extraordinary significance has been distorted by Mr Arshi and his group to serve their purpose. According to their misinterpretation, the Prophet Abraham, may Allah's be upon him, was actually mistaken and understood the meaning of his dream incorrectly. In the 'ecstasy of the wine of love', the great Prophet, they believe, misunderstood the meaning of his own dream and went out to slaughter his son for the sake of God, whereas the Divine purpose was that he should have no worldly designs for his son and should dedicate him entirely to the service of the Divine mission. Thus, when he was about to commit the 'great mistake', he was warned by God, which led to the 'mighty sacrifice', i.e. Ismāʿīl's dedication in the service of the Divine mission. However, the greatest hurdle in the way of this misinterpretation is the reaffirmation by the Lord that the Prophet Abraham had *indeed fulfilled* his dream. The author of the tract tried to remove that hurdle through yet another distortion. He crudely mistranslates 37: 105 that acclaims the Prophet Abraham's unparalleled act of love as: 'You sought to fulfil the vision.' He did not bother to pause for a moment and see how his insolent attempt rendered the rest of the verse meaningless, in which the Lord solemnly promises: *Thus do We reward the doers of good.*

Through wilful distortions like these we can see how the avenues of proper understanding of the holy Qur'an are blocked in matters of great moral and religious significance. The unique historical event that stands out as the Prophet

Abraham's most glorious achievement was thus reduced to a blunder, and the quality meant to enable the believers to understand the true spirit of Islam – total submission to the will of God – and generate within them a penchant for selflessness and sacrifice was rendered absolutely meaningless.

Let us now take note of yet another distortion of Mr Arshi's. Allah Most Blessed and Exalted says:

وَلِكُلِّ أُمَّةٍ جَعَلْنَا مَنسَكًا لِّيَذْكُرُوا۟ ٱسْمَ ٱللَّهِ عَلَىٰ مَا رَزَقَهُم مِّنۢ بَهِيمَةِ ٱلْأَنْعَـٰمِ ۗ ... ﴿٣٤﴾

For every people We have laid down a ritual of sacrifice that they pronounce the name of Allah over the cattle He has provided them.
(*al-Ḥajj* 22: 34)

There can be hardly any doubt about the meaning of this verse, which tells us in unequivocal terms that blood sacrifice is an act of worship and it has not been prescribed by any human being but by the Lord Himself. However, Mr Arshi mistranslates the verse: 'See, how We have prescribed for every people the way of worship that they may celebrate the name of God while slaughtering the domestic animals We gifted to them'. This is how the Qur'anic term *mansak*, which means a solemn 'ritual of sacrifice', has been distorted and reduced to denote the daily practice of animal slaughter, on which Muslim butchers routinely recite the invocation *Allāhu akbar*. From such distortions, we come to realize how immensely blessed the Muslim *ummah* has been by the All-Merciful Lord, Who took upon Himself to preserve the holy Qur'an in letter and spirit. Had it not been so, self-serving and misguided 'scholars' might have succeeded in bringing out a distorted version of the Book on the basis of the material they have gathered from the otherwise high-sounding foreign sources.

Distortions like these also betray a lack of understanding or bias in a section of our 'scholars' against established Islamic norms and values. The sole purpose of their writings is apparently to mislead innocent readers who do not have direct access to the commentaries of the holy Qur'an or the books of Hadith or jurisprudence. Such wilful distortion in matters of religious significance reflect nothing but intellectual impoverishment and dishonesty and an incorrigibly twisted frame of mind. (*Tarjumān al-Qur'ān*, January 1938)

15 *Ṣawm* and Self Restraint

One of the many spiritual, social and ethical benefits of *ṣawm* is that it injects within the human being the power of self-restraint. In order to fully comprehend this, let us first know what self-restraint means and then try to understand the type of self-restraint Islam demands and finally see how *ṣawm* develops this potential.

The quality of self-restraint means that a man's 'self' should be in full command over his body and physical potential. His grip on his personal desire and emotion should be so strong so as to keep them totally under his control. The self's status in the human body is the same as that of a sovereign for the state. The body and its limbs are the tools of the self. All his physical and intellectual capabilities are there to serve the self. The human psyche's position is nothing beyond that of an agent's. It submits its pleas concerning its desires and emotions to the human self. It is up to the self to decide how to use and to what end the available tools and potential and which one of the psyche's pleas to approve and which ones to disapprove. If the self is so weak that it cannot have its way in its body's kingdom and instead submits meekly to its psyche's demands and personal whims, it could only signify the helplessness of the self and the loss of its control over its kingdom. It is like a horseman who instead of riding the horse lets the horse ride over him. Such a weak person cannot lead a successful life in this world. Those who leave their footprints on the sands of time are they who succeed in gaining full command over their physical potential, who master their personal desires, whims, emotions and aspirations and are not enslaved by them, who are endowed with strong willpower and firm resolve.

However, there is a very big difference between the self that becomes its own lord and master and the self that follows the dictates of its Lord and Master like His true subject. For a meaningful and successful life, it is necessary for the self to be controlled. The self that gets out of control and ignores even the authority of its supreme Sovereign has little regard for the dictates of any law governing human manners and morals. Nor does it care much for its accountability of the Hereafter. Eventually such a self gathers all powers of the body and the psyche to itself to emerge as a hot-headed and ruthless despot, a Pharaoh, a Nimrod, a Hitler, a Mussolini and the like. Islam is for inculcating the spirit of self-restraint in human beings so that they may surrender the power of their selves entirely to their Lord and Creator, and make allegiance to the Divine law the goal of their lives, considering themselves accountable to Him for their words and deeds. Such a *muslim* (i.e. totally subservient to the Lord's will) and *mu'min* (i.e. faithful and firmly believing) self is expected to have full command over its body and its physical, emotional and intellectual potential so it can grow as a potent force for reform and rejuvenation in the world. According to the Islamic viewpoint, this is the meaning and connotation of self-restraint. Now, let us see how *ṣawm* generates this potential in human beings.

When we look at the basic demands of the human body and the self, we notice that three of them are fundamental in nature and the most powerful of them all. The first is the demand for food on which life depends for survival. The second is the urge for sex, which is the sole means for self-preservation. The third basic demand is that of rest, essential to regaining lost energies. If these demands are kept well within their limits, they remain natural urges, but once they cross the limits of permissibility, a man is enslaved by his own self. Each of these three fundamental demands then multiplies into a series of unending demands pulling a man in different directions and away from his life's objectives and principles, and the dictates of his own conscience. Once the self becomes weaker under the control of such demands, the appetite for food turns the human being into the slave of his stomach, the surging desire for sex debases him to the lowest of the low, and the wish for leisure leaves him devoid of the will to work. Then he is no longer the sovereign of his body and psyche, but a subject to these and his task remains only to carry out their orders by fair means or foul.

Ṣawm takes these three fundamental demands of human psyche into the regimen of its routine and trains the self to control them. It tells the self, which has declared its faith in God, that the Lord has prohibited food and drink and any gratification of sexual desire even through lawful means from pre-dawn until sunset. *Ṣawm* also tells him that his Lord's pleasure lies in not letting tiredness and exhaustion overtake him in the evening after the day-long fast. Instead, He would like to see the believer line up for prayers at the mosque for a much longer period of time than in the days outside of Ramadan. When he retires to bed, he is cautioned against getting lost in sweet dreams as he is to wake up in the dead of night when his body wants him to remain in bed. That is the time for him to have *suḥūr*, the light meal in the latter part of the night that will provide his body with the energy needed for the rest of the day. These instructions are conveyed to him and then he is left to act accordingly.

No police force, secret agency or external pressure is brought to bear upon him, compelling his observance of these commands. There is no power on earth other than Allah Most Blessed and Exalted to monitor him in this respect, or to ensure that he carries out the Divine instructions in letter and spirit. If the self of the Lord's faithful subject is true to its faith and it has the will to control the animal instincts, it will then be capable of exercising the desired restraint according to the regulations prescribed for this blessed month.

This is not a one-day exercise. In fact, a single day is not enough for such drills. It is a thirty-day course, spread over 720 hours each year. The programme has been designed so that one has to get up from bed in the later part of the night to have *suḥūr,* stop eating and drinking from pre-dawn to sunset, break one's fast immediately after sunset, spend part of the night offering *tarāwīḥ* prayers and then repeat the same pattern the next day. Through this month-long exercise, the individual becomes fully trained in his allegiance and obedience to his Lord and how to rule over his own body and psyche. It is a programme that begins with the age of puberty and continues until death. A particular month has been earmarked for this during the year to revive the spirit of self-control, to strengthen the human self's grip over his psyche (or the mental faculties), and to create a collective spirit and a healthy social environment to promote righteousness in society.

The entire exercise is meant to enable a Muslim's self to regain control over its hunger, thirst, sexual desire and urge for leisure not only during the month of Ramadan, but also to let him retain this capability during the remaining eleven months of the year. By regaining control over the three fundamental and most frequent demands of human nature, the objective of this exercise is that a person becomes capable of controlling and checking all his feelings, sentiments, desires and aspirations, and be strong enough to make the best use of the God-given potential of his mind and body in the service of his Lord as long as he lives. Thus, he is trained to seek his Lord's pleasure through his quest for all that is good, to avoid all that is bad, and to keep in check his every desire and sentiment so that these do not cross the limits prescribed for them by his Lord. In this way, he is no longer at his psyche's mercy that can lead him this way or that. Instead, the reins of authority remain in his hands and he acts for the sake of the Almighty's pleasure as instructed by Him. His willpower is not now so weak that he feels incapable of resisting the demands of his body and ignoring what his Lord rules as being mandatory for him. He rules over the kingdom of his physical existence like a sovereign having full command over his subjects, assigning to them whatever task he may wish, as enjoined by his supreme Sovereign, the Lord and Master of the heavens and the earth. This is the potential *ṣawm* is intended to create and promote. Anyone who fails to achieve this capability unnecessarily inflicts upon himself hunger, thirst and nightly exertion.

This has been explained in depth by the holy Qur'an and the holy Prophet's traditions. Allah Most Exalted proclaims:

يَـٰٓأَيُّهَا ٱلَّذِينَ ءَامَنُوا۟ كُتِبَ عَلَيْكُمُ ٱلصِّيَامُ كَمَا كُتِبَ عَلَى ٱلَّذِينَ مِن قَبْلِكُمْ لَعَلَّكُمْ تَتَّقُونَ ﴿١٨٣﴾

> *Believers! Fasting is enjoined upon you, as it was enjoined upon those before you, that you become God-fearing.*
>
> (*al-Baqarah* 2: 183)

Our master the Messenger of Allah, may Allah bless him and give him peace, said:

> He who does not stop telling lies and acting upon them, God has no need for him to leave his food and his drink.
>
> (Bukhārī)

> There are many who fast, but get nothing out of it except thirst and hunger. And there are many who stay awake at night praying to the Lord, but get nothing from it other than sleeplessness.
>
> (Dārquṭnī)

(Radio Pakistan, 15 July 1948).

16 The Night of Acquittal from Sin (*Laylat al-Barā'ah*)

Laylat al-Barā'ah, or Shab-i-Barā'at as it is popularly termed in the Subcontinent, is generally celebrated by Muslims as a festival. Some rituals and fanfare are associated with it and the event is virtually akin to Muharram in this respect. However, factually speaking, it is no event at all. There is no sanction in either the holy Qur'an or the holy Prophet's Sunnah regarding what has come to be known as Laylat al-Barā'ah. It was neither observed by the holy Prophet's Companions nor subsequently by those who followed them amongst the luminaries of Islam and the Muslim *ummah.*

As we all know, Islam is not a 'religion' of fanfare and festivities. It is the religion of truth, the religion of nature, in which nothing conflicts with reason. It relieves man of the enslavement of unnecessary rites and rituals, customary extravaganzas and worthless preoccupations that entail wastage of time, energy and money. Instead, it invites the attention of its followers to the concrete facts of life and seeks to involve them in preoccupations that may lead to their well-being in this world and the Hereafter. Such a religion cannot be expected to earmark a full day every year to the preparation of a certain type of sweet dish or for fireworks. Moreover, Islam as a way of life can never approve of an activity that unnecessarily costs a person his time and money and often so many precious lives. Had such rites and rituals been there during the days of the holy Prophet, he would have definitely ordered them to stop. After all he did ban many such frivolous pastimes of the pre-Islamic days.

When we try to find any authentic reference about the observance of a particular night in the month of Sha'bān as the Night of Salvation or Acquittal from Sin, we discover neither any Qur'anic injunction nor a Prophetic Tradition in this context. According to the only hadith available to us, the Mother of the Faithful Sayyidah 'Ā'ishah Ṣiddīqah once got up in the middle of the night of 15 Sha'bān and did not find the holy Prophet at home. Worried, she set out to look for him and finally discovered him at the cemetery al-Baqī' in Madinah. On her enquiry, the holy Prophet, may Allah bless him and give him peace, told her that it was the night when Allah Most Glorified and Exalted specially focused His blessings on the earth and pardoned the sins of human beings, be they as enormous in number as the wool on the Kalb tribe's sheep.

Imam Tirmidhī, an eminent and well-known traditionist, has declared the narration weak (*ḍaʿīf*), because according to his research its chain of narrators does not reach up to Sayyidah ʿĀ'ishah. According to some other traditions, found in less authentic compilations, everything pertaining to life and death and human fate is decided on this so-called Night of Acquittal from Sin. According to the established parameters of the science of Prophetic Tradition (*ʿilm al-ḥadīth*), the above-mentioned narrations on this are weak and the sequence of their narrators is broken. Therefore, we do not find them in the more authentic and well-revered compilations, like those of Imam Bukhārī, Imam Muslim, Imam Mālik and others. Even if we take them as authentic, what we may at best deduce from these traditions is that the night is meant for offering prayers individually and seeking God's pardon from sins. Nonetheless, there is nothing in them to suggest that the night of 15 Shaʿbān has been declared an occasion to celebrate as we do or that collective worship has been prescribed for the community on that night.

What we come to know from the well-established traditions of the holy Prophet, available in *Ṣaḥīḥ al-Bukhārī*, *Ṣaḥīḥ Muslim*, or the *Muwaṭṭa'* of Imam Mālik and other authentic collections, is that the Prophet of God, may Allah bless him and give him peace, especially used the month of Shaʿbān to prepare for the holy month of Ramadan. A new fervour for gaining blessings could be noticed in him as the holy month came nearer. Ramadan is the month when Allah Most Glorified and Exalted elevated our master the Messenger of Allah as His Prophet. The revelation of the holy Qur'an began in this month. This is why the holy Prophet devoted himself to the Lord's worship to an extraordinary degree not just during Ramadan but in the preceding month of Shaʿbān. The Mothers of the Faithful the Ladies ʿĀ'ishah and Umm Salamah reported that in the eleven months before Ramadan it was only during Shaʿbān that the holy Prophet, may Allah bless him and give him peace, spent about the whole month fasting. However, this practice was exclusive to the Prophet alone because of his deep spiritual bond with the 'month of Qur'an'. As for Muslims in general, he advised them not to fast during the second half of Shaʿbān lest it became common practice and assumed the status of an obligatory ritual before Ramadan, thus imposing an unnecessary burden on them, unsanctioned by their Lord.

Islam has taken special care not to let anyone impose upon something additional upon himself that God has not enjoined. It permits no self-made custom, rite, ritual or collective activity to gain the status of a mandatory act of worship that people must observe. God alone knows what is best for His servants to observe and to what extent something has to be practised and followed. If we invent our own set of rituals, transgress the limits prescribed by Him and start to observe them as something obligatory, we will unnecessarily make our lives more difficult. Earlier nations committed the same folly of inflicting on themselves queer sets of rites, rituals and customs, which subsequently enveloped them like a cocoon and became more important to them than the duties made obligatory by their Lord. The holy Qur'an likens such self-imposed customs and rituals to iron chains, and the great message of the holy Prophet enjoins us to break these chains and to set humanity free from all unnecessary bondage. This is why the Islamic Shariah has prescribed a set of very easy and simple acts of worship and has done away with all cumbersome rites and rituals. There are no festivals in Islam other than Eid al-Fitr and Eid al-Adha, no pilgrimage other than hajj, and no mandatory offerings other than *zakāh*. According to the golden principles of Islam, nobody has the right either to add to or to reduce the obligatory duties that the Lord has determined once and for all.

In the early days of Islam, those who were aware of the spirit and temperament of the Islamic Shariah strictly observed this principle. They very carefully refrained from inventing rites and rituals in the name of religion. They also cut at the roots of things that were emerging as potential rituals. They knew that a practice started with true sincerity in the beginning as a thing of virtue and reward in the Hereafter would gradually gain in importance over the customary acts of worship sanctioned by Prophetic Tradition (Sunnah, plural *sunan*), then over essential (*wājib*) and eventually over obligatory duties (*farā'iḍ*). With the passage of time, the ignorant would often turn an otherwise healthy practice into a highly ignoble rite by mixing unhealthy items with the originally innocuous thing of 'virtue'. Such rites and customs eventually become a curse for society and a great obstacle in the way of social progress and development. This is the reason why Muslim jurists and the early scholars took extreme precaution against the addition of anything new to the duties enjoined by the Shariah. There has been a consensus among them on the following fundamental principle:

كُلُّ مُحْدَثَةٍ فِى الدِّينِ بِدعَةٌ، وَ كُلُّ بِدعَةٍ ضَلَالَةٌ، وَكُلُّ ضَلَالَةٍ فِى النَّارِ.

> To introduce anything extraneous into religion is innovation (*bid'ah*) and innovations are misguidance and misguidance leads to Hell.

Unfortunately, however, the centuries that followed witnessed extreme negligence, especially on part of the *ulema*, and Muslim societies gradually became entangled in a mishmash of self-made rites and rituals just like other world communities. One of the main reasons for this perversion was that the communities which subsequently embraced Islam were not given proper education and training in Islamic fundamentals, manners and morals. They entered Islam along with their age-old un-Islamic notions, customs and traditions. They had for centuries been used to a culture of fun and festivities, rites and rituals as though their religious life held no charm for them without these frivolous festivities. Instead of feeling relieved that Islam had freed them from the shackles of those cumbersome and unhealthy customs and traditions, their main concern became how to enchain themselves once again with the same shackles. That is how they retained some of the rites and rituals of the 'Age of Ignorance' by giving them a partial facelift to suit their new Islamic environment. Additionally, they invented some new ones to satisfy their *jāhilī* urge for fun and festivity.

Sadly enough, the role played by those claiming to be well grounded in Islamic learning was equally questionable. Instead of seeking refuge in the Qur'an and the Sunnah to have a better understanding of the social order that Islam has devised for man, they sought on one pretext or another to justify as Islamic the continuation of pre-Islamic customs or the adoption of new rites and rituals that they invented. They tried to blow out of all proportion even a slightest hint of support for their irreligious approach. Therefore, sincere efforts are needed by well-meaning religious scholars to relieve society of such self-inflicted customs and traditions and to liberate it from the outworn shackles of the past, from which Allah Most Exalted in His infinite mercy had freed the Muslim *ummah.* (Radio Pakistan, July 1948)

Appendix I: ʿ*Ibādah*–The Means as well as the Ends

The meaning and significance of ʿ*ibādah* in Islam has been explained in depth in the preceding pages. As an addendum to the discourse, the addition of some further explanatory notes of Sayyid Mawdūdī on the subject in his magnum opus *Tafhīm al-Qur'ān* would be beneficial. In his epoch-making exegesis, he describes how ʿ*ibādah* is not just the means to achieve proximity to Allah Most Blessed and Exalted, it is also the very objective that every believer must set in his heart to achieve. As an ʿ*abd* (bondsman) of his Lord, the sole purpose of his life is ʿ*ibādah*. An edited version of those notes is reproduced below. — Editor.

> *(O Prophet), it is We Who have revealed this Book to you with truth. So serve only Allah, consecrating your devotion to Him. Indeed, religion is exclusively devoted to Allah.*
>
> (*al-Zumar* 39: 2–3)

We have been asked to 'serve' Allah, consecrating our devotion to Him alone. It has been emphatically stressed that 'religion is entirely consecrated' to Allah and hence those who worship deities other than the One and Only God, considering them as means to bring the worshippers closer to the Almighty, are given to sheer lying. *Glory be to Him. He is Allah, the One, the Overpowering.*

The word ʿ*ibādah* in Arabic means obedience, allegiance, servitude, bondsmanship and unquestioning surrender to the will of the One Who is Supreme and to follow His dictates in all commands and prohibitions. By commanding us to serve Allah exclusively, it has been impressed upon us in these verses that this bondsmanship (ʿ*ibādah*) must be the sole objective of our life. The Lord needs no intermediary to reach Him, as to every human being He is *nearer than even his jugular vein.* Hence, all that is needed from us is our sincere devotion and consecration of our religion entirely to Him. There is none to share with Him in worship. This is best explained by the Prophetic Tradition (hadith), according to which a person asked the holy Prophet, may Allah bless him and give him peace: 'Often we spend in charity to also earn a good name in society. Can we expect reward from the Almighty on such spending?' The Prophet replied:

'Allah Most Exalted does not accept any deeds except those which have been exclusively dedicated to Him' (اِنَّ اللهَ تَعَالىٰ لَا يقبَلُ اِلاَّ مَن اَخلَصَ لَهُ). The holy Prophet then recited:

إِنَّآ أَنزَلْنَآ إِلَيْكَ ٱلْكِتَـٰبَ بِٱلْحَقِّ فَٱعْبُدِ ٱللَّهَ مُخْلِصًا لَّهُ ٱلدِّينَ ۝٢

(O Prophet), it is We Who have revealed this Book to you with truth. So serve only Allah, consecrating your devotion to Him.
(*al-Zumar* 39: 2) (*Tafhim al-Qur'ān*, vol. 4, nn. 3 and 4, pp. 353–6)

وَمَا خَلَقْتُ ٱلْجِنَّ وَٱلْإِنسَ إِلَّا لِيَعْبُدُونِ ۝٥٦ مَآ أُرِيدُ مِنْهُم مِّن رِّزْقٍ وَمَآ أُرِيدُ أَن يُطْعِمُونِ ۝٥٧ إِنَّ ٱللَّهَ هُوَ ٱلرَّزَّاقُ ذُو ٱلْقُوَّةِ ٱلْمَتِينُ ۝٥٨

I created the jinn and humans for nothing else but that they may serve Me; I desire from them no provision, nor do I want them to feed Me. Surely Allah is the Bestower of all provision, the Lord of all power, the Strong.

(*al-Dhāriyāt* 51: 56–58)

The point stressed here is that Allah has created man to serve Him to the exclusion of everyone else. Man should serve Him by virtue of the fact that He is man's Creator. Since Allah Most Blessed and Exalted alone is his Creator, what justification can there be for serving others? *ʿIbādah* has not been used here just to mean different acts of worship like *ṣalāh*, *ṣawm*, etc. The fact that the Lord created the jinn and humankind for nothing else but that they may serve Him obviously makes it incumbent upon them not only to worship Him alone, but also to shun all other allegiances and servitudes unless these are subservient to His allegiance and servitude. They must bow in humility before none but Him, obey nobody else's command but His, beg for favours from none but Him, inculcate the spirit of *taqwā* for no one else but Him, and follow no way of life other than the one revealed by Him to the Last of His prophets.

That Allah Most Exalted has mentioned only the jinn and humans for His service does not mean that the rest of his creatures are free to worship, obey, and be in service of whomsoever they please. Factually speaking, everything that exists in this universe, whether animate or inanimate, is eternally bound in an unbreakable bond of service to the Lord. However, the jinn and humans are the only two beings among his creatures to have been blessed with freedom of choice. They are free to obey or disobey their Lord and upon their correct exercise of this option depends their reward or punishment. Therefore, the right course of action for them is not to misuse this freedom and to remain faithfully in service of their Lord the Creator the way all other creatures, including their own physical frame, are obediently pursuing His path. (*Tafhīm al-Qur'ān*, vol. 5, nn. 53–54, pp. 155–6)

قُلْ يَـٰٓأَيُّهَا ٱلْكَـٰفِرُونَ ﴿١﴾ لَآ أَعْبُدُ مَا تَعْبُدُونَ ﴿٢﴾ وَلَآ أَنتُمْ عَـٰبِدُونَ مَآ أَعْبُدُ ﴿٣﴾ وَلَآ أَنَا۠ عَابِدٌ مَّا عَبَدتُّمْ ﴿٤﴾
وَلَآ أَنتُمْ عَـٰبِدُونَ مَآ أَعْبُدُ ﴿٥﴾ لَكُمْ دِينُكُمْ وَلِىَ دِينِ ﴿٦﴾

Say: 'O unbelievers! I do not worship those that you worship; neither do you worship Him Whom I worship; nor will I worship those whom you have worshipped; nor are you going to worship Him Whom I worship. To you is your religion, and to me, my religion.'

(*al-Kāfirūn*, 109: 1–6)

This chapter is a declaration of the eternal divide between those who believe in One God and His Apostle, our master Muhammad, the Messenger of Allah, may Allah bless him and give him peace, and those who are unbelievers and have opted to disdain Islam and the Prophet of Islam.

Addressed to those who refused to believe in the prophethood and teachings of the holy Prophet, the message contained in the chapter is universal: it is neither for the believers to worship those whom the unbelievers worshipped, nor did the unbelievers worship the One True God Whom the Prophet and his followers are bound to worship under all circumstances and in all times and conditions. The holy Prophet has been told to reject the unbelievers' worship because worshipping God alongside other deities does not constitute worship at all.

Thus, it has been reaffirmed once and for all that in matters of religion there can be nothing in common between the holy Prophet and his followers and those who follow the path of unbelief (*kufr*). (*Tafhīm al-Qur'ān*, vol. 6, nn. 1–2 and 5, pp. 503–9)

Appendix II: Sayyid Mawdūdī and *Taṣawwuf*

Before examining Sayyid Mawdūdī's approach to *taṣawwuf*, a brief overview of its origins and development is given below to place his views on the subject into some kind of context.

During the second and eighth centuries AH (the eighth to fourteen centuries CE), there emerged in the world of Islam a chain of great spiritual leaders and guides, with whom flourished the great Islamic revolutionary movement of *taṣawwuf*. The movement initially provided valuable spiritual support to the glorious struggle of the fighters for the cause of Allah (*mujāhidūn fi sabīl Allāh*), i.e. for the supremacy of Islam and its way of life. The seven-century history of *taṣawwuf* is marked by laudable achievements in the realm of character-building and the projection of the Islamic message and mission (*da'wah*), especially in areas that had freshly entered the benign fold of Islam. However, the movement could not sustain its true spirit and subsequently lost its way in almost becoming a hereditary system of pseudo-spiritualism. It became much more like the traditional 'mysticism' of other religions with its eyes set on material gains and socio-political interests. Let us have a brief overview of the origin and development of this movement.

The term *taṣawwuf* is one of the most misunderstood religious terms in Islamic literature. It is often translated as 'Islamic mysticism' and equated with asceticism and monasticism, which have no relevance to Islam at all, either in theory or in practice. Etymologically, words like *taṣawwuf*, *ṣūfi*, and al-Ṣūfiyyah are derivatives from the word *ṣūf*, which means 'wool'. Historically, the appellations *ṣūfi*, al-Ṣūfiyyah, and *taṣawwuf* are of later origin and find no presence in the Islamic lexicon of the holy Qur'an and the Prophetic traditions, or even in the enormous literature on Islam and the Islamic way of life produced during the glorious days of the Companions, the Followers, or the Followers of the Followers. Neither do we come across these terms in the books of Islamic law produced during the first and second centuries of the Hijrah.

The earliest eminent religious figure to whom various Sufi chains attribute their affiliation is Imam Abū Sa'īd al-Ḥasan al-Baṣrī (21–110 AH/642–728 CE). He was the son of Peroz, a Persian prisoner of war from the conquest of the

Battle of Maysān. Peroz later embraced Islam and was known as Abū al-Ḥasan. His mother Khayriyyah was also of Persian origin. Imam Ḥasan was blessed to have the honour of being brought up in the house of the Mother of the Believers, Umm Salamah, in which he rose to the highest pedestal of Islamic learning as a traditionist. He was a close friend of Caliph ʿUmar bin ʿAbd al-ʿAzīz (60–101 AH/680–720 CE) and during his rule served as the chief justice (*qāḍī*) of Basra in a voluntary capacity. Ḥasan al-Baṣrī was known for his piety and virtues as a traditionist (*muḥaddith*), and a missionary with a revolutionary spirit. He openly opposed the dynastic rule and the way of governance of the Umayyad Caliph Yazīd bin ʿAbd al-Mālik and the Governor of Iraq Ḥajjāj bin Yūsuf. However, he is not known to have established a Sufi chain or asked his disciples and followers, who were in the thousands, to follow a particular way of life other than those of the Companions, the Followers and other Islamic personalities. What he proposed through his sermons, addresses, and lifestyle was piety, simplicity, uprightness, and sincere devotion and dedication to Islam as a message and mission.

In later years, the earliest known Islamic preachers, whom their devotees now know by the title of Sufis, similarly lived an exemplary life of virtue, piety and simplicity. Nevertheless, they too are not known to have discarded any other form of clothing to don only the coarse clothes made of raw wool (*ṣūf*). Neither did they found a Sufi order (*ṭarīqah*), as it is known today. Some of the early leading Islamic missionaries, who are held in high esteem by the Sufis, as well as the Muslim *ummah* in general, were Ibrāhīm ibn Adham (100–164 AH/718–782 CE), al-Sayyid Abū Maḥfūẓ Maʿrūf al-Karkhī (132–200 AH/750–815 CE), Fuḍayl ibn ʿAyāḍ (d.187 AH/803 CE), Abū Yazīd al-Bistāmī (d. 261 AH/874 CE), Junayd al-Baghdādī (d. 297 AH/910 CE), and al-Sayyid ʿAbd al-Qādir al-Jīlānī (470–561 AH/1077–1166 CE).

The common feature in the lives of these great Islamic spiritual leaders was that they lived a life of extreme piety and virtue. Their sole mission was to propagate the teachings of the holy Qur'an and the glorious Tradition of our master the Messenger of Allah, may Allah bless him and give him peace. They neither added any new aspect or pattern to their mission nor lived an isolated life with a group of disciples and devotees. They definitely established centres of Islamic *daʿwah* and taught those who were influenced and inspired by their preaching and pious way of life to avoid idolatry and associating others in Allah's divinity (*shirk*), worship the One and Only God, follow the injunctions of the Book of God and the teachings of the holy Prophet, may Allah bless him and give him peace, and be true bondsmen of Allah Most Glorified and Exalted. They elevated their followers from the materialistic approach to life, the life of self-love and craze for worldly gain, to the higher pedestal of spirituality and the love of God and His Prophet, may Allah bless him and give him peace. In a nutshell, such were the teachings of these great spiritual leaders, as may be gleaned from the collections of their writings, epistles, sermons and biographies.

Originating from the world of Islam's civilizational centres in Basra and Baghdad, the movement, led by the followers of these great missionaries, gradually spread to Persia, Khorasan, Sīstān, and Central Asia as a whole, and then further east to South Asia and even to East Asia; the movement also spread through the Middle East to North and Sub-Saharan Africa and Muslim Spain, and under the Ottomans to South-Eastern Europe. They were guided by their illustrious spiritual leaders (sheikhs) to establish centres for Islamic *da'wah*. These centres soon became hubs for the message and mission of Islam and training centres of spirituality. The majority of the people who thronged to those centres included non-Muslims, who were taught in the basics of religion and Islamic ethics. These eminent Islamic preachers or later-day Sufis evolved some novel training methods, which were not repugnant to Islamic teachings. Some famous Sufis who were pioneers of the Islamic movement in South Asia were: Khwājah Abū al-Ḥasan ʿAlī ibn ʿUthmān al-Hujwīrī (379–469 AH/990–1077 CE), Khwājah Muʿīn al-Dīn Chishtī (527–627 AH/1131/2–1230 CE), and Sayyid Mawdūdī's ancestors Khwājah Sayyid Mawdūd Chishtī (d. 527 AH/1132/3 CE), his father Sayyid Nāṣir al-Dīn Abū Yūsuf, who was the grandson and disciple of Khwājah Sayyid Aḥmad Abdāl Chishtī (d. 355 AH/965 CE), the founder of the Chishtī Sufi order.

Some of the means of spiritual training adopted by these Sufis soon became very popular, as they reflected the centuries-old local traditions of the native hermits and Yogis. The Islamized versions of the native traditions of *giyān-dhiyān* were meditation (*murāqabah*) and the forty-day retreat (*chillah nashīnī*) to a solitary place praying, reading the holy Qur'an, fasting, and meditating upon the hard facts of life and the Hereafter. A certain school within Sufism also adopted the mode of devotional music, for which they arranged special sittings, called *maḥāfil al-samā'* or assemblies of recitation and listening to devotional songs in praise of Allah Most Glorified and Exalted and His Messenger, may Allah bless him and give him peace. The instruments used were strictly of simple and sedate nature and never of a high-pitch erotic or repulsive kind and hence they did not disturb the spiritual environment of the *maḥāfil*. These instruments traditionally used by the singers were a kind of drum (*ṭablah* or *ṭabal*), a sort of fiddle (*sārangī*), and a three-stringed instrument (*sitār*). These *maḥāfil* were not known to exist before the twelfth century CE and were introduced by a certain Sufi school in the Subcontinent to attract non-Muslims to Islam. In addition to providing spiritual training, these centres also offered free meals to the deserving, a welfare activity that remains an essential part of the major shrines of the Subcontinent even today.

The phase of Sufism that followed the departure of eminent Sufis in later years showed a marked deviation from its earlier tradition. Many of the centres established by them for spiritual training and welfare work were gradually turned by their successors into hereditary estates, to be milked for material gains and worldly comforts. The very ideals for which their predecessors, the epitomes of piety and virtue, stood for throughout their lives were reduced to some formal practices to be observed, especially on the anniversaries of their deaths, to attract devotees and collect donations. Islam has certainly nothing to do with such activities wrongfully perpetrated in the name of *taṣawwuf*.

Sayyid Mawdūdī is generally believed to have been entirely opposed to *taṣawwuf* as an institution. However, as the scion of the house of Chishtī Sufi order, with lineal family and spiritual connections to its earliest founders, Sayyid Mawdūdī was not in fact absolutely opposed to the Sufi tradition. To elaborate further on the point made above, the tradition that started as a movement for spiritual rejuvenation gradually lost its way and became a means for self-promotion, power, money and prestige. The simple life of the Sufis turned into the pompous lifestyle of their successors at the cost of their devotees. Some un-Islamic practices of the pirs and their disciples included extracting compulsory donations from even the hand-to-mouth rural folk, and the obligatory prostration of respect (*sajdah taʿẓīmī*) at the feet of the pirs, for everyone seeking their audience and blessing.[1] Their spiritual centres were turned into shrines (*āstānah*) that were dens of exploitation, monetary extortion, and exercises in grabbing land and property. Such practices are the notable features of the pirs and their shrine-keepers today, and are not only contrary to the true Sufi tradition and its teachings, but very much repugnant to the injunctions of the holy Qur'an and the Sunnah. Sayyid Mawdūdī never condoned such practices and hence a section of the so-called Sufis, better to say

---

[1] They claim sanction for this idolatrous act by drawing upon the analogy of the angels, including Satan, being ordered by the Almighty Lord to prostrate before Adam as mark of respect to him, as His loftiest creation. These 'divines' know fully well that they are neither Adam nor are their devotees angels or Satan. Moreover, that was an exclusive act ordered by God and thereafter no *sajdah* was ever allowed by the Almighty to anyone but Himself. Even His prophets, including our master the Messenger of Allah, may Allah bless him and give him peace, never permitted their followers to prostrate before any human or material object, but only to Allah Most Glorified and Exalted alone. — Editor.

the pirs and their disciples, have tried to create a misunderstanding about his stance on *taṣawwuf*.

Sayyid Mawdūdī was one of the greatest Islamic reformers in contemporary times. He was a prolific writer who expounded the teachings of the Qur'an and the Sunnah, and founded one of the most dynamic movements of Islamic resurgence in the modern age. As a scion of the house of Khwājah Sayyid Mawdūd Chishtī, he was well-qualified to lay claim to the leadership of the Chishtī Sufi order, and then to lead a materially prosperous life as 'Pir Mawdūdī'. But he never did that. In fact, he told some of his more ardent followers, who were not in the dozens but in the thousands, not to call him 'Pir' or 'Murshid' Mawdūdī. Let us now examine from his own words and see what his stance actually was towards *taṣawwuf* and whether it was backed by logic and sound reasoning or was just an emotional and personalized approach. — Editor.

Taṣawwuf, as we understand it today, is not the name of a particular phenomenon. So many things have been mixed up with it instead and are taken as part of *taṣawwuf*. The type of *taṣawwuf* that we approve of as genuine is one thing and the one we reject is another, while the category of *taṣawwuf*, which we would like to reform is another.

The type of *taṣawwuf* we find in the lives of the Sufis in the early days of Islam, such as Ibrāhīm bin Adham, Maʿrūf al-Karkhī and others, may Allah have mercy on their souls, was not an exclusive philosophy of life or a mode of living away from Islam. Their views and practices were based on the teachings of the Book of God and the Tradition of our master the Messenger of Allah, may Allah bless him and give him peace. Their objective was the same as that of Islam and true Muslims, which is sincere devotion to Allah Most Glorified and Exalted and the quest for nearness to Him:

وَمَآ أُمِرُوٓاْ إِلَّا لِيَعۡبُدُواْ ٱللَّهَ مُخۡلِصِينَ لَهُ ٱلدِّينَ حُنَفَآءَ ... ﴿٥﴾

> *And they have been commanded no more than this: to worship Allah, devoting themselves exclusively to Him.*
>
> (*al-Bayyinah* 98: 5)

We not only approve and reaffirm our faith in this form of *taṣawwuf*, but are also keen to see its revival and propagation.

The second category of *taṣawwuf* is the one that is the admixture of alien philosophies, like those of the adherents of Neoplatonic Illuminationism (Ishrāqiyyūn), the followers of Stoicism (Riwāqiyyūn) or of the Zoroastrian or Vedantic schools. This category has co-opted the ways and practices of Christian monks and the Hindu Yogis. Consequently, so many idolatrous thoughts and practices have crept in this type of *taṣawwuf.* The Shariah (or Divine law), the practical method (*ṭarīqah*), and spiritual awareness (*maʿrifah*) have been turned into three distinct phenomena that are not only separate but often opposed to each other. Instead of spiritually preparing the man to perform his duties as the Lord's deputy on earth, he is groomed for an entirely different role. We reject this type of the so-called *taṣawwuf* and also consider it imperative to do away with it, the way we are determined to eliminate modern-day Jāhiliyyah.

There is another type of *taṣawwuf* as well that has some characteristics of the first and some of the second category. It was evolved by those divines who were sincere and well-intentioned in their mission but whom were not quite free from the influence of alien practices of the past and those of their own times. They tried their best to rid the pristine form of Islamic *taṣawwuf* from the adulterations of the *jāhilī* ways, but could not practically keep away from the impact of the alien philosophies and practices of old and in their own age. That which was in their view in conformity with the Qur'an and the Sunnah or not directly in conflict with the teachings of Islam was adopted and made part of their Sufi practice. However, they could not delve deeper to find out if the ways and means they adopted were in any way helpful in furthering the Islamic cause and the dictates of the Lord as well as man's spiritual advancement. Islam has so distinctly enjoined us how to prepare man for the discharge of his duties towards God and also to His subjects, as is evident from the following verse:

وَكَذَٰلِكَ جَعَلْنَٰكُمْ أُمَّةً وَسَطًا لِّتَكُونُوا۟ شُهَدَآءَ عَلَى ٱلنَّاسِ وَيَكُونَ ٱلرَّسُولُ عَلَيْكُمْ شَهِيدًا ... ﴿١٤٣﴾

And it is thus that We appointed you to be the community of the middle way so that you might be witnesses to all mankind and the Messenger might be a witness to you.

(*al-Baqarah* 2: 143)

It is this last category of *taṣawwuf* that we neither totally approve of nor entirely reject. Let me sincerely request its exponents and elders to kindly undertake its thorough reappraisal in light of the teachings of the Qur'an and the Sunnah and to accordingly improve its ethos and practices. Furthermore, my word of advice to them is not to condemn and castigate unilaterally those who try to remove the inaccuracies and shortcomings of this category to bring it into conformity with Islamic teachings. (*Tarjumān al-Qur'ān*, February 1952)

Sayyid Mawdūdī wrote a review of the book *Khātimah* by an eminent sheikh of the Chishtī order Khwājah Muhammad al-Ḥusayni Gīsū Darāz (d. 825 AH/

1422 CE), whom ʿAllāmah Sayyid Sulaymān Nadwī called the sultan of the pen (*sulṭān al-qalam*) because of the number and quality of his books on the message and mission of Islam. — Editor.

In theory and practice, the correct picture of what *taṣawwuf* stands for can be seen in the books authored by the eminent friends of God (*awliyā' Allāh*, singular *waliyy*) like him [i.e. Khwājah Gīsū Darāz]. They are the true representatives of *taṣawwuf*. (*Tarjumān al-Qur'ān*, Jamādā II–Rajab 1356 AH/1937 CE).

How well-versed Sayyid Mawdādī was in *taṣawwuf*, both as a science and as an institution, can be gauged from the following observations of his. — Editor.

I have often benefitted from the company of the Sufis. It has been my practice for a fairly long time not to miss any opportunity to visit a respected personality and to spend some time in his company. I myself belong to a family of Sufis and the chain of allegiance and guidance (*al-bayʿah wa al-irshād*) that continued up to my late father. I have also studied *taṣawwuf* to a certain level and tried to seek the attention of many Sufis as well. Hence, the views and opinions expressed by me about *taṣawwuf* and the Sufis may not be taken as being the views and opinions of the one who is an absolute stranger to this domain. I have seen both the brighter and darker sides of *taṣawwuf* and the Sufis and have arrived on certain conclusions. I certainly do not wish to impose my considered views on all and sundry, but would definitely like to observe that none should the mistake of summarily rejecting these views on the basis that they are of a superficial nature. I would not hesitate even today to benefit from a perfect spiritual guide and my every opinion in this context is subject to review. (*Tarjumān al-Qur'ān*, Dhū al-Qaʿdah–Dhū al-Ḥijjah 1370 AH/1951 CE)

This brief examination should remove the cobwebs woven round the subject and help a right-thinking scholar or even the layperson to have a sounder understanding of Sayyid Mawdūdī's views on *taṣawwuf*. For a detailed reference on the subject, it is recommended that the book by Abū Manẓūr Shaykh Aḥmad (ed.), *Mawlānā Mawdūdī awr Taṣawwuf* (Sargodha: Jahān-i-Nau Publications, 1957) be consulted. — Editor.

Index